Risks in Agricultural Supply Chains

NATIONAL BUREAU *of* **ECONOMIC RESEARCH**

A National Bureau of Economic Research

Conference Report

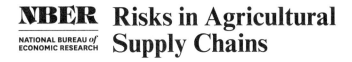

NBER Risks in Agricultural
NATIONAL BUREAU *of*
ECONOMIC RESEARCH Supply Chains

Edited by **Pol Antràs and David Zilberman**

The University of Chicago Press

Chicago and London

The University of Chicago Press, Chicago 60637
The University of Chicago Press, Ltd., London
© 2023 by National Bureau of Economic Research
Published 2023
Printed in the United States of America

32 31 30 29 28 27 26 25 24 23   1 2 3 4 5

ISBN-13: 978-0-226-82922-7 (cloth)
ISBN-13: 978-0-226-82923-4 (e-book)
DOI: https://doi.org/10.7208/chicago/9780226829234.001.0001

Library of Congress Cataloging-in-Publication Data

Names: Antràs, Pol, 1975– editor. | Zilberman, David, 1947– editor.
Title: Risks in agricultural supply chains / edited by Pol Antràs and
    David Zilberman.
Other titles: National Bureau of Economic Research conference report.
Description: Chicago : The University of Chicago Press, 2023. | Series:
    A National Bureau of Economic Research Conference report |
    Includes bibliographical references and index.
Identifiers: LCCN 2023007259 | ISBN 9780226829227 (cloth) |
    ISBN 9780226829234 (ebook)
Subjects: LCSH: Food supply—Risk management. | Food security—
    Risk management.
Classification: LCC HD9000.5 .R575 2023 | DDC 338.1/9—dc23/
    eng/20230510
LC record available at https://lccn.loc.gov/2023007259

Relation of the Directors to the Work and Publications of the NBER

1. The object of the NBER is to ascertain and present to the economics profession, and to the public more generally, important economic facts and their interpretation in a scientific manner without policy recommendations. The Board of Directors is charged with the responsibility of ensuring that the work of the NBER is carried on in strict conformity with this object.

2. The President shall establish an internal review process to ensure that book manuscripts proposed for publication DO NOT contain policy recommendations. This shall apply both to the proceedings of conferences and to manuscripts by a single author or by one or more co-authors but shall not apply to authors of comments at NBER conferences who are not NBER affiliates.

3. No book manuscript reporting research shall be published by the NBER until the President has sent to each member of the Board a notice that a manuscript is recommended for publication and that in the President's opinion it is suitable for publication in accordance with the above principles of the NBER. Such notification will include a table of contents and an abstract or summary of the manuscript's content, a list of contributors if applicable, and a response form for use by Directors who desire a copy of the manuscript for review. Each manuscript shall contain a summary drawing attention to the nature and treatment of the problem studied and the main conclusions reached.

4. No volume shall be published until forty-five days have elapsed from the above notification of intention to publish it. During this period a copy shall be sent to any Director requesting it, and if any Director objects to publication on the grounds that the manuscript contains policy recommendations, the objection will be presented to the author(s) or editor(s). In case of dispute, all members of the Board shall be notified, and the President shall appoint an ad hoc committee of the Board to decide the matter; thirty days additional shall be granted for this purpose.

5. The President shall present annually to the Board a report describing the internal manuscript review process, any objections made by Directors before publication or by anyone after publication, any disputes about such matters, and how they were handled.

6. Publications of the NBER issued for informational purposes concerning the work of the Bureau, or issued to inform the public of the activities at the Bureau, including but not limited to the NBER Digest and Reporter, shall be consistent with the object stated in paragraph 1. They shall contain a specific disclaimer noting that they have not passed through the review procedures required in this resolution. The Executive Committee of the Board is charged with the review of all such publications from time to time.

7. NBER working papers and manuscripts distributed on the Bureau's web site are not deemed to be publications for the purpose of this resolution, but they shall be consistent with the object stated in paragraph 1. Working papers shall contain a specific disclaimer noting that they have not passed through the review procedures required in this resolution. The NBER's web site shall contain a similar disclaimer. The President shall establish an internal review process to ensure that the working papers and the web site do not contain policy recommendations, and shall report annually to the Board on this process and any concerns raised in connection with it.

8. Unless otherwise determined by the Board or exempted by the terms of paragraphs 6 and 7, a copy of this resolution shall be printed in each NBER publication as described in paragraph 2 above.

Contents

Preface

This volume is the latest in a sequence supported by a cooperative agreement between the Economic Research Service (ERS) at the US Department of Agriculture and the National Bureau of Economic Research (NBER). We are grateful to ERS for making this project possible, and in particular to Dr. Spiro Stefanou, the Administrator of ERS, for his interest in this topic and his encouragement of this project. We also thank NBER President James M. Poterba, who has actively supported research on topics on agricultural economics. We are very grateful to all of the authors and discussants who participated in this project, many of whom redirected their research activities to focus on the important issues associated with agricultural supply chains.

Many members of the NBER staff played key roles in making this project a success. Denis Healy oversaw the grant administration at NBER and was the key contact with Utpal Vasavada at ERS, who was a terrific administrative partner. Carl Beck and the NBER conference staff managed all of the meeting logistics with great efficiency and earned the gratitude of all the conference participants. Helena Fitz-Patrick did an outstanding job in managing the production process for this volume, and in working with all of the contributors to meet deadlines and keep the volume on track. She handled all the communication with the University of Chicago Press; the staff there were also a delight to work with.

Introduction

Pol Antràs and David Zilberman

There has been a growing awareness of the importance of agricultural supply and value chains and the need to understand the interactions within and between these supply chains to understand the performance of agricultural markets, their dependence on exchange rates and macro policies, and especially their vulnerability to risk. The performance of agricultural supply chains has received the attention of the Agricultural Economics literature. Zilberman, Lu, and Reardon (2019) emphasize the importance of economic considerations in the design of supply chains to implement agricultural innovation and establish the agricultural market structure with multiple illustrations. Barrett et al. (2020) survey the rich literature on the transformation of agricultural value chains, especially in developing countries. However, the COVID-19 pandemic and concerns about the vulnerability of agricultural systems to climate change emphasize the importance of establishing a solid research agenda on assessing the vulnerability of agricultural and food supply chains to various risks, behavioral responses to this risk, and the use of policy instruments to enhance resilience and mitigate the impacts of shocks to agricultural systems. The workshop and this book are initial steps to develop an integrated research agenda on agricultural supply chains' resilience to risk and policies to enhance it.

The workshop, co-sponsored with the USDA, benefited from the recent

Pol Antràs is the Robert G. Ory Professor of Economics at Harvard University and a research associate of the National Bureau of Economic Research.

David Zilberman is a Distinguished Professor who holds the Robinson Chair in the Department of Agricultural and Resource Economics at the University of California, Berkeley.

For acknowledgments, sources of research support, and disclosure of the authors' material financial relationships, if any, please see https://www.nber.org/books-and-chapters/risks-agricultural-supply-chains/introduction-risks-agricultural-supply-chains.

literature on the impact of the pandemic in agriculture and from the growing efforts supported by the USDA to collect and analyze data on agricultural vulnerability. The chapters in the book are a mixture of conceptual studies and especially promising empirical directions of research on agricultural supply chain resilience to risk. The book addresses supply chain vulnerability to stress broadly defined, but has a big emphasis on the impact of the recent pandemic.

The analysis of risks facing agricultural value chains expands the range of phenomena we must analyze. They include risks from accumulating stock pollution, such as the buildup of greenhouse gases, the accumulation of contaminants in water, and risks faced by industry and consumers from transitory random shocks. The latter shocks include economic shocks, e.g., recession, biophysical and medical shocks (pandemics), and climate and weather shocks (tsunamis, earthquakes, etc.). The heterogeneity of these shocks necessitates a diversity of analytic approaches and modeling. The chapters also differ in how they analyze the economic impact of the risk-causing phenomena. These are early studies in important emerging literature, and we wanted to introduce the reader to these diverse lines of inquiry.

We broadly distinguish between two types of contributions to this volume: *general studies* attempting to make broad points with data from several settings and time periods, and studies that are more focused on the *recent shocks* (such as COVID-19). We next describe each of these in turn.

General Studies

The general studies fall into several categories. The chapters by Sunghun Lim, and by Reardon and Zilberman, review the structural transformation of supply chains and present methodologies to quantify them and predict future directions. Steinbach presents an econometric study on the vulnerability of global food supply chains to exchange rate vulnerability. An essay by the former Californian secretary of agriculture, A. G. Kawamura, provides a practitioner's perspective on new technological opportunities, emerging economic challenges, and the evolution of agricultural supply chains. There are two methodological studies, one by Taylor and Heal on the use of spatial satellite data to assess the vulnerability of agricultural water and marine systems with an application to fertilizer externalities and their implications for algal blooms; and the other by Lu, Nguyen, Rahman, and Winfree on the use of agent-based modeling to determine the dynamics of crop supply chains under risk. We next describe these chapters in a bit more detail.

In "Symbiotic, Resilient, and Rapidly Transforming Food Supply Chains in LMICs: Supermarket and E-commerce Revolutions Helped by Wholesale and Logistics Co-pivoting," Reardon and Zilberman provide an overview of the findings of large emerging literature on the evolution and transformation of food supply chain evident in developing countries. Food supply chains are transforming rapidly from traditional to modern supply chain, and the transformation is affected by trade liberalization and globalization (Reardon et al. 2019). The evolution of food supply chain responds to change in technologies and is symbiotic with innovation supply chain, and results in the emergence of new markets where economic considerations affect market structure and capacity. Food supply chain has capacity to adapt to long-term risk by investment in new technologies, diversification of locations and activities, and modification of trade patterns. They adjust to short-term shocks by pivoting to new exchange strategies, digitization, and product innovation. Innovations tend to emerge in response to shocks. The literature on the supermarket revolution, as supermarkets spread throughout the world in the last century, illustrates long-term adaptation and changes to supply chain. The emerging literature on the response of the food sector to the pandemic illustrates some of the pivoting and changes in response to short-term shocks.

Following this survey chapter, we have several mostly empirical studies on various aspects of transformation on supply chain and information systems. In "Global Agricultural Value Chains and Structural Transformation," Sunghun Lim studies the impact of participation in agricultural value chains (AGVCs) on the structure of production in the participating agrarian economies. Does participating in AGVCs lead to subsequent growth in manufacturing? Does it lead to an expansion of the service center? The author provides answers to these questions using a panel data set covering 155 countries for the period 1991–2015. Building on the EORA Multi-Region Input-Output tables (MRIOs) generated by the UNCTAD-Eora Global Value Chain database, Lim begins by computing country-year measures of AGVC participation following standard tools in global input-output analysis (see Borin and Mancini 2019; Wang et al. 2017). He then studies the extent to which high AGVC participation has predictive power for both GDP and employment shares in agriculture, services, and manufacturing. His results suggest that AGVC participation increases GDP and employment in the agricultural and service sector, while decreasing them in the manufacturing sector. Counter to conventional wisdom about structural transformation, Lim's evidence indicates that modern agrarian economies appear to be leapfrogging the manufacturing sector to directly develop their agriculture and services sectors through their participation in AGVCs.

Lim then digs deeper and studies whether positioning in AGVCs matters for structural transformation. After decomposing the total AGVC participation into upstream participation and downstream participation in AGVCs, he finds that the core leapfrogging result applies for both upstream and downstream participation. However, he finds some divergence on the relative effect of upstream and downstream participation on the share of GDP and employment in the agricultural sector, and he interprets this result as suggestive that upstream AGVC participation leads to more labor-intensive agriculture than downstream AGVC participation.

In "Exchange Rate Volatility and Global Food Supply Chains," Sandro Steinbach analyzes the impact of exchange rate risk on global food supply chains. The conventional wisdom is that an increase in exchange rate uncertainty causes an increase in revenue uncertainty, which will hamper the exchange of goods and services across international borders. Nevertheless, several authors (Johnson 1969; Franke 1991; De Grauwe 1988) have identified a number of mechanisms under which exchange rate volatility can actually enhance international trade flows. It is then perhaps not too surprising that the extant literature on the impact of exchange rate volatility on international trade has failed to produce unambiguous and robust results (see, for instance, Tenreyro 2007), though the majority studies point toward a negative impact. Steinbach's paper contributes to the ongoing debate by investigating the relationship between exchange rate volatility and global food supply chains employing product-level trade flows for 781 agricultural and food products and for a balanced panel of 159 countries for 2001 to 2017. The author estimates a sectoral gravity model and addresses concerns related to endogeneity, heteroskedasticity, zero trade flows, sampling, and reverse causality. Furthermore, both the short-run and the long-run effects of exchange volatility are studied.

The paper finds evidence for interesting heterogeneous effects of exchange rate volatility on global food supply chains both across products and across time horizons. While the mean trade effects are positive for short-run and long-run volatility, these effects vary substantially according to product and industry characteristics. More specifically, Steinbach finds that the majority of agricultural products are positively affected by short-run exchange rate volatility, whereas aquaculture and horticulture products are negatively impacted by both short-run and long-run exchange rate volatility. Furthermore, he finds a positive association between exchange rate volatility and trade flows for upstream products (according to the measure in Antràs et al. 2012) and a negative association for downstream products. Finally, Steinbach demonstrates that if one adopts alternative specifications that do not account for several sources of bias, one finds negative and significant effects of exchange rate volatility, in line with the bulk of previous studies. In sum, the results of the paper enhance our understanding of the implications of exchange rate volatility, which is a primary source of international risk exposure for global food supply chains.

In "Fertilizer and Algal Blooms: A Satellite Approach to Assessing Water Quality," Charles A. Taylor and Geoffrey Heal study the impact of the use of fertilizer in agricultural supply chains on water quality in the form of aquatic hypoxic zones and algal blooms. Nutrient pollution is one of the most challenging environmental problems of our age, and is caused by excess nitrogen and phosphorus, coming primarily from fertilizer use but also from human and industrial waste. These nutrients feed the growth of phytoplankton, thus producing algal blooms, which are considered to produce harmful environmental and health effects when concentrations achieve sufficient density. Nevertheless, as Taylor and Heal point out, the economic impacts of hypoxia and algal blooms and the related external cost of fertilizer are difficult to quantify because of the challenges in linking accumulated downstream pollution to specific upstream sources. A second challenge to rigorous estimation of the social cost of fertilizer is the lack of a temporally consistent, administrative-level data set on water quality.

In their paper, the authors make creative use of a novel satellite-derived measure of algal bloom intensity that spans 30-plus years and encompasses lakes, rivers, and coastal aquatic resources across US counties. More specifically, Taylor and Heal construct a county-level measure of algal bloom intensity derived from over three decades of Landsat satellite imagery and processed using computing power available through Google Earth Engine. Their "bloom algorithm" is based on the near-infrared (NIR) band with an atmospheric correction for shortwave radiation (SWIR).

They then show that their constructed bloom intensity is higher in agricultural regions. There is significant geographic variation in where bloom intensity increased and decreased the most from 1984 to 2020, but there seems to be a general upward trend in the upper Great Plains and along the 100th meridian.

In their econometric results, Taylor and Heal study how bloom intensity is shaped by various factors, including fertilizer use. To compute an annual and county-level measure of fertilizer use, the authors employ data from the US Geological Survey (USGS) on nitrogen and phosphorus use from 1987 to 2012. The underlying data are based on fertilizer product sales compiled by the Association of American Plant Food Control Officials (AAPFCO). Their findings provide strong and robust evidence for the effect of fertilizer use on water quality. Specifically, fertilizer-associated farm pollution drives water quality impairment both locally and downstream from the fertilizer use, and these impacts occur across short-term, medium-term, and long-term horizons. Their findings are of utmost policy relevance, especially given that fertilizer use is mostly exempt from federal regulation under the Clean Water Act despite being the major source of water quality impairment in the US.

In "Demand Shocks and Supply Chain Resilience: An Agent-Based Modeling Approach and Application to the Potato Supply Chain," Liang Lu, Ruby Nguyen, Md Mamunur Rahman, and Jason Winfree address some of the implications that emerge from demand shocks on agricultural food supply systems. Existing literature put a lot of emphasis on understanding the risks in the supply side of the agricultural supply chain. Yet, the COVID-19 pandemic reveals the risks from demand side and their impact throughout the food supply chain. In the case of the pandemic, there is evidence that surpluses and shortages arose from the quick transition of demand from restaurants, hotels, and schools to cooking at home: for example, potato shortage on supermarket shelves and farmers' dumping potatoes at the same time. The paper develops an agent-based model to assess the impact of demand shock on food supply chain based on the case of Idaho's potato supply chain. Five types of agents (farmers, shippers, processors, retailers, and logistics companies) are modeled in this multi-echelon potato supply chain. The model allows for simulating how agents along the supply chain respond to sudden demand changes (demand shocks happening early or late in the growing season). Results showed that not only the magnitude but also the timing of the demand shock have different impacts on various stakeholders of the supply chain. When a demand drop occurs early in the season, even after the disruption period, the fresh potato price is comparatively low for the remaining time of the season. Meanwhile, since the supply chain gets a long period to absorb the surplus inventory, the amount of disposed potatoes is small. When demand drop occurs late in the season, the supply chain cannot absorb the surplus supply of potatoes within a short period. Therefore, farmers have no choice but to dispose of unsold potatoes before the new harvesting season starts. Early demand rise resulted in a 139 percent price hike compared to the baseline scenario, while the late demand rise scenario was responsible for a 56 percent price hike only.

In "The Performance and Future of Ag Supply Chains," A. G. Kawamura, previous secretary of agriculture of California, a farmer and a thinker, presents an essay about factors that affect agricultural supply chain in the present, including his perceptions about the future. His experience suggests that we live in an era of very fast agricultural technologies that are associated with dramatic changes in the structure of agricultural business and supply chain. He views these changes as driven by three forces: (1) globalization, the opening to China, and the large new market opportunities, as well as potential competition facing US agriculture; (2) new technologies resulting from revolutionary discoveries in information science, biology, and robotics; (3) concern about the environment and development, in particular climate change. The UN Sustainable Development Goals provide targeting for policy makers in government, NGOs, and industry. Environmental considerations are added to concern about quality and price in consumer choices. These rapid changes lead to the evolution of agricultural technologies and the structure of the industry, with new forms of farming, ranging from small organics to large industrial producers, allowing them to pursue diverse consumers. The only certainty in the food sector is change. Kawamura is aware that agrifood is subject to continuous scrutiny that led to change but is quite satisfied with the resilience of the food systems in response to the COVID-19 pandemic.

The above studies identify how the structure of supply chains and their performance are affected by risk consideration, shocks, and new information. The major shocks between 2018 and 2022—the COVID-19 pandemic, African swine fever, and changes in international trade agreement—provide evidence of the impact of shock in the supply chain. They are discussed in the next section.

Studies on Recent Shocks

Several of our studies assess economic challenges associated with recent shocks. The study by Delgado, Ma, and Wang assesses the impact responses to the outbreak of African swine fever (ASF) in China on prices and consumption. The chapter by Ma and Lusk is an investigation of the impact of the US meat supply chain's concentration on its resilience to shocks like the current pandemic. This study is especially relevant,9 given the proposals for new regulations on the structure of the meat sector. The study by Ramsey, Goodwin, and Haley addresses the disruptions in the labor market of the food sector as a result of the pandemic. This study assesses the labor impacts of the pivot away from sit-in restaurants to take-home food, the emergence of food delivery services, and the vulnerability of food processing workers to COVID-19. Finally, the study by Arita, Grant, Sydow, and Beckman assesses the resilience of the global agricultural trade to the pandemic. It teases the impact of the pandemic compared to other shocks and demonstrates how they vary across sectors and countries.

In "Exploring Spatial Price Relationships: The Case of African Swine Fever in China," Michael Delgado, Meilin Ma, and H. Holly Wang exploit a natural experiment to study spatial mechanisms behind the dynamics of market integration. In particular, the paper is focused on a temporary ban on inter-province shipping of live hogs induced by the 2018 outbreak of African swine fever (ASF) in China. This is a particularly interesting setting because China is the world's largest producer and consumer of pork, and furthermore, pork consumption is concentrated in large cities in coastal provinces, while its production is in rural areas. Inter-province transportation of live hogs has thus been a dominant feature of the Chinese hog market. In response to the ASF outbreak, the central government immediately imposed an inter-province shipping ban for live hogs, which greatly disrupted market integration across provinces. The ban was lifted a few months later when cases diminished.

The authors assemble a unique data set of weekly provincial hog prices, and they employ state-of-the-art spatial network econometric techniques (c.f., de Paula et al. 2018) to estimate the strength of price co-movement across provinces pre and post the ban. More specifically, Delgado and co-authors identify a pre-ban period, a ban period, and a post-ban period and study price integration during those periods. The methodology parameterizes the price links across provinces to facilitate estimation of those connections via generalized method of moments (GMM), while controlling for province- and time-specific factors.

Their first finding is that the hog market was highly integrated across provinces prior to the ban, with longer geographical distances between two provinces not significantly weakening the strength of their price linkage. The shipping ban dramatically broke down spatial integration (see their figure 7.2). Although the ban only lasted a few months, the authors document that even during the post-ban period, longer distances remained a significant obstacle to spatial price linkage, implying faster reintegration of hog prices between proximate provinces than remote ones. The authors then use variables such as geographic distance and the length of time period under ban for any pair of provinces to explain the slow market reintegration process measured by the price relationships previously estimated. The authors' preferred interpretation of the results is that the slow reintegration of markets was due to the interplay between arbitrage opportunities and imperfect information. More specifically, they ascribe the slow recovery of integration to producers' and processors' reluctance to reassume trading with distant partners, compared with partners nearby, given the incomplete public information regarding ASF. The authors conclude that information transparency is a key factor in fostering market integration in the aftermath of shipping bans used to curb animal pandemics like ASF.

In "Concentration and Resilience in the US Meat Supply Chains," Meilin Ma and Jayson L. Lusk analyzed to what extent a less concentrated meat processing sector is less vulnerable to shocks including shutdown of plants. Their analysis is based on a model of meat supply chain that includes competitive livestock production and retailing, and a rather concentrated meat processing sector. They used simulations to assess the impacts of different changes in the structure of the meat packing sector—in particular, impact of shocks and changes on the wedge between consumer and animal producer prices and the welfare effects on various sectors. The analysis consisted of simulations that assessed the impact of changes on three possible structures of the industry: processing done by large plants; processing done by small plants; and the current model, which is a mix of the two. The system was calibrated assuming linear demand and marginal cost curves, as well as the fact that larger processors have higher fixed costs but lower marginal costs. The results suggest the complex relationship between structure and resilience. For example, when the industry is facing 10–30 percent risk of plants' shutdown, more concentrated packing assures a higher probability of obtaining higher level of output and higher expected outcome, while less concentrated packing assures that output doesn't fall below a minimum threshold of 40 percent. A more concentrated packing sector structure may result in higher variability of responses to shock than a more diffused structure. However, at least in the case of beef, expected total welfare tends to be lower under more diffused structure than under concentrated structure because the latter allows taking advantage of economy of scale. These results are consistent with other findings reported in the survey by Azzam and Schroeter Jr. (1995).

This study is the first one to assess the resilience to external shock of the meat sector, and suggests the need for more research, using both simulations and, perhaps, econometric studies comparing regions or different time periods. There is a place for ex-ante studies that may assess the role of technological innovations in processing and other parts of the meat sector in ensuring resilience and improving welfare. The framework can be expanded to analyze some of the multiple policies suggested to reform the meat sector.

In "Labor Dynamics and Supply Chain Disruption in Food Manufacturing," A. Ford Ramsey, Barry K. Goodwin, and Mildred M. Haley analyze the dynamics of wage and employment in the food manufacturing and animal processing sector and use the estimate to assess outcomes during the pandemic.

The authors estimated both wages and employment in the food manufacturing and animal slaughter industries using county-level data. Food manufacturing has a higher rate of employment and less variability than the animal slaughter industries, perhaps because of higher reliance on migrant workers in the animal slaughter sector. However, regions with higher food manufacturing prices have higher animal slaughter wages. The wages and employment tend to increase by the extent of use of the productive capacities of the industry and by the price of output. Higher volatility of wages tends to increase average wages, but higher volatility of employment tends to reduce average wages. The paper finds that wages in food manufacturing and animal slaughtering in the early part of 2020 were slightly higher than what was expected given the magnitude of the shock, but later in the year, the deviation from predicted prices was smaller. That suggests manufacturers needed to induce employees to work during the early part of the pandemic in 2020, but later in the year, the volatility of wages declined, and the availability of labor increased. The analysis suggests that the pandemic had significant impact on labor in food processing sectors early in the pandemic, but the labor situation recovered relatively fast. The analysis relied on county data, but further insight can be gained using plant-based data and distinguishing between different types of employment and labor relationships and contracting.

In "Has Global Agricultural Trade Been Resilient under COVID-19? Findings from an Econometric Assessment of 2020," Shawn Arita, Jason Grant, Sharon Sydow, and Jayson Beckman show that overall the pandemic has half the effect on agricultural trade (5–10 percent reduction) than trade in nonagricultural commodities, but impacts vary by agricultural sectors. While some effects can be obtained by comparing ag trade patterns of 2019 and 2020, econometric analysis enables separating the impacts of the pandemic from impact of animal diseases (African swine fever, ASF) and policy (US-China trade agreement). For example, the overall trading in pork increased in 2020 because of the reduced severity of ASF, despite some reduction due to the pandemic. Furthermore, the analysis also shows that quarantines and trade and movement restrictions resulting from COVID-19 have had stronger impact than the disease itself. The analysis suggests that the impact of the pandemic was more significant on the demand than the supply side. Non-food items like skin hides, ethanol, and rubber suffered the steepest reduction in trade because of the pandemic, while most commodities didn't suffer much, and trade in rice actually increased. It seems that low-income and less-developed countries were more vulnerable to the pandemic, and COVID-19 contributed to reduction in income. Transfer policies in developed and some developing countries reduced the impact of COVID-19 on agricultural trade. Finally, the trade reduction because of COVID-19 occurred mostly early in the pandemic, and smaller disruptions continued throughout the year, indicating signs of adjustment and recovery.

The analysis suggests that global agriculture trade was resilient to COVID-19, and major impacts were more on luxury non-food groups than on essential food commodities. The impact of COVID-19 on agricultural trade and the resulting welfare of individual groups should be further studied with more detailed data on outcomes within countries.

Conclusions

Agriculture and other industries consist of a web of interrelated supply chains, which evolve and adapt in response to changes in technology, policy, and biophysical and medical shocks. This book hopes to provide an important launching pad for the emerging research agenda on the vulnerability of agricultural and food markets to shock. In addition, it supplies methodological and empirical foundations for economists, and valuable information for policy makers and the general public, especially when relating to the impact of COVID-19 and other shocks in the late 2019 and early 2020s. Economic research can and should gain understanding of the evolution and the economics of supply chain, how product supply chains are linked to innovation policies and institutions, and how the evolution of supply chain shapes markets, trade patterns, and economic welfare (Zilberman et al. 2022). Agriculture and natural resources can provide important past lessons and case studies on the economics of supply chain and its implications for major policy issues associated, for example, with climate change, food security, biodiversity, and economic development.

This book contributes to emerging literature on the economics of agriculture and food supply chains and their responses to risks. It suggests that the agrifood sector is facing multiple categories of risks. Unfortunately, some of them have not received much attention from economic research. Thus hopefully, the works presented here will inspire further research on the economics of supply chains and the response to diverse categories of risks by firms and supply chains. The analysis of these risks requires access to new sources of data and multidisciplinary understanding that will further enrich the economic stock of knowledge.

While much of the activities in agriculture are increasingly outside the farm gate, the USDA has provided mostly data and information about agriculture. This information has contributed immensely to the development of economics, and for agricultural policy and analysis. However, at present, significant information gathering and data collection are needed to understand the behavior and evolution of food and agricultural supply chains. There would be substantial value to USDA pursuing such an effort, and the design and management of this information collection will require creative research that will challenge and enhance the capabilities of economics and the data sciences.

References

Antràs, Pol, Davin Chor, Thibault Fally, and Russell Hillberry. 2012. "Measuring the Upstreamness of Production and Trade Flows." *American Economic Review Papers and Proceedings* 102 (5): 412–16.

Azzam, Azzeddine M., and John R. Schroeter Jr. 1995. "The tradeoff between oligopsony power and cost efficiency in horizontal consolidation: An example from beef packing." American Journal of Agricultural Economics 77 (4): 825–836.

Barrett, Christopher B., Thomas Reardon, Johan Swinnen, and David Zilberman. 2020. "Agri-food Value Chain Revolutions in Low- and Middle-Income Countries." *Journal of Economic Literature* 58: 1–67.

Borin, Alessandro, and Michele Mancini. 2019. "Measuring What Matters in Global Value Chains and Value-Added Trade." The World Bank.

De Grauwe, Paul. 1988. "Exchange Rate Variability and the Slowdown in Growth of International Trade." IMF Staff Papers 35: 63–84.

de Paula, Aureo, Imran Rasul, and Pedro Souza. 2018. "Recovering Social Networks from Panel Data: Identification, Simulations and an Application." Working paper. https://ssrn.com/abstract=3322049.

Franke, Günter. 1991. "Exchange Rate Volatility and International Trading Strategy." *Journal of International Money and Finance* 10: 292–307.

Johnson, Harry G. 1969. "The Case for Flexible Exchange Rates." *Federal Reserve Bank of St. Louis Review,* 12–24.

Reardon, T., R. Echeverría, J. Berdegué, B. Minten, S. Liverpool-Tasie, D. Tschirley, and D. Zilberman. 2019. "Rapid Transformation of Food Systems in Developing Regions: Highlighting the Role of Agricultural Research and Innovations." *Agricultural Systems* 172 (June): 47–59. https://doi.org/10.1016/j.agsy.2018.01.022.

Tenreyro, Silvana. 2007. "On the Trade Impact of Nominal Exchange Rate Volatility." *Journal of Development Economics* 82: 485–508.

Wang, Zhi, Shang-Jin Wei, Xinding Yu, and Kunfu Zhu. 2017. "Measures of Participation in Global Value Chains and Global Business Cycles." NBER Working Paper 23222. Cambridge, MA: National Bureau of Economic Research.

Wohlgenant, Michael K. 2013. "Competition in the US Meatpacking Industry." *Annual Review of Resource Economics* 5 (1): 1–12.

Zilberman, David, Liang Lu, and Thomas Reardon. 2019. "Innovation-Induced Food Supply Chain Design." *Food Policy* 83: 289–97.

Zilberman, D., T. Reardon, J. Silver, L. Lu, and A. Heiman. 2022. "From the Lab to the Consumer: Innovation, Supply Chain, and Adoption with Applications to Natural Resources." *Proceedings of the National Academy of Science of the USA (PNAS)* 119(23)e2115880119. Published online June1. https://doi.org/10.1073/pnas.2115880119.

Symbiotic, Resilient, and Rapidly Transforming Food Supply Chains in LMICs
Supermarket and E-commerce Revolutions Helped by Wholesale and Logistics Co-pivoting

Thomas Reardon and David Zilberman

1.1 Introduction

1.1.1 FSCs in Developing Countries Are Transforming Rapidly

FSCs (food supply chains) in developing countries (referred to here as LMICs, low- and middle-income countries) have been transforming rapidly in the past several decades (Reardon et al. 2019; Barrett et al., forthcoming). FSCs are transforming along three stages: from "traditional" to "transitional" to "modern" (Reardon et al. 2012b). The main changes are spatial lengthening, consolidation, technological intensification, and movement along the product cycle from niche to commodities to differentiated products (and thus introduction of innovations).

While most attention concerning transformation is paid to food trade and global value chains, the domestic FSCs are also crucial. On the one hand, domestic FSCs are important and have grown quickly. Only about 10 percent of national food consumption in developing countries is imported and 5 percent of food output is exported, so 90 percent of their food is from domestic sources. Most of that food comes via supply chains: about 80 percent of all national food consumption is purchased; only about 20 percent is subsistence farming. The FSCs have grown extremely rapidly, such as 800

Thomas Reardon is a University Distinguished Professor at Michigan State University, and a nonresident fellow of the International Food Policy Research Institute.

David Zilberman is a Distinguished Professor who holds the Robinson Chair in the Department of Agricultural and Resource Economics at the University of California, Berkeley.

For acknowledgments, sources of research support, and disclosure of the authors' material financial relationships, if any, please see https://www.nber.org/books-and-chapters/risks -agricultural-supply-chains/symbiotic-resilient-and-rapidly-transforming-food-supply -chains-lmics-supermarket-and-e-commerce.

percent in Africa and 1,000 percent in Southeast Asia in the past 25 years (Reardon et al. 2019).

On the other hand, domestic FSCs have transformed rapidly during globalization (somewhat at odds with the common image that trade and "global value chains" are the main face of globalization in the developing country food economy). Reardon and Timmer (2007) give an example of the "supermarket revolution" and contend that:

> The primary impact of globalization on domestic food markets came not through the trade effect, but through direct changes wrought on domestic food markets by FDI liberalization. . . . Spurred by massive retail sector foreign direct investment (FDI) to which was added competitive investments from domestic capital, a profound retail transformation has occurred in the past decade—the "supermarket revolution."

1.1.2   FSCs Face Long-Term Risks and Short-Term Shocks and Develop Resilience or Pivoting Strategies Based on Symbiotic Relationships

As supply chains grow, introduce their innovations to the market, and transform in structure and conduct, they face two kinds of challenges in developing countries: (1) long-term conditions and problems like high transaction costs and risks; (2) short-term shocks like climate disasters and COVID-19. To deal with these two sets of challenges, supply chains (and their individual actors, the farms and firms) undertake two strategies, one that can be thought of as the internal design of the supply chain and one as linkages between supply chains, as follows.

First, supply chain firms make choices about the design of their own supply chains in order to develop new markets for the product or service which is innovative in the new setting. To develop their supply chains over time, they have to, as the Chinese say, "cross the river by feeling the stones." They have to adapt or "pivot" to deal with long-term problems and still achieve rapid growth and resilience. Reardon, Henson, and Berdegué (2007) note that ". . . firms undertake 'proactive fast-tracking strategies' . . . These strategies reveal that the leading retailers saw demand and supply-side conditions in food markets as 'endogenous' rather than 'exogenous'—things they could influence to their own gain." Examples they give are of outsourcing procurement to sidestep fragmented, transaction-costly traditional market sources.

Zilberman, Lu, and Reardon (2019) cast this endogenous design of supply chains as a set of specific choices: technological, institutional (contract or spot markets, standards), and organizational (make or buy). The aggregate of these micro design choices then affects the meso market environment of these variables. Note that part of the choices involve choices of linkages with complementary supply chains, to which we turn next.

Second, symbiotic relationships are formed among supply chains for co-adaptation and growth and transformation of FSCs, with the concepts heuristically laid out in Reardon, Henson, and Berdegué (2007) and Reardon and Timmer (2012). As lead segments in PSCs pivot to long-term challenges and sudden shocks (like COVID-19), they work out arrangements with complementary supply chains[1] that need to "co-innovate" or "co-pivot." Those terms are used by Reardon and Swinnen (2020) and Reardon et al. (2021c) as an illustration of this (reviewed below) when during COVID-19 retailers (small and large) in developing countries had to quickly pivot to e-commerce and relied on co-pivoting by delivery intermediary and logistics supply chains. In section 1.3 we will explore this in more depth, especially related to our illustrative foci in retail (supermarkets and e-commerce).

To show the breadth of applicability of the concept of "symbiotic supply chains" introduced in the literature on food supply chains in the past 25 years, it suffices to note literature emphasizing this symbiosis across a range of situations: supermarkets and (logistics) lateral supply chains (in Asia, Reardon, Timmer, and Minten 2012; in Central and Eastern Europe and China, Reardon and Swinnen 2004; in Latin America, Reardon and Berdegué 2002); processors and input and finance supply chains in Slovakia (Gow and Swinnen, 1998); supermarkets and farm input and R&D&E supply chains in Indonesia (Reardon, Henson, and Berdegué 2007); supermarkets and large processors in dairy in Brazil (Farina et al. 2005), and R&D&E innovation supply chains and product supply chains (Zilberman et al. 2022).

A central message of this paper is that food supply chain transformation and inter-supply chain symbiosis (and co-adaptation) are intimately connected: (1) transformation of PSCs requires "pivoting" by the firms— new investments and innovations and adapting to long-term challenges and opportunities and short-term shocks (like COVID-19); (2) the quest for transformation calls forth or induces complementary supply chains (lateral, farm inputs, and R&D&E) to co-pivot, to co-adapt and co-innovate, to enable the pivoting. FSC resilience is based on these two pillars.

The balance of the paper provides illustrations of these concepts for the rapid rise of the supermarket revolution (section 1.2) and the rise of e-commerce and its acceleration during SAR1 and SARS2 (COVID-19) (section 1.3). We show that the explosive rapidity of the take-off of these retail transformations was considered surprising, predicted improbable, in the earlier literature, but that their rapid rise and numerous pivots to address the unique challenges of developing country food economies were dependent in large part initially on a transfer of innovations from developed countries but then on a series of co-pivots by symbiotic supply chains—wholesale

1. Supply chains complementary to product supply chains include: (1) farm inputs; (2) "lateral supply chains" like the supply of logistics, finance, energy, and labor feed the nodes of the product and input supply chains; and (3) the R&D&E (research and development and extension) supply chains feed the other supply chains. Together these three and the product supply chain form a "dendritic" (tree form) cluster of complementary supply chains (Reardon et al. 2019).

and delivery intermediaries, logistics supply chains, large processors, and farm input supply chains.

1.2 The Supermarket Revolution in LMICs: Fast-Tracked Diffusion via Supply Chain Symbioses Involving Resilience to *Long-Run* Challenges

1.2.1 Surprisingly Rapid Diffusion of Supermarkets

1.2.1.1 The Supermarket Revolution Was Predicted to Be Improbable in LMICs—Before It Happened

Supermarkets have been around for a half century in a number of developing countries. Goldman (1974) noted the emergence of domestic supermarket chains in a number of countries due to various demand side factors (rising incomes, urbanization, increasing opportunity cost of women's time in large cities). However, he noted at that time that this was a very limited phenomenon—limited mainly to large cities, upper middle or rich consumer segments, and was an affair nearly exclusively of domestic-capital chains.

Goldman, and other retail researchers in the 1960s to 1980s, contended that supermarkets were destined to not "take off" in developing countries for two sets of reasons. On the demand side, they maintained that the poor and even the middle class would not be induced to switch from shopping at "mom and pop" stores and open markets—to buy flour here, fruit there, meat another place, and so on—to shop in supermarkets.

They had several reasons for their demand-side contention. (1) They reasoned that as shopping in supermarkets was meant to save women's time, and women worked little outside the home and so their opportunity costs of time were low, only the upper class would shop in supermarkets, and it would scarcely penetrate the middle class, let alone the poor. In a similar vein, they observed that at the time the poor did not tend to buy processed foods, as they had low opportunity costs of processing them at home. (2) They also maintained that supermarkets sold large units that required lumpy outlays that the poor could not afford at one go. (3) They also observed that supermarkets at that time charged high food prices compared to traditional shops, and so the poor would not be drawn to them. (4) They observed in those decades that supermarket chains in the US and Europe had large stores and were located mainly in the outskirts of cities and required cars to get to, that the poor in developing countries, who tended to live in center city or in slums, would not be able to go out to them, even if the supermarkets reduced their prices.

On the supply side, Goldman and others contended that traditional supply chain conditions in developing countries as observed in the 1960s to 1980s would present such a risky and high transaction cost procurement situation for supermarket chains that they would not be able to generate a cost or quality advantage over traditional retailers. Their procurement supply chains would be mired in traditional conditions and forced thus to equality with traditional retailers. These very conditions, exacerbated with FDI regulations restricting investment by foreign firms especially in the "downstream" segments of the value chains, were seen as dissuading foreign direct investment (FDI) from modern retailers in the US and Europe.

1.2.1.2   The Supermarket Revolution "Took Off" against Predictions— And Diffused Rapidly in Waves

In the 1990s and 2000s private-sector modern retail took off in the supermarket revolution. This surprising takeoff in the 1990s is documented by a body of literature that emerged mainly in the 2000s (e.g., Reardon et al. 2003; Traill 2006). The diffusion of modern food retail rolled out in broadly three waves in different regions. (1) The first wave, with takeoff in the early 1990s, was in East Asia (outside Japan and China), South America, South Africa, and Central Europe. The share of modern retail in food retail went from roughly 5–10 percent in 1990 to some 50–60 percent by the late 1990s. (2) The second wave, in the mid- to late 1990s, was in Southeast Asia (outside transition countries like Vietnam), Central America, and Mexico. The share of modern retail in food retail reached some 20–50 percent by the late 1990s. (3) The third wave, in the late 1990s and 2000s, was mainly in China, Vietnam, India, and Russia. The share of modern retail in food retail climbed to some 5–20 percent by the end-2000s in a rapid rise. In Africa outside South Africa, mainly in eastern and southern Africa, modern retail is by the 2010s just starting in most countries.

The spread of supermarkets that started mainly in the 1990s continued rapidly in the 2000s and 2010s, especially in Asia and Latin America. For Latin America, Popkin and Reardon (2018) analyzed Planet Retail data for food sales of the top 100 chains in 12 countries from 2002–2016. The sales increased about 400 percent from 2002 to 2011. For Asia, Reardon, Timmer, and Minten (2012) used the same method and data source for 9 countries and 195 leading chains and found roughly a 400 percent increase from 2002 to 2009. The sales growth rates strongly exceeded GDP/capita growth rates, meaning that we were observing a structural change in retail away from small shops and wet markets.

This rapid growth occurred in three spatial sets of waves. The first set was waves over countries per region. For example, Reardon, Timmer, and Minten (2012) show that the first wave countries (South Korea and Taiwan), i.e., those that had started their surge of supermarket growth in the 1980s/1990s, had by the 2000s the slowest sales growth rate; one expects this as countries near the modern retail saturation point. They found the second wave countries (Indonesia, Malaysia, Philippines, and Thailand), with their retail takeoff in the 1990s, showed moderate sales growth rates; while the third wave countries (China, India, and Vietnam) showed very rapid yearly sales growth rates. This is the "catch-up" or convergence phenomenon. Popkin and Reardon (2018) showed similar waves over countries and catch-up trends in Latin America.

The developing regions themselves show these waves, with the first wave among East Asian and South American countries, the second among Southeast Asian, Central American/Mexico, and Central European countries, and the third wave in the transition such as China and Vietnam and Eastern Europe, and the emerging fourth wave mainly in Africa (Reardon and Timmer 2012).

Within a given country, waves of supermarket diffusion occur from large to small cities and then to rural areas, from more urban and richer to less urban and poorer zones, and from richer to middle to poorer consumers. The diffusion also occurs in waves over products, from non-food to processed food, to semi-processed food such as milk, to perishables such as produce, meat, and fish (Reardon et al. 2003).

The same spatial, socioeconomic, and product waves of supermarket penetration had been seen over the 20th century in the US, starting from a similar traditional retail system to that found in developing countries. The most salient difference was that retail change in the US had been much more gradual than it was in developing countries from the 1980s/1990s on.

1.2.2   How Supermarket Chains "Pivoted" to Fast-Track Their Spread

Recall from above that the constraints to a supermarket revolution hypothesized by the retail literature before 1990s revolved around four perceived traits of supermarkets as disadvantages in developing countries: (1) their accessibility (outside city center because "big box," and need for a car) is too low for most consumers; (2) their prices are too high for most consumers if they relied on imports, and just the same as traditional retail (or higher if they had to pay taxes) if they had to use the traditional markets to source; (3) they are agglomerations of products that save time, which does not need to be saved by poor households; (4) they were thought to mainly sell processed foods, which also represent time-savers; (5) their possible food safety advantages were not perceived as they had change attributes faced by consumers; (6) their quality was no higher and possibly lower than traditional markets with high turnover.

Demand side and supply side factors combined to allow supermarket chains to "fast-track" their diffusion.

On the demand side, roughly in the late 1980s/1990s and certainly in the 2000s and 2010s (with the period a function of the wave and region), income and employment characteristics, especially of urban areas, began to change quickly, and urbanization itself soared, such as in Asia (Reardon, Timmer, and Minten 2012) and Latin America (Popkin and Reardon 2018). Women's participation in the workforce outside the home increased and with it their opportunity costs of home-preparation and home-processing of food and of shopping; incomes rose. With these factors, the demand for processed food rapidly increased, not just in Asia (Pingali 2007) and Latin America (Popkin and Reardon 2018) but also in Africa (Reardon et al. 2021a). Bus systems and ownership of motorbikes and cars spread.

Important for supermarket diffusion, sensitivity to food safety issues increased, because both urbanization and greater consumption of perishables led to more worries. However, the perception that supermarket chains were more careful with food safety increased (Reardon, Henson, and Gulati 2010). Food crises, like bird flu and some produce scares, have sensitized urban consumers (for Thailand, see Posri and Chadbunchachai 2006; for Tianjin China, see Zhang 2005; for Vietnam, see Moustier et al. 2006; for chicken and ducks after the shock of bird flu, see Phan and Reardon 2007).

On the supply side, the essence of the rapid and surprising takeoff and spread of supermarkets is that modern retailers found ways to "fast-track" solutions to the problems of high prices, low accessibility, and undifferentiated quality and safety over time (Reardon et al. 2003), as follows.

First, chains drove up their accessibility by diversifying formats away from "big box" stores on the periphery of cities and creating small-format stores (but still using procurement with economies of scale over the small outlets in a chain) that could nestle into city centers and fit into tertiary cities and be reachable by bus and foot and motorbike. This made them accessible to the poor (Reardon and Berdegué 2002 for Latin America, for example). As discussed below, they implemented e-commerce and delivery, which made them even more accessible and diminished the local shops' prior advantage of proximity (Lu and Reardon 2018).

Second, chains drove down their consumer prices to wrest the price advantage from traditional retail. They did this by creating economies of scale in procurement, buying in large quantities, and storing in distribution centers (DCs). DCs served as an aggregation mechanism that helped retailers step around traditional wholesale markets and traditional wholesaler dominated supply chains. This was accomplished in symbiosis with emergent specialized/dedicated wholesalers and 3PLS, as discussed further below.

Chains did this first and most successfully for processed and semiprocessed foods such as flour, oil, noodles, and dairy (such as in Delhi, Minten, Reardon, and Sutradhar 2010), and then second and gradually successfully for fresh foods like chicken and meat; finally, they have begun competing on fresh produce especially for basic staples like kale in Kenya (Minten and Reardon 2008; Minten, Reardon, and Sutradhar 2010).

Third, supermarket chains, as well as large processors such as dairy firms, instituted private standards of quality and safety for suppliers. This was done for two reasons. The first was to differentiate themselves and their products and services in the eyes of consumers from traditional retailers and processors in terms of quality and safety and to compete with one another on product differentiation along the product cycle. The second was to impose practices that reduced costs and risks and increased consistency in procurement and processing and farming, such as dairy (Reardon et al. 1999; Farina and Reardon 2000; Henson and Reardon 2005; Swinnen 2007).

Private standards were imposed formally via contracts and via informal "relational contracts" (Macchiavello 2022; Macchiavello, Reardon, and Richards 2022) between retailers and processors and specialized/dedicated wholesalers (discussed below) and farmers. Traditional retailers and small processors did not have the leverage or bargaining power to impose such standards on firms and farms in their procurement supply chains, as they had to buy from the spot market.

Moreover, "resource provision contracts" between supermarket chains or large processors on the one hand and farmers on the other allowed fast-tracking of modernization and meeting of private standards (Reardon et al. 2009). These contracts included provisions for assistance to farmers (and others) who face "idiosyncratic market failures" such as lack of access to credit, to technological information, to special inputs, and to services such as delivery. Modern food industry firms working with traditional supply chain actors that needed to upgrade quickly often have had to use such contracts and provide such assistance, such as for sugar beet farming in Slovakia (Gow and Swinnen 1998), horticultural export farming in Mexico (Key and Runsten 1999), dairy in Central and Eastern Europe (Dries and Swinnen 2004, 2010), and melon farming for Carrefour in Indonesia (Reardon, Henson, and Berdegué 2007, discussed more below).

Finally, two sources of expertise, innovation, investment funds, and complementary actions flowed like surging rivers into the midstream and downstream segments of the transforming food supply chains, enabling and fast-tracking the above pivoting strategies to overcome long-term risks and transaction costs and create advantages for modern firms.

On the one hand, foreign direct investment (FDI) flowed massively into developing country food supply chains. In an earlier period, these flows had been mainly by agribusinesses like Dole to establish plantations, such as bananas in Central America, and create export platforms; this was termed "vertical FDI." In the 1990s on, the FDI shifted to being mainly "horizontal FDI," where FDI was mainly by supermarket chains and large processors to buy or establish firms, as Nestlé did at a vertiginous pace in the late 1980s and 1990s in Brazil's dairy sector (Farina and Reardon 2000). The "push factor" for FDI from Europe and the US was that profits in those mature food markets had been competed down and products and approaches (like chains) that had been niches then commoditized in those markets were ripe for transfer to developing country markets as new profitable niche innovations to be commoditized there (Awokuse and Reardon 2018). This FDI was facilitated by the diffusion of FDI liberalization (along with trade liberalization), part of "globalization" following GATTs in the 1980s and structural adjustment in the 1990s on (Reardon et al. 2003).

On the other hand, there emerged a host of "specialized/dedicated wholesalers" (Reardon and Berdegué 2002) and 3PLS (third party logistics firms) that formed symbiotic supply chains of their services that dovetailed with the needs of retailers and large processors to implement the strategies above. To this symbiosis we turn next.

1.2.3   Symbiotic Value Chain Firms (in Wholesale and Logistic Services) Co-Pivoting to Enable the Supermarket Revolution

Given the steep challenges in developing countries discussed above of transferring and developing a new way of retailing via chains that require massive procurement systems, consistent quality and safety, and prices and accessibility competitive with traditional retailers, it was usually impossible for modern retailers to "go it alone." Reardon, Henson, and Berdegué (2007) emphasized that the retailers' solution was to pursue a symbiosis of the supermarket's supply chain and the supply chains of services (wholesale and logistics) and processing so they could work together to solve the problems. To wit:

Beside the retail investments that have been extensively treated in recent literature, these proactive strategies focus on improving the "enabling conditions" via (i) procurement system modernization and (ii) local supply chain development. One important strategy retailers have used to facilitate (i) and (ii) is to form symbiotic relationships with modern wholesale, logistics, and processing firms (Reardon, Henson, and Berdegué 2007).

Here we briefly illustrate the innovative ways that this symbiosis occurred.

First, retailers and processors worked together to co-innovate new processed products that would confer a "product cycle" advantage over traditional competitors. For example, Carrefour and other large retailers in Brazil worked with Nestlé and Parmalat to create new dairy beverages (e.g., mixing with tropical fruit juices) geared to the Brazilian market (Farina and Reardon 2000).

Second, retail chains "follow sourced" services from home market partners to fast-track solutions in new markets instead of being held back by relying on local traditional services. (Recall that pre-1990, retail researchers argued that supermarket development would be held back by such a limitation.) For example, modern retailers from the US and Western Europe starting in Central Europe in the 1990s and early 2000s called on multinational logistics (3PLS) companies from the US and Western Europe to undertake FDI ("follow source") in Central Europe and set up regional procurement networks with series of DCs (Dries, Reardon, and Swinnen 2004); Carrefour in Brazil called on Penske Logistics of the US to do the same in partnership with Cotia Trading (a Brazilian specialized/dedicated wholesaler, a term treated next) (Reardon and Berdegué 2002). Tesco in China called on its purveyor (processor and wholesaler) of semi-processed vegetables for its European operations to follow it to China to set up fresh-cuts operations instead of relying on local companies to work out that supply (Reardon,

Henson, and Berdegué 2007). In these cases, the FDI partner often bought and upgraded local companies to assemble a new supply chain.

Third, "specialized/dedicated" wholesalers emerged to service the special needs of supermarket chains (Reardon and Berdegué, 2002):

> Supermarkets tend to find that the traditional wholesalers provide inadequate service since they lack standards, mix items of different grades, and have significant bargaining power in the wholesale markets because wholesaling is usually quite concentrated per product rubric. Supermarkets tend to continue to procure from wholesale markets only where they cannot make adequate arrangements direct with producers through their own distribution centers, or where new types of wholesalers emerge to meet their needs. (380)

In the 1990s and 2000s some of these specialized wholesalers emerged as traditional wholesalers and then built DCs and set up sorting and packing operations to distribute to and for supermarkets (e.g., Bimandiri in Indonesia; Reardon, Timmer, and Minten 2012). Some of them started as export firms and then opened a division to serve supermarkets as the latter emerged (as in the case of WingMau in Hong Kong; Hu et al. 2004).

Fourth, arrangements among firms leading value chains of inputs and products and services multiplied during the supermarket revolution to address particular challenges for which no individual firm had a full solution. For example, in Indonesia, Carrefour wanted to innovate in its melon retail by sourcing and selling a new variety of melon (seedless mini melons) attractive to the emerging educated urban singles who wanted high-quality fruit but not in large sizes. No farmer was growing these, no wholesaler had them in stock, and stores were waiting to sell them. Carrefour then worked up a five-player arrangement with a specialized wholesaler (Bimandiri) that would work with the farmers' cooperative; with a farmer cooperative that was doing traditional watermelons but had a subset of farmers skilled enough to grow the new melons; with Syngenta, which had the seeds and a credit facility for the farmers; and with the government's R&D&E department that agreed to a program focused on training farmers in the growing of these new melons (Natawidjaja et al. 2007).

A variant on the above adds in NGOs that are focused on helping small farmers enter modern markets. Such an arrangement can:

> . . . involve a "symbiosis" between NGOs and governments to partner with these private sector-led efforts to assist in provision of resources and services needed by small farmers, but with the promise of the latter gaining access to specific and demanding modern markets. This approach is mutually beneficial. NGOs are often seeking to help their beneficiary farmers move from low remuneration non-quality-differentiated and demand-constrained local produce markets to modern markets linked to urban and export demand, as illustrated by the Dutch NGO Himalayan Action Research Centre in India, working with the Mother Dairy/Safal chain. (6)

1.3 The E-Commerce Revolution: Fast-Tracked Diffusion via Supply Chain Symbioses Involving Resilience to *Short Run-Run* Shocks and Pivots

1.3.1 Diffusion of E-Commerce in Developing Countries

The emergence and diffusion of e-commerce in developing countries can be seen as an extension, like a branch from a tree, of the supermarket revolution (Lu and Reardon 2018). It was driven by demand and supply factors (synthesizing from Reardon et al. 2021b, 2021c).

The demand-side factors driving e-commerce diffusion were threefold. First, the same demand factors that drove the supermarket revolution are relevant for e-commerce, especially the rising opportunity cost of time to go out shopping. This drove the quest to shop in the "one stop shop" of supermarkets, as well as having food delivered. As developing country cities become increasingly crowded and congested, consumers' interest in shopping from home increases. The latter undoes the location advantage of small shops.

Second, there has been an extremely rapid spread of cell phones in particular, as well as home computers in developing countries in the past two decades.

Third, while food safety shocks (such as bird flu, discussed above) spurred a shift to shopping at supermarkets, human disease shocks have been important to accelerating the diffusion of e-commerce. Yang and Wang (2013) note that Alibaba's e-commerce (taobao.com) was started in May 2003 with SARS as an important inducement. COVID-19 is related to SARS, and has been a strong inducement to the acceleration of e-commerce in developing (and developed) countries in 2020–2021. For example, Vardhan (2020) presents Euromonitor survey data showing food e-commerce upticks in yearly growth rates in various countries, comparing growth rates over 2019 with growth rates over 2020: Indonesia, 60 percent versus 120 percent; South Africa, 20 percent versus 100 percent; Brazil, 15 percent versus 100 percent; Mexico, 15 percent versus 80 percent; India, 30 percent versus 70 percent; Nigeria, 20 percent versus 50 percent; and China, 10 percent versus 20 percent.

The supply side factors driving e-commerce diffusion were several. First, there was a diffusion of the technologies and business organization needed for e-commerce. The computer revolution of the 1950s to 1960s put technology in play that was adapted to digitalization of internal processes of firms starting in the 1970s (such as SAP). In the 1980s and 1990s, supermarket chains and processors, especially in the US and Europe, began to digitalize their procurement systems toward B2B.

In developing countries that were starting to export to these chains, especially China, B2B firms arose, such as Alibaba, the fruit of FDI by Japanese Softbank and US Yahoo in 1999. In the 1990s Amazon innovated with e-commerce, B2C, starting with nonfoods and then into packaged foods and later into fresh foods. With SARS and consumer lockdowns in China, Alibaba started e-commerce using a good part of the Amazon model. From there the diffusion of e-commerce in developing countries proceeded rapidly (from a low base) in the 2000s and 2010s. As noted above, it was accelerated with the COVID shock. These new firms could adopt technology that was already on the shelf, already in the form of software and hardware ready to be applied.

Second, e-commerce spread due to organizational innovations. E-commerce firms bought or started brick and mortar supermarket chains (like Amazon buying Whole Foods) to enter fresh food sales. Supermarket chains bought or started e-commerce (like Walmart buying Flipkart in India). E-commerce firms competed with supermarkets for e-commerce, thus propelling rapid diffusion. Startups grew and were acquired, thus multinationalizing, as Alibaba bought Lazada in Southeast Asia. FDI was crucial to the process, as it had been in the supermarket revolution.

Third, as in the supermarket revolution, e-commerce operators, whether "pure" or amalgams with physical stores, realized that a key component of the business was fulfillment of orders and delivery to consumers. The larger firms could "make," but many others had to "buy" this service. Crucial then was the co-pivoting of delivery intermediaries, such as Instacart, that created symbiotic relationships (Reardon et al 2021c). We turn to that next.

1.3.2   Symbiotic Supply Chains: Delivery-Intermediaries and 3PLS Co-Pivoting with Retailers/E-Commerce

Several lines of business innovation emerged over the past decade and accelerated with COVID-19. First, delivery intermediaries have been crucial partners in symbiotic relationships (similar to the role specialized/dedicated wholesalers played upstream in the supermarket revolution but these intermediaries play downstream between the retail and consumer). Reardon et al. (2021b) write:

> "Delivery intermediaries" . . . offer a range of services from intermediation itself (representing the retailer to the consumer) to assembling the functional elements of the transaction (communication, payment, logistics, sometimes credit and advertising and value-added such as packing). These services are thus outsourced by the retailer to the delivery intermediary. The delivery intermediary provides an app that handles an order from a customer to a client store (a supermarket or a small shop), restaurant, or an e-commerce distribution center, and the delivery intermediary processes the payment and arranges delivery. The payment function may rely on partnering with an e-payment firm; the delivery may rely on partnering with a logistics firm such as Uber or DHL (12).

> Second, as in the supermarket revolution, 3PLS co-pivoting has been crucial to the diffusion of e-commerce. For example, passenger logistics firms like Bykea in Pakistan and Uber in India added food delivery dur-

ing COVID-19 and maintain it after. Rapid delivery services like Getir in Turkey have set up divisions to help small retailers with e-commerce apps as well as logistics for hyper local delivery.

1.4   Conclusions

We focused in this paper on showing how rapid transformation of developing country food systems has been based on fundamental innovation and pivoting by firms like retailers and processors to adapt to long-term challenges like high transaction costs, and short-term shocks like COVID-19.

Moreover, we showed that that pivoting was necessary but not sufficient. It was crucial that symbiotic supply chains adapted and co-pivoted with the retailers and processors to enable the overall set of innovations and resilience. Important players in this were specialized/dedicated wholesalers, delivery intermediaries, and 3PLS. More research on the economics of the latter segments is a crucial agenda.

The diffusion of these growth and resilience strategies over firms and supply chains is a function of inter-firm, inter-spatial, and inter-temporal heterogeneity. We have painted this with broad brush strokes in this short paper, with elements of theory and examples. Much more work needs to be done to understand the resilience mechanisms of supply chain actors and their consequences for agri-food industrial organization. Macchiavello, Reardon, and Richards (2022), Zilberman et al. (2022), and Barrett et al. (2022) contend that a crucial agenda for such an understanding lies in more cross-pollination between empirical industrial organization economics (EIO) and food value chain transformation in developing regions.

References

Awokuse, T., and T. Reardon. 2018. "Agrifood Foreign Direct Investment and Waves of Globalization of Emerging Markets: Lessons for U.S. Firms." *Economic Review—Federal Reserve Bank of Kansas City.* Special Issue 2018: Agriculture in a Global Economy, October: 75–96. https://www.kansascityfed.org/~/media/files /publicat/econrev/econrevarchive/2018/si18awokusereardon.pdf.

Barrett, C.B., T. Reardon, J. Swinnen, D. Zilberman. 2022. "Agri-food Value Chain Revolutions in Low- and Middle-Income Countries." Journal of Economic Literature 60 (4): 1316–1377. https://doi.org/10.1257/jel.20201539.

Barrett, C. B., T. Reardon, J. Swinnen, and D. Zilberman. Forthcoming. "Structural Transformation and Economic Development: Insights from the Agri-food Value Chain Revolution." *Journal of Economic Literature.* https://www-aeaweb-org .proxy1.cl.msu.edu/articles?id=10.1257/jel.20201539&&from=f.

Dries, L., T. Reardon, and J. Swinnen. 2004. "The Rapid Rise of Supermarkets in Central and Eastern Europe: Implications for the Agrifood Sector and Rural Development." *Development Policy Review* 22 (5): 525–56.

Dries, L., and J. F. M. Swinnen. 2004. "Foreign Direct Investment, Vertical Integration, and Local Suppliers: Evidence from the Polish Dairy Sector." *World Development* 32 (9): 1525–44.

Dries, L., and J. F. M. Swinnen. 2010. "The Impact of Interfirm Relationships on Investment: Evidence from the Polish Dairy Sector." *Food Policy* 35 (2): 121–29.

Farina, E., and T. Reardon. 2000. "Agrifood Grades and Standards in the Extended MERCOSUR: Conditioners and Effects in the Agrifood System." *American Journal of Agricultural Economics* 82 (5): 1170–76.

Farina, E. M. M. Q., G. E. Gutman, P. J. Lavarello, R. Nunes, and T. Reardon. 2005. "Private and Public Milk Standards in Argentina and Brazil." *Food Policy* 30 (3): 302–15.

Goldman, A. 1974. "Outreach of Consumers and the Modernization of Urban Food Retailing in Developing Countries: Low Outreach Is an Important Barrier to the Establishment of a More Modern, More Economical Supermarket System in Developing Countries." *Journal of Marketing* 38 (October): 8–16. https://doi.org/10.1177/002224297403800403.

Gow, H. R., and J. F. M. Swinnen. 1998. "Up- and Downstream Restructuring, Foreign Direct Investment, and Hold-Up Problems in Agricultural Transition." *European Review of Agricultural Economics* 25 (3): 331–50. https://doi.org/10.1093/erae/25.3.331.

Henson, S., and T. Reardon. 2005. "Private Agri-Food Standards: Implications for Food Policy and the Agri-Food System." *Food Policy* 30 (3): 241–53.

Hu, D., T. Reardon, S. Rozelle, P. Timmer, and H. Wang. 2004. "The Emergence of Supermarkets with Chinese Characteristics: Challenges and Opportunities for China's Agricultural Development." *Development Policy Review* 22 (4): 557–86.

Key, N., and D. Runsten. 1999. "Contract Farming, Smallholders, and Rural Development in Latin America: The Organization of Agroprocessing Firms and the Scale of Outgrower Production." *World Development* 27 (2): 381–401.

Lu, L., and T. Reardon. 2018. "An Economic Model of the Evolution of Food Retail and Supply Chains from Traditional Shops to Supermarkets to E-commerce." *American Journal of Agricultural Economics* 100 (5): 1320–1335. https://doi.org/10.1093/ajae/aay056.

Macchiavello, R. 2022. "Relational contracts and development." Annual Review of Economics 14: 337–62. https://doi.org/10.1146/annurev-economics-051420-110722.

Macchiavello, R., T. Reardon, T. J. Richards. 2022. "Empirical industrial organization economics to analyze developing country food value chains." Annual Review of Resource Economics 41: 193–220. https://doi.org/10.1146/annurev-resource-101721-023554.

Minten, B., T. Reardon, and R. Sutradhar. 2010. "Food Prices and Modern Retail: The Case of Delhi." *World Development* 38 (12): 1775–1787.

Minten, B., and T. Reardon. 2008. "Food Prices, Quality, and Quality's Pricing in Supermarkets vs Traditional Markets in Developing Countries." *Review of Agricultural Economics* 30 (3): 480–90.

Moustier, P., T. A. Dao, A. B. Hoang, B. T. Vu, M. Figuie, and T.G.T. Phan. 2006. "Supermarkets and the Poor in Vietnam." Malica Project (Markets and Ag Linkages for Cities in Asia) and M4P (Making Markets Work Better for the Poor), Hanoi.

Natawidjaja, R., T. Reardon, and R. Hernandez. Shetty, S. with T. I. Noor, T. Perdana, E. Rasmikayati, and S. Bachri. 2007. "Horticultural Producers and Supermarket Development in Indonesia." UNPAD/MSU/World Bank. World Bank Report No. 38543. Indonesia: World Bank.

Phan, T. G. T., and T. Reardon. 2007. "Urban Consumer Preferences for Poultry from Supermarkets versus Traditional Retailers in the Era of Avian Influenza in Ho Chi Minh City, Vietnam." Report to USAID and Paper published in the FAO/MARD Proceedings of the Workshop. 'The Future of Poultry Farmers in Vietnam after Highly Pathogenic Avian Influenza', March. Hanoi.

Pingali, P. 2007. "Westernization of Asian Diets and the Transformation of Food Systems: Implications for Research and Policy." *Food Policy* 32: 281–98.

Popkin, B. M., and T. Reardon. 2018. "Obesity and the Food System Transformation in Latin America." *Obesity Reviews* 19 (8): 1028–1064. https://doi.org/10.1111/obr.12694.

Posri, W., and S. Chadbunchachai. 2006. "Consumer Attitudes towards and Willingness to Pay For Pesticide Residue Limit Compliant 'Safe' Vegetables in Northeast Thailand." *Journal of International Food and Agribusiness Marketing* 19 (1): 81–101.

Reardon, T., C. B. Barrett, J. A. Berdegué, and J. Swinnen. 2009. "Agrifood Industry Transformation and Farmers in Developing Countries." *World Development* 37 (11): 1717–1727.

Reardon, T., and J. A. Berdegué. 2002. "The Rapid Rise of Supermarkets in Latin America: Challenges and Opportunities for Development." *Development Policy Review* 20 (4): 317–34.

Reardon, T., K. Z. Chen, B. Minten, and L. Adriano. 2012b. *The Quiet Revolution in Staple Food Value Chains in Asia: Enter the Dragon, the Elephant, and the Tiger*. Asian Development Bank and IFPRI, December.

Reardon, T., J-M. Codron, L. Busch, J. Bingen, and C. Harris. 1999. "Global Change in Agrifood Grades and Standards: Agribusiness Strategic Responses in Developing Countries." *International Food and Agribusiness Management Review* 2 (3/4): 421–35.

Reardon, T., S. Henson, and J. Berdegué. 2007. "'Proactive Fast-Tracking' Diffusion of Supermarkets in Developing Countries: Implications for Market Institutions and Trade." *Journal of Economic Geography* 7 (4): 1–33.

Reardon, T., S. Henson, A. Gulati. 2010. "Links between supermarkets and food prices, diet diversity and food safety in developing countries." Chapter 7 in Trade, food, diet and health: Perspectives and policy options, edited by C. Hawkes, C. Blouin, S. Henson, N. Drager, L. Dubé. Oxford: John Wiley & Sons.

Reardon, T., C. P. Timmer, and B. Minten. 2012. "The Supermarket Revolution in Asia and Emerging Development Strategies to Include Small Farmers." *PNAS: Proceedings of the National Academy of Science of the USA* 109 (31): 12332–12337.

Reardon, T., C. P. Timmer, C. B. Barrett, and J. Berdegue. 2003. "The Rise of Supermarkets in Africa, Asia, and Latin America." *American Journal of Agricultural Economics* 85 (5): 1140–146.

Reardon, T., R. Echeverría, J. Berdegué, B. Minten, S. Liverpool-Tasie, D. Tschirley, and D. Zilberman. 2019. "Rapid Transformation of Food Systems in Developing Regions: Highlighting the Role of Agricultural Research and Innovations." *Agricultural Systems* 172 (June): 47–59. https://doi.org/10.1016/j.agsy.2018.01.022.

Reardon, T., and J. Swinnen. 2020. "COVID-19 and Resilience Innovations in Food Supply Chains." In *COVID-19 & Global Food Security*, edited by J. Swinnen and J. McDermott, 132–36. Washington, DC: IFPRI. https://doi.org/10.2499/p15738coll2.133762_30 https://ebrary.ifpri.org/utils/getfile/collection/p15738coll2/id/133762/filename/133971.pdf.

Reardon, T., and J. F. M. Swinnen. 2004. "Agrifood Sector Liberalization and the Rise of Supermarkets in Former State-Controlled Economies: A Comparative Overview." *Development Policy Review* 22 (5): 515–23.

Reardon, T., and C. P. Timmer. 2007. "Transformation of Markets for Agricultural Output in Developing Countries since 1950: How Has Thinking Changed?" In *Handbook of Agricultural Economics. Vol. 3: Agricultural Development: Farmers, Farm Production and Farm Markets*, edited by R. E. Evenson and P. Pingali, 2808–2855. Amsterdam: Elsevier.

Reardon, T., A. Heiman, L. Lu, C. S. R. Nuthalapati, R. Vos, and D. Zilberman. 2021c. "'Pivoting' By Food Industry Firms To Cope With COVID-19 in Developing Regions: E-commerce and 'Co-pivoting' Delivery-Intermediaries." *Agricultural Economics* 52 (3), June. https://doi.org/10.1111/agec.12631.

Reardon, T., B. Belton, L. S. O. Liverpool-Tasie, L. Lu, C. S. R. Nuthalapati, O. Tasie, and D. Zilberman. 2021b. "E-Commerce's Fast-Tracking Diffusion and Adaptation in Developing Countries." *Applied Economic Perspectives and Policy*. March 2. https://doi.org/10.1002/aepp.13160.

Reardon, T., and C. P. Timmer. 2012. "The Economics of the Food System Revolution." *Annual Review of Resource Economics* 4: 225–64.

Reardon, T., D. Tschirley, L.S.O. Liverpool-Tasie, T. Awokuse, J. Fanzo, B. Minten, R. Vos, M. Dolislager, C. Sauer, R. Dhar, C. Vargas, A. Lartey, A. Raza, and B. M. Popkin 2021a. "The Processed Food Revolution in African Food Systems and the Double Burden of Malnutrition." *Global Food Security* 28: 100466. https://doi.org/10.1016/j.gfs.2020.100466.

Swinnen, J. F. M. 2007. *Global Supply Chains, Standards and the Poor: How the Globalization of Food Systems and Standards Affects Rural Development and Poverty*. Wallingford, Oxon, UK: CABI Press.

Traill, W. B. 2006. "The Rapid Rise of Supermarkets?" *Development Policy Review* 24 (2): 163–74. https://doi.org/10.1111/j.1467-7679.2006.00320.x.

Vardhan, V. 2020. "Impact of the COVID-19 Pandemic on Retailing in Emerging Countries." Powerpoint presentation published by Euromonitor International, October.

Yang, G., and R. Wang. 2013. "The Institutionalization of an Electronic Marketplace in China. 1998–2010." *Journal of Product Innovation Management* 30 (1): 96–109.

Zhang, X. 2005. "Chinese Consumers' Concerns about Food Safety: Case of Tianjin." *Journal of International Food and Agribusiness Marketing* 17 (1): 57–69.

Zilberman, D., L. Lu, and T. Reardon. 2019. "Innovation-Induced Food Supply Chain Design." *Food Policy* 83: 289–97. http://dx.doi.org/10.1016/j.foodpol.2017.03.010.

Zilberman, D., T. Reardon, J. Silver, L. Lu, A. Heiman. 2022. "From the Lab to the Consumer: Innovation, Supply Chain, and Adoption with Applications to Natural Resources." Proceedings of the National Academy of Science of the USA (PNAS). 119(23)e2115880119. Published online June1. https://doi.org/10.1073/pnas.2115880119.

2

Global Agricultural Value Chains and Structural Transformation

Sunghun Lim

2.1 Introduction

Global value chains (GVCs) have changed the nature of production around the world. Historically, firms produced goods from start to finish in one country, and countries traded finished goods with other countries. Nowadays, however, it is uncommon for international trade transactions to be based on the exchange of finished goods. Rather, sales of individual components of products and value-added intermediate services dominate most of what is being traded, and over 70 percent of today's international trade involves GVCs wherein services, raw materials, parts, and components cross borders—often numerous times. Once those services, raw materials, parts, and components are incorporated into final products, those final products are shipped to consumers all over the world. As a result, "Made in" labels have become symbols of a bygone era because the disintegration of production processes across borders has gradually spread in the modern economy (Antràs 2016).

Sunghun Lim is an assistant professor of International Agricultural Trade in the Department of Agricultural Economics and Agribusiness at Louisiana State University.

I thank Marc F. Bellemare, Pol Antràs, David Zilberman, and Davide Del Prete for helpful suggestions which made for a much improved manuscript. I also thank the conference participants at the NBER Conference on Risks in Agricultural Supply Chains as well as the FAO Trade and Markets Division International Workshop, the Federal Reserve Bank of Kansas City, the Royal Economic Society, European Association of Agricultural Economists, Agricultural Economic Society, PacDev, and the Agricultural Applied Economics Association for comments. Any remaining errors are the author's responsibility. For acknowledgments, sources of research support, and disclosure of the author's material financial relationships, if any, please see https://www.nber.org/books-and-chapters/risks-agricultural-supply-chains/global -agricultural-value-chains-and-structural-transformation.

In modern production, a single finished product often results from a multi-national supply chain wherein each step in the process adds value to the final product—a so-called global value chain. Global value chain refers to the sequence of dispersed activities in several countries involved in transforming raw materials into final consumer products, including production, marketing, distribution, and support to the end users (Gereffi and Fernandez-Stark 2011). In other words, a GVC is a sequence of all functional activities required in the process of value creation by more than one country.

Since the mid-1900s, agricultural GVCs (hereafter AGVCs) have grown rapidly. From the 1950s to the 1980s, agricultural industries were in a period of pre-globalization, shifting from traditional, small-scale, and informal to larger-scale, more formal industries. Since the early 1990s, when trade liberalization expanded with China's emergence as a major participant in world trade, countries have modernized their agricultural GVCs (Reardon et al. 2009). Moreover, through rapid vertical integration, leading global grocery processors and retailers have emerged as dominant players in AGVCs by linking farmers upstream with customers downstream (Sexton 2013).

Here I investigate how AGVC participation transforms the structure of agrarian economies. Since Kuznets and Murphy (1966), structural transformation—wherein a country reallocates its economic activities from the agricultural sector to the manufacturing and services sectors— has received a lot of attention in policy debates surrounding economic growth in both developed and developing countries. Although the rise of GVCs has changed modern agricultural production systems, it is unclear whether and how the rise of AGVCs has affected the economic structure of participating countries (Barrett et al. 2019). One scenario is that countries allocate more economic resources to the agricultural sector from the non-agricultural sector because more AGVC participation might increase agrarian export volume by adding value in supply chains. A second scenario is that countries reallocate economic resources from the agricultural sector to non-agricultural sectors such as manufacturing or services. This scenario is often supported by the view that some countries outsource agricultural production from other countries and focus more on food processing and labeling in downstream value chains.

I begin by assessing whether AGVC participation affects structural transformation at the country level. To do so, I use data on 155 countries over the period 1991–2015 to look specifically at whether participation in AGVCs changes the GDP and employment shares of the agricultural, manufacturing, and services sectors. In order to measure AGVC participation at the country level, I first apply the bilateral gross exports decomposition method developed recently by Wang et al. (2017) to the EORA multi-region input-output tables. I then rely on country and year fixed effects to look at whether AGVC participation is associated with changes in the GDP and employment shares of each sector.

I find that, on average, in the response to greater AGVC participation, a country tends to become more agrarian. Both GDP share and employment share in the agricultural sector are positively associated with an increase in AGVC participation. However, individual countries also tend to become less industrial and more services-based. Both GDP and employment shares in manufacturing decrease as the country increases its participation in AGVCs, while in the services sector more participation in AGVCs is positively and significantly associated with the GDP share and the employment share. These findings suggest that modern agrarian economies are leapfrogging the manufacturing sector to directly develop their services sector through greater participation in AGVCs. This result runs counter to conventional wisdom about structural transformation. In examining the heterogeneous effects of AGVC participation, I find that the core results of structural transformation appear to be driven by high-income countries.

I further analyze whether positioning in AGVCs matters for structural transformation. After decomposing the total AGVC participation into upstream participation and downstream participation in AGVCs, I find that the core leapfrogging result remains robust both upstream and downstream. However, when GDP shares are the outcomes under consideration, upstream participation in AGVCs is associated with a more agrarian economy; when employment shares are the outcomes, downstream participation in AGVCs is associated with a more agrarian economy. This finding implies that upstream (downstream) participation leads to more labor- (capital-) intensive agriculture.

The contribution of this study is threefold. First, it contributes broadly to the literature on the consequences of trade liberalization. Since the late 1940s, world trade has rapidly liberalized, along with successive rounds of trade negotiation by the General Agreement on Tariffs and Trade (GATT) and its successor, the World Trade Organization (WTO). Unlike the manufacturing and services sectors, the agricultural sector tends to be heavily protected by national agricultural policies in many developing countries (Reardon and Timmer 2007; Sheldon, Chow, and McGuire 2018). By providing evidence that trade liberalization via AGVCs transforms the structure of economies, this study sheds light on the importance of AGVC for economic development.

This work also contributes more directly to the literature on agricultural value chains by looking at the relationship between agricultural trade and agricultural value chains. In the literature, numerous studies have studied the effects of participation in agricultural value chains by rural households, which stand at the very beginning of those value chains, on a myriad of economic outcomes such as income, food security, and productivity (Mergenthaler, Weinberger, and Qaim 2009; Minten, Randrianarison, and Swinnen 2009; Bellemare 2012; Cattaneo et al. 2013; Montalbano, Pietrelli, and Salvatici 2018). Although that literature is abundant, there are few empirical studies looking at the effect of participation in agricultural GVCs from the other end of agricultural value chains, viz. international trade (Balié et al. 2019a). This is because conventional trade data do not accurately present the extent of GVC participation, and measuring the extent of GVCs is in itself challenging (Koopman, Wang, and Wei 2014). The new method developed by Wang et al. (2017) combined with newly released multi-regional input-output (MRIO) data produces empirical evidence that can deepen our understanding of the relationship between agricultural value chains and trade from a global perspective.

Lastly, this study contributes to the literature on structural transformation by documenting that modern economies can transform their economies by going directly from agriculture to services via AGVCs. In the early literature, structural transformation was regarded as the key channel toward sustainable growth (Kuznets and Murphy 1966; Syrquin 1988). As economies developed, poor countries would reallocate their economic activities from agriculture to manufacturing and then services to attain higher levels of productivity, and historically that is how rich countries saw their economies evolve (Rogerson 2008). As a result, manufacturing was prioritized as a key driver of structural transformation in poor agrarian countries (e.g., East Asia in the 1980s). More recent studies, however, provide evidence that the conventional structural transformation narrative has been less common for developing economies over the last two decades (Diao, McMillan, and Rodrik 2019; Newfarmer, Page, and Tarp 2019). With the rise of GVCs, many developing countries need to make more complex decisions about whether to prioritize manufacturing or to attempt to leapfrog manufacturing and go straight to services, which influences those countries' agricultural policies (Dasgupta and Singh 2007; Rodrik 2016). While numerous studies have discussed this new paradigm of structural transformation, few studies empirically show what drives the leapfrogging. The empirical findings here illustrate that.

The rest of the paper is organized as follows. Section 2.2 presents the data and discusses the descriptive statistics. Section 2.3 presents the empirical framework and the estimation results of the effects of AGVC participation on structural transformation. Section 2.4 assesses whether and how positioning in AGVCs is associated with structural transformation. Section 2.5 further explores the heterogeneous effects of AGVC participation by countries' income level and Section 2.6 concludes with policy implications.

2.2   Data and Descriptive Statistics

2.2.1   Agricultural Global Value Chains

In the trade literature, there have been two barriers to mapping GVCs. First, unlike conventional trade data that account for the final product transaction, measuring GVCs requires industry-level data, which enable one to track all value-added activities by the industry or country involved in global production. National accounts data (e.g., gross import or export of final products) are not suitable for measuring GVCs because those data lack information on the value added of intermediate input transactions. National input-output account data that describe value-chain linkages across industries can be considered as an alternative, but they only include value-added transactions within a country, not across countries (Johnson 2018). In contrast, a multi-country, input-output table that combines the national input-output tables of various countries at a given point in time provides a comprehensive map of international transactions of goods and services (Inomata 2017). Second, there is lack of agreement on a uniform way to measure GVCs. Researchers have struggled to conceptually define what types of value-added activities should be included (Hummels, Ishii, and Yi 2001; Johnson and Noguera 2012; Johnson 2018). International trade in value-added goods and services has become more complicated to track because GVC flows are heterogeneous, varying by commodity and by industry. As a result, decomposition of gross exports into various sources of value added is methodologically challenging.

To overcome these difficulties, I employ the EORA Multi-Region Input-Output ables (MRIOs) generated by the UNCTAD-Eora Global Value Chain database, to measure AGVC participation by adopting the new analytical conceptual framework proposed by Borin and Mancini (2019).[1] The framework captures all complicated sources of value-added activities across more than two countries, which are often missing in other measures of GVCs. It also provides an empirical method to extract value-added exports from gross exports, which enables users to identify each value-added activity by using cross-country input-output data.

Following the extensive literature on GVCs (Koopman, Wang, and Wei 2014; Los and Timmer 2018; Wang et al. 2017; Belotti, Borin, and Mancini 2020), I decompose gross exports into three broad value-added activities. First, domestic value added (DVA) refers to the value of exports that is created by domestic production factors and contributes to gross domestic product (GDP) for each country. Second, foreign value added (FVA) is the value of exports that originates from imported inputs. FVA is considered a component of backward GVC participation (downstream). Lastly, domestic value added embedded in other countries' exports (DVX) refers to the domestic value added in intermediate goods that are further re-exported by the partner country. DVX is considered a component of forward GVC participation (upstream).

---

1. For similar analytical frameworks that have been developed to measure supply and demand contributions of countries and sectors in GVCs, see Koopman, Wang, and Wei (2014); Los and Timmer (2018); Wang et al. (2017).

To measure GVC participation (D_{it}) for country i in year t, I follow Borin and Mancini (2019):

(1) $$GVC\ Participation_{it} = \frac{DVX_{it} + FVA_{it}}{Gross\ Export_{it}}.$$

Similarly, upstream participation is measured by $DVX_{it}/Gross\ Exports_{it}$ and downstream participation is measured by $DVX_{it}/Gross\ Exports_{it}$.

To calculate total AGVC participation, I use the *agriculture* industry classification to measure agricultural GVCs and the *food & beverage* industry classification to measure food GVCs, respectively. The total AGVC participation is therefore defined as

(2) $$AGVC\ participation_{it}^{Total} = \frac{DVX_{it}^{agr} + DVX_{it}^{food} + FVA_{it}^{agr} + FVA_{it}^{food}}{Gross\ Export_{it}^{agr} + Gross\ Export_{it}^{food}}.$$

Using the general cross-country input-output table from the UNCTAD-Eora Global Value Chain database, I measure country-level GVC participation for 155 countries in the period 1991–2015. Specifically, I generate AGVC participation, foreign value added (FVA), and domestic value added first exported then returned home (DVX) for the agriculture industry and the food industry, respectively, by a STATA command of *icio* following Belotti, Borin, and Mancini (2020).

Table 2.1 reports summary statistics of AGVC participation for 155 countries in the period 1991–2015. Across countries, the mean total AGVC participation was 31.7 percent; agricultural GVC participation (33.2 percent) was slightly larger than food GVC participation (30.9 percent). Total AGVC participation is almost equally distributed between downstream (15.67 percent) and upstream (16.09 percent). However, in decomposing AGVC participation into agriculture and food industries, I find upstream participation (22.29 percent) is approximately twice as great as downstream participation (10.91 percent) in agriculture, while downstream participation (19.28 percent) in the food industry is 1.6 times greater than upstream participation (11.62 percent). In other words, GVCs in food and beverages likely have a larger share of backward linkages in production and relatively fewer forward linkages because the food and beverage industry involves a higher degree of foreign value added including processing, distributing, and labeling. The different pattern of average GVC participation between the agriculture and food industries is robust across years in the period 1991–2015 (see figure 2A.1).

Figure 2.1 shows the geographical distribution of AGVC participation in the year 2015. European countries and sub-Saharan African (SSA) countries show a relatively high level of GVC participation in both the agriculture and food industries. Also, European countries are more involved in downstream participation (backward linkages), while African countries are more involved in upstream participation (forward linkages) (see figure 2.2). This

Table 2.1 Summary statistics: agri-food GVC participation (1991–2015, *N*=155 countries)

	N	Mean	S.D.	Min	Max	p25	Median	p75
Total								
AGVC participation (%)	3200	31.763	9.912	9.088	85.507	25.015	30.534	37.428
Downstream participation (FVA, %)	3200	15.671	10.132	.082	76.929	7.959	12.886	21.819
Upstream participation (DVX, %)	3200	16.091	7.47	3.578	53.649	11.06	14.79	19.894
Agricultural Industry								
AGVC participation (%)	3200	33.208	10.687	8.506	74.923	25.456	32.526	39.844
Downstream participation (FVA, %)	3200	10.913	7.51	.078	63.581	5.492	8.755	14.639
Upstream participation (DVX, %)	3200	22.296	8.303	4.149	67.814	16.602	22.388	27.178
Food Industry								
AGVC participation (%)	3200	30.91	10.273	9.693	87.333	23.474	29.544	36.639
Downstream participation (FVA, %)	3200	19.288	10.508	.133	80.974	11.458	16.827	25.16
Upstream participation (DVX, %)	3200	11.621	5.894	2.394	41.82	7.588	10.465	14.395

Note: Data source from the UNCTAD-Eora Global Value Chain (GVC) database. GVC is measured by a GVC share of a country's gross exports following Koopman, Wang, and Wei (2014). Downstream participation is measured by the foreign value added (FVA); upstream participation is measured by the domestic value added (DVX). "*Total*" includes both agricultural industry and food industry by calculating

$$TotalAGVCparticipation = \frac{DVX_{agr} + DVX_{food} + FVA_{agr} + FVA_{food}}{GrossExport_{agr} + GrossExport_{food}}.$$

(a) Agriculture sector

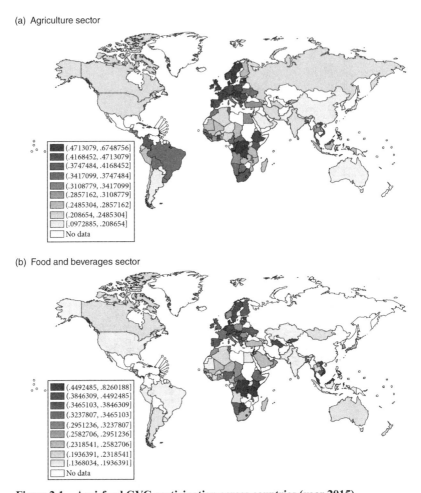

(b) Food and beverages sector

Figure 2.1   Agri-food GVC participation across countries (year 2015)

Note: GVC participation rates in 2015. Panels (a) and (b) display GVC participation rate across countries in agriculture sector and food and beverages sector, respectively.

AGVC participation pattern is likely to be driven by increasing demand from Europe for raw commodities produced in SSA in order to produce more processed food in Europe (Balié et al. 2019a,b; Feyaerts, Van den Broeck, and Maertens 2020).

In table 2A.1, I further provide summary statistics of AGVC participation by income level. Following the World Bank classification, I calculate total AGVC participation, downstream participation, and upstream participation for four income groups: low, lower-middle, upper-middle, and

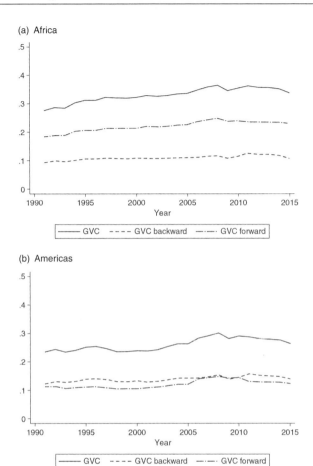

Figure 2.2   Agricultural GVC participation by region (1991–2015)

Note: For individual regions, I use the UN Standard Country Codes for Statistical Use (Series M, No. 49), a standard for area codes used by the United Nations for statistical purposes. Africa (Northern African, Sub-Saharan Africa); Americas (Northern America, Latin America and the Caribbean); Asia (Eastern Asia, Southern Asia, South-eastern Asia, Central Asia, Western Asia); Europe (Southern Europe, Eastern Europe including Northern Asia, Western Europe). Oceania (four countries) is excluded from the analysis.

high income.[2] I find three stylized facts: First, high-income countries' total AGVC participation (37.12 percent) is about 20 percent greater than that of relatively low-income countries. Second, as countries' income increases, downstream participation increases and upstream participation decreases.

2. The World Bank classifies economies for analytical purposes into four income groups by using gross national income (GNI) per capita data in US$ at year 2010: low income (≤ 1,005); lower middle income (1,006–3,975); upper middle income (3,976–12,275); high income (> 12,275).

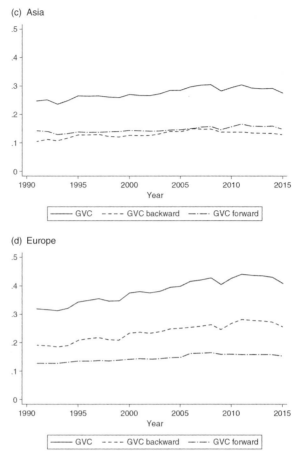

Figure 2.2   (continued)

Third, relatively low-income countries participate more in the upstream agriculture industry than relatively higher-income countries, while relatively high-income countries participate more in the downstream food industry than relatively low-income countries.

2.2.2   Structural Transformation

The structural transformation of countries involves a variety of features. Following Timmer (2009), structural transformation is characterized within a country by the following economic changes: (i) a falling share of agriculture in economic output and employment, (ii) a rising share of urban economic activity in industry or services, (iii) migration from rural to urban areas, (iv) a demographic transition from high birth rates to low death rates, and (v) declining female labor market participation in agriculture and rising female labor market participation in services.

In the growth and development literature, three measures of national economic activity by sectors (agriculture, manufacturing, and services) have been widely used: (i) GDP shares, (ii) employment shares, and (iii) final consumption shares (Herrendorf, Rogerson, and Valentinyi 2014). For instance, one can measure structural transformation in a country by looking at whether the share of agricultural activities decreases while the share of non-agricultural activities increases over the years.

I use GDP shares of agriculture, manufacturing, and services in each country as the main measure of structural transformation. To perform robustness checks, I use employment share by sector. I exclude final consumption shares as an alternative measure of structural transformation, however, for two reasons: First, it is difficult to obtain credible expenditure estimates for numerous developing countries (Ravallion 2001). Second, measuring final consumption in the services sector has been proven to be perpetually challenging, and estimates are believed to be low, in both developing and developed countries (Landefeld, Seskin, and Fraumeni 2008). Thus, the measure of structural transformation is limited to production.

I use the World Development Indicators (WDI) database for GDP and employment shares in the agriculture, manufacturing, and services sectors, respectively.[3] Table 2.2 reports GDP and employment shares by sectors for 155 countries from 1991 to 2015. Panel A shows that, on average, countries' GDP and employment shares in the agriculture sector decrease while GDP and employment shares in the services sector increase. In Panel B, we see that the economies of relatively high-income countries are more concentrated in the services sector and that relatively low-income countries focus their economic activities in the agriculture sector.

2.2.3 Other Control Variables

To account for potential confounders, I include a broad set of country-level demographic, socioeconomic, and trade covariates, guided by the considerable empirical literature on determinants of structural transformation. To control for demographics, I include population share by age group and gender. To control for urbanization (Michaels, Rauch, and Redding 2012), I also include both rural and urban population shares. To control for differences in economic composition across countries, I include GDP, GDP growth, net trade proportion of GDP, inflation GDP deflator, proportion

---

3. The agriculture sector corresponds to ISIC divisions 1–5, which include forestry, hunting, and fishing, as well as cultivation of crops and livestock production. Industry corresponds to ISIC divisions 10–45 including value added in mining, manufacturing, construction, electricity, water, and gas. Services correspond to ISIC divisions 50–99 including value added in wholesale and retail trade, transport, and government, financial, professional, and personal services such as education, health care, and real estate services.

Table 2.2   **Summary statistics: employment and GDP share by sector (N=155 countries)**

	N	Employment Share (%)				GDP Share (%)			
		Mean	S.D.	Min	Max	Mean	S.D.	Min	Max
Panel A: By time period									
1995–2002									
Agriculture sector (%)	3036	31.36	24.8	.22	92.37	14.21	12.66	.09	79.04
Manufacturing sector (%)	3036	20.74	9.06	1.86	43.13	27.98	10.29	3.24	84.8
Services sector (%)	3036	47.9	18.41	5.36	83.96	50.64	11.81	10.57	85.61
2003–2009									
Agriculture sector (%)	2844	27.85	23.63	.18	90.93	11.51	11.75	.05	72.24
Manufacturing sector (%)	2844	20.18	8.09	1.95	40.53	28.41	11.99	4.15	74.11
Services sector (%)	2844	51.97	18.18	6.66	86.62	52.61	11.67	20.76	90.29
2010–2015									
Agriculture sector (%)	2589	25.84	22.53	.19	88.22	10.98	11.13	.05	58.65
Manufacturing sector (%)	2589	19.74	7.87	2.06	54.14	27.75	12.25	4.56	74.81
Services sector (%)	2589	54.42	18.05	8.77	87.91	53.52	11.86	25.63	91.92
Panel B: By Income-level, 1995–2015									
Low Income									
Agriculture sector (%)	1674	64.73	16.93	29.31	92.37	31.92	10.55	14.06	79.04
Manufacturing sector (%)	1674	9.37	5.72	1.86	31.55	20.22	6.75	3.24	45.98
Services sector (%)	1674	25.9	12.96	5.34	62.41	42	8.76	12.44	67.59
Lower-Middle Income									
Agriculture sector (%)	2565	39.92	15.22	8.66	86.82	16.93	8.21	3.76	51.85
Manufacturing sector (%)	2565	18.22	6.25	2.8	38.3	30.28	11.2	14.16	84.8
Services sector (%)	2565	41.86	11.39	10.39	66.5	46.56	9.69	10.57	72.59
Upper-Middle Income									
Agriculture sector (%)	2685	21.3	12.04	.26	59.7	7.89	4.62	1.83	36.41
Manufacturing sector (%)	2685	23.33	6.17	9.44	40.29	31.16	9.78	8.41	66.16
Services sector (%)	2685	55.38	11.18	18.9	78.8	53.24	9.34	21.76	75.41
High Income									
Agriculture sector (%)	2676	5.23	3.92	.18	22.88	2.3	1.45	.05	7.98
Manufacturing sector (%)	2676	25.9	6.73	9.19	54.14	28.11	12.64	6.72	74.81
Services sector (%)	2676	68.87	8.72	43.99	87.91	60.94	10.47	25.25	91.92

Note: The World Bank defines four income categories based on GNI per capita in US$ in the year 2010: low income (≤ 1,005); lower middle income (1,006–3,975); upper middle income (3,976–12,275); high income (> 12,275). GDP and employment share data are sourced from the World Development Indicator database.

of export/import of goods and services, and self-employed rate. To control for differences in agricultural production across countries, I further include a subset of agrarian covariates, including land area (agricultural land area, arable land, land under cereal production) and agricultural production by commodity (cereal, fisheries, livestock, and food). For all of these variables, I use the WDI database at the country level from 1991 to 2015.

Combining these covariates, I further control for differences in trade activities across countries. Using Mario Larch's Regional Trade Agreements Database, I include a subset of trade agreement variables—regional trade agreement (RTA), customs union (CU), free trade agreement (FTA), partial scope agreement (PTA), and economic integration agreement (EIA)—in the form of the numbers of each agreement and binary variables for each country in a year.[4] Table 2A.2 displays the list of all time-varying control variables in the sample.

2.3   AGVC Participation and Structural Transformation

In section 2.3.1, I present the preferred empirical specification based on standard linear regression methods with country and year fixed effects. I next discuss the identification strategy by explaining how the empirical approach addresses the main sources of endogeneity in section 2.3.2. In section 2.3.3, I discuss the core estimation results.

2.3.1   Baseline Regression Model

The equation of interest is

$$(3) \qquad y_{it} = \alpha + \beta AGVC_{it} + X_{it}\delta + \gamma_i + \mu_t + \varepsilon_{it},$$

where y_{it} is a sector share (agriculture, manufacturing, or services) for country i in year t. This is a percentage outcome, taking on a value between 0 and 100; D_{it} is the treatment variable (i.e., the level of participation in agricultural GVCs of country i in year t); X_{it} denotes time-varying control variables; γ_i denotes a vector of country fixed effects; $\mu\alpha_t$ denotes a vector of year fixed effects. λ_i is a country-specific time trend and it is an error term with mean zero. I estimate equation 3 using ordinary least squares.

Country fixed effects (γ_i) are included to control for time invariant unobserved heterogeneity within each country i. Year fixed effects (μ_t) control for all the country-invariant unobserved heterogeneity within each year. I cluster the standard errors by country following the recommendations in Abadie et al. (2017). The goal in this study is to estimate β to show the effect of participation in agricultural GVCs on structural transformation by testing the null hypothesis H_0: $\beta = 0$ versus the alternative hypothesis H_A: $\beta \neq 0$.

2.3.2   Endogeneity Issues

Because the extent of GVCs participation by a country is not randomly assigned, and therefore the treatment is not exogenous to structural transformation measured in GDP shares by sector, it is important to discuss potential threats to identification. I discuss the identification strategy by addressing three broad sources of endogeneity: unobserved heterogeneity, measurement error, and reverse causality.

---

4. Mario Larch's Regional Trade Agreements Database includes all multilateral and bilateral regional trade agreements as notified to the World Trade Organization (WTO) from 1950 to 2019 (Egger and Larch 2008). See https://www.ewf.uni-bayreuth.de/en/research/RTA-data /index.html.

2.3.2.1   Unobserved Heterogeneity

To properly identify the average treatment effect, a linear regression should include all potential confounders—i.e., all of the variables that cause both the outcome and the treatment. Although it is generally not feasible to account for all omitted variables, in many cases it is important to identify and include potential unobserved confounders.

In the empirical framework, multiple tactics are deployed to minimize unobserved heterogeneity. First, the country fixed effects used in the baseline specification are expected to control for the time-invariant factors in each country. The time-invariant factors include country-specific geographical conditions and socio-cultural backgrounds, such as language or history, which have been deemed determinants of trade volumes or economic growth. Country fixed effects also control for initial economic conditions (e.g., levels of GDP in the initial year in the panel data) in each country, which often determine the pattern of structural transformation of a country (De Vries, Timmer, and De Vries 2015; Hnatkovska, Lahiri, and Végh 2016; Bustos, Caprettini, and Ponticelli 2016). Second, year fixed effects purge the error term of its correlation with the treatment variable owing to factors that are constant across all countries in a given year. For example, progress on structural transformation might have been slowed in 2008–2009 because of the global financial crisis.

Further, I include a broad set of country-level demographic and economic covariates, guided by the considerable empirical literature on structural transformation (Michaels, Rauch, and Redding 2012; Bustos, Caprettini, and Ponticelli 2016; Duarte and Restuccia 2010; Alvarez-Cuadrado and Poschke 2011). To control for demographics, I include population shares by age group, gender, rural population, and urban population. To control for differences in economic composition across countries, I also include GDP growth, inflation GDP deflator, GDP, trade share in GDP, exports of goods and services, and self-employed share. One might be concerned that the extent of participation in agricultural GVCs is endogenous because of changes in trade policy within a country, trade competitiveness with other countries, or domestic agricultural price policy. To control for time-varying trade policy and competitiveness conditions, a vector X_{it} also contains regional trade agreements, customs unions, free trade agreements, partial scope agreements, and economic integration agreements. Various agricultural covariates are also included to control for time-varying production conditions.

Although most of unobserved confounders that mar the identification of the causal effect of GVC participation on the measures of structural transformation can be captured by the various means described above, the identifying assumption one needs to make in order to make a causal statement about the relationship between GVC participation and structural transformation is that whatever unobserved confounders are left do not significantly bias the estimate of β. This is an assumption that I am unwilling to make, and so for the remainder of this paper I talk about the association between GVC participation and structural transformation, and interpret the estimates as only suggestive of a causal relationship.

2.3.2.2   Measurement Error

Another source of endogeneity is measurement error, especially in fixed-effects regressions such as those used here, wherein one should avoid overly strong claims when interpreting estimates given that the data might have systematic errors, such as under- or over-reporting. In measuring the extent of GVCs, missing information on the division between intermediate and final goods can be a source of measurement error. This is because there are heterogeneous product codes in cross-border supply chains. Although there are a few trials to measure the extent of GVCs in the literature, the existing measures are still not free from the measurement error issue.

The treatment variable is the extent of agricultural GVC participation in each country, and it is measured using the recent measure developed by Wang et al. (2017). Their measure eliminates the aforementioned missing information source by decomposing value-added production activities in cross-border production. Also, it provides measures of upstream and downstream GVC participation, which show a much more detailed GVC involvement than other measures (see Antràs and Chor 2018). Thus, I rely on the proven validity of the measure of GVCs (Antràs, De Gortari, and Itskhoki 2017; Antràs and Chor 2018; Balié et al. 2019a) to obviate concerns about measurement error in the treatment variable.

Another concern is measurement error related to the measures of structural transformation. Recall that I use the GDP (or employment) share of each of the three sectors of the economy (i.e., agriculture, manufacturing, services) for each country over the years as a primary measure of structural transformation. The longitudinal data I use were assembled from the statistical offices in 155 countries. Although the estimates of GDP (or employment) shares are reliable in most developed countries, they are likely to be measured with error in many developing countries (Jerven 2013; De Vries, Timmer, and De Vries 2015). For example, in various African countries, large measurement errors in estimating GDP are due to the low quality of statistical management—a phenomenon that has been referred to as "Africa's statistical tragedy" (Devarajan 2013; Jerven and Johnston 2015).

There is no evidence, however, that GDP (or employment) shares are systematically over-or under-estimated; the measurement error I face in this case is classical measurement error, and so the estimate of β may suffer from attenuation bias. This implies that a rejection of the null hypothesis provides stronger evidence than in the absence of measurement error and that the estimate $\hat{\beta}$ is the lower bound (in absolute value) of the true coefficient of β.

Table 2.3   The effects of AGVC participation on structural transformation, total

	Structural transformation measured by GDP or employment share by sector (%)					
	Agriculture		Industry		Service	
	(1)	(2)	(3)	(4)	(5)	(6)
Panel A: GDP Share						
AGVC participation (%)	.11***	.039***	−.179***	−.338***	.003	.112***
	(.013)	(.014)	(.02)	(.023)	(.022)	(.025)
N	3200	3200	3200	3200	3200	3200
R^2	.958	.97	.95	.966	.959	.971
Panel B: Employment Share						
AGVC participation (%)	.206***	.006	−.365***	−.151***	.159***	.144***
	(.022)	(.016)	(.021)	(.019)	(.017)	(.019)
N	3200	3200	3200	3200	3200	3200
R^2	.983	.995	.895	.95	.99	.993
Country & Year FE	yes	yes	yes	yes	yes	yes
Covariates		yes		yes		yes

Note: All regression specifications include country fixed effects and year fixed effects. Country-level characteristics include population bins (by age, by gender, rural and urban population ratio), agricultural production conditions (arable land, agricultural land, total land area, food production index, livestock production index, land under cereal production, total cereal production, total fisheries production), and economic characteristics (GDP, GDP growth, inflation GDP deflator, trade proportion [%], exports of goods and services, self-employment total). Trade policy controls include the number of 5 types of trade agreements and a binary variable for each trade agreement (RTA, CU, FTA, PSA, EIA). A full list of variables included in the regression can be found in table 2A.2. Standard errors clustered at the country level are in parentheses. *** $p < 0.01$; ** $p < 0.05$, * $p < 0.1$.

2.3.2.3   Reverse Causality

The third endogeneity concern stems from reverse causality. If structural transformation leads to changes in participation in agricultural GVCs and y_{it} and D_{it} are thus jointly determined, the estimate of β would thus be biased. Structural transformation is, however, unlikely to be a dominant influence on GVC participation. Indeed, for a given country in a given year, trade activity occurs before GDP is calculated; therefore reverse causality, wherein GDP shares drive participation in agricultural GVCs, is not a concern.

2.3.3   Estimation Results

Table 2.3 reports the core results for 155 countries for the period 1991–2015. Panel 1 and panel 2 in table 2.3 present the estimation results for GDP shares and the employment shares, respectively. Estimation results for the agricultural sector, the industry sector, and the services sector are reported in columns (1)(2), (3)-(4), and (5)-(6), respectively with country and year fixed effects of equation 3. In columns (1), (3), and (5), I exclude time-varying control variables, while columns (2), (4), (6) are the full specifications as in equation 3.

Panels A and B show that, as a country's participation in AGVCs increases, that country tends to become more agrarian on average. Both GDP share and employment share in the agricultural sector are positively associated with an increase in AGVC participation. That country also tends to become less industrial. Columns (3)-(4) show that, in response to a 1 percentage point increase in the AGVC participation rate, the industry sector GDP share decrease ranges from 0.179 to 0.338. Surprisingly, the estimation results in columns (5)-(6) show that more participation in AGVCs is positively and significantly associated with the GDP share and employment share in the services-based sector.

This result points to a hollowing out of the middle of the economic structure (i.e., the industrial sector). More importantly, it points to a leapfrogging by the average economy over the industrial sector. This finding suggests that modern agrarian economies are moving directly from agriculture to developing their services sector as a consequence of greater participation in AGVCs. This core result runs counter to conventional wisdom about structural transformation.

Recall that the AGVC participation measure in this study includes two agri-food sectors (*agriculture* and *food & beverage*). To check whether the patterns of structural transformation are different in different agri-food sectors, I separate total agricultural GVCs into agriculture and food sectors and report the estimation results in table 2.4.

In all cases, the core results are robust. Increased participation in AGVCs—measured by either GDP shares or employment shares, and looking at either agriculture or the food industry—is associated with a hollowing out of the middle industrial sector of the economy. However, column (2) shows that the GDP share or employment share in the agricultural sector increases only in the agricultural industry while the effects in the food and beverage industry remain the same. This finding implies that GVC participation in the food and beverage industry leads countries more directly to structural transformation as they leapfrog the industrial sector and develop the services sector instead.

2.4   Does Positioning in AGVCs Matter for Structural Transformation?

Here I further assess whether positioning in AGVCs is associated with structural transformation. As described in section 2.2.1, downstream participation is measured by the foreign value added (FVA), while upstream participation is measured by the domestic value added (DVX). After decomposing total AGVC participation into upstream (forward linkages) and downstream (backward linkages) participation, I run the following regression similar to equation 3 to analyze whether the type of GVC participation (or positioning) matters for structural transformation:

Table 2.4   The effects of AGVC participation on structural transformation by industry

	Structural transformation measured by GDP or employment share by sector (%)					
	Agriculture		Industry		Service	
	(1)	(2)	(3)	(4)	(5)	(6)
Panel A: Agriculture Industry						
Panel A.1: GDP Share						
AGVC participation (%)	.115***	.055***	−.255***	−.315***	.046*	.095***
	(.018)	(.019)	(.023)	(.025)	(.025)	(.027)
N	3200	3200	3200	3200	3200	3200
R^2	.954	.966	.948	.962	.961	.972
Panel A.2: Employment Share						
AGVC participation (%)	.164***	.033*	−.402***	−.198***	.238***	.165***
	(.027)	(.018)	(.025)	(.02)	(.019)	(.019)
N	3200	3200	3200	3200	3200	3200
R^2	.984	.995	.886	.951	.992	.994
Panel B: Food & Beverage Industry						
Panel B.1: GDP Share						
AGVC participation (%)	.067***	.012	−.103***	−.247***	−.002	.084***
	(.009)	(.01)	(.018)	(.02)	(.019)	(.022)
N	3200	3200	3200	3200	3200	3200
R^2	.96	.974	.951	.967	.957	.97
Panel B.2: Employment Share						
AGVC participation (%)	.16***	−.006	−.265***	−.083***	.105***	.089***
	(.018)	(.014)	(.018)	(.017)	(.015)	(.017)
N	3200	3200	3200	3200	3200	3200
R^2	.981	.995	.899	.949	.989	.992
Country & Year FE	yes	yes	yes	yes	yes	yes
Covariates		yes		yes		yes

Note: All regression specifications include country fixed effects and year fixed effects. Country-level characteristics include population bins (by age, by gender, rural and urban population ratio), agricultural production conditions (arable land, agricultural land, total land area, food production index, livestock production index, land under cereal production, total cereal production, total fisheries production), and economic characteristics (GDP, GDP growth, inflation GDP deflator, trade proportion [%], exports of goods and services, self-employment total). Trade policy controls include the number of 5 types of trade agreements and a binary variable for each trade agreement (RTA, CU, FTA, PSA, EIA). A full list of variables included in the regression can be found in table 2A.2. Standard errors clustered at the country level are in parentheses. *** $p < 0.01$; ** $p < 0.05$, * $p < 0.1$

$$(4) \quad y_{it} = \alpha + \beta_1 GVC_{it}^{up} + \beta_2 GVC_{it}^{down} + X_{it}\delta + \gamma_i + \mu_t + \varepsilon_{it} ,$$

where GVC_{it}^{up} is upstream participation, as measured by DVX (%) and GVC_{it}^{down} is downstream participation, as measured by FVA (%).

Table 2.5 presents the estimation results of AGVC positioning. Panels A, B, and C report estimation results for total AGVC participation, agricul-

Table 2.5   **The effects of AGVC positioning on structural transformation**

| | Dependent variable: Structural transformation (share by sector) | | | | | |
| | GDP share (%) | | | Employment share (%) | | |
	Agr (1)	Ind (2)	Srv (3)	Agr (4)	Ind (5)	Srv (6)
Panel A: Total						
Upstream participation	3.916***	−33.867***	11.626***	1.095	−15.564***	14.458***
(DVX, %)	(1.437)	(2.272)	(2.526)	(1.597)	(1.939)	(1.89)
Downstream	2.905	−34.675***	30.424***	19.626***	−36.352***	16.717***
participation (FVA, %)	(3.362)	(5.315)	(5.909)	(3.735)	(4.535)	(4.42)
N	3200	3200	3200	3200	3200	3200
R^2	.97	.966	.971	.995	.95	.993
Panel B: Agriculture Industry						
Upstream participation	6.11***	−33.875***	4.826*	−.024	−14.954***	14.975***
(DVX, %)	(2.01)	(2.636)	(2.878)	(1.936)	(2.133)	(2.067)
Downstream	3.844	−24.664***	22.519***	12.547***	−33.292***	20.747***
participation (FVA, %)	(2.766)	(3.627)	(3.96)	(2.663)	(2.935)	(2.843)
N	3200	3200	3200	3200	3200	3200
R^2	.966	.962	.972	.995	.952	.994
Panel C: Food Industry						
Upstream participation	1.797*	−25.193***	9.324***	.58	−9.874***	9.277***
(DVX, %)	(1.054)	(2.032)	(2.251)	(1.369)	(1.767)	(1.73)
Downstream	10.434***	−31.989***	23.222***	18.783***	−33.939***	15.136***
participation (FVA, %)	(3.179)	(6.13)	(6.793)	(4.129)	(5.333)	(5.219)
N	3200	3200	3200	3200	3200	3200
R^2	.974	.967	.97	.995	.95	.992
Country & Year FE	yes	yes	yes	yes	yes	yes
Covariates	yes	yes	yes	yes	yes	yes

Note: Following Koopman, Wang, and Wei (2014), downstream participation is measured by the foreign value added (FVA); upstream participation is measured by the domestic value added (DVX). "*Total*" includes both agricultural industry and food industry by calculating

$$TotalAGVCparticipation = \frac{DVX_{agr} + DVX_{food} + FVA_{agr} + FVA_{food}}{GrossExport_{agr} + GrossExport_{food}}.$$

All regression specifications include country fixed effects and year fixed effects. Country-level characteristics include population bins (by age, by gender, rural and urban population ratio), agricultural production conditions (arable land, agricultural land, total land area, food production index, livestock production index, land under cereal production, total cereal production, total fisheries production), and economic characteristics (GDP, GDP growth, inflation GDP deflator, trade proportion [%], exports of goods and services, self-employment total). Trade policy controls include the number of 5 types of trade agreements and a binary variable for each trade agreement (RTA, CU, FTA, PSA, EIA). A full list of variables included in the regression can be found in table 2A.2. Standard errors clustered at the country level are in parentheses. *** $p < 0.01$; ** $p < 0.05$, * $p < 0.1$

tural industry, and food industry, respectively. One thing that immediately jumps out is that both upstream and downstream participation in AGVCs is associated with a leapfrogging of the industrial sector to directly develop the services sector. When considering GDP shares as outcomes, upstream participation in AGVCs is associated with a more agrarian economy. When considering employment shares as outcomes instead, it is downstream participation in AGVCs that is associated with a more agrarian economy. This finding suggests that upstream (downstream) participation leads to more labor- (capital-) intensive agriculture.

2.5   Treatment Heterogeneity by Income Level

This section examines the heterogeneous effects of AGVC participation by country income level. Following the World Bank Analytical Classifications, I use four income categories that are based on GNI per capita in US$ in 2010 (i.e., low income 1,005; lower middle income 1,006–3,975; upper middle income 3,976–12,275; high income >12,275). Table 2.6 reports the estimation results.

The estimation results in table 2.6 suggest that our average findings from the core results involve heterogeneity. Panels C and D appear to show that the core results of structural transformation in response to greater AGVC participation are driven by high-income countries. Outside of that high-income category, the findings seem to be highly dependent on the type of country considered. For example, employment shares in low-income and low-middle-income countries in particular seem to follow the conventional structural transformation narrative.

2.6   Concluding Remarks

This paper is the first to investigate the relationship between the extent of a country's participation in agricultural GVCs and the structural transformation of its economy. I have looked at the relationship between agricultural GVC participation on the one hand and at how the reallocation of economic activities affects the shares of GDP and employment in the agricultural, manufacturing, and services sectors on the other hand. Using cross-country data from 155 countries for the period 1991–2015, I find that modern economies leapfrog the manufacturing sector, choosing instead to reallocate economic activity to their agricultural and services sectors as their participation in agricultural GVCs becomes more extensive. This result is robust, and the results seem driven by high-income countries rather than by developing countries. This runs counter to conventional wisdom about structural transformation.

The findings in this study can help inform agricultural trade policy in two ways. First, policy makers may wish to focus on participation in global

Table 2.6   **The effects of AGVC participation on structural transformation by income**

	Dependent variable: Structural transformation (share by sector)					
	GDP share (%)			Employment share (%)		
	Agr (1)	Ind (2)	Srv (3)	Agr (4)	Ind (5)	Srv (6)
Panel A: Low-income countries						
AGVC	15.428	−28.038***	28.357***	−20.004***	10.133***	9.861***
Participation (%)	(11.43)	(6.707)	(10.065)	(6.147)	(3.454)	(3.359)
N	558	558	558	558	558	558
R^2	.829	.873	.753	.976	.958	.986
Panel B: Low-middle income countries						
AGVC	4.499	−46.479***	16.537***	−7.38**	1.62	5.744**
Participation (%)	(3.558)	(4.106)	(4.302)	(3.112)	(1.732)	(2.523)
N	855	855	855	855	855	855
R^2	.9	.933	.903	.983	.962	.986
Panel C: Middle-high income countries						
AGVC	15.446***	−31.863***	−20.097***	17.949***	−28.387***	10.457**
Participation (%)	(3.693)	(5.522)	(6.231)	(4.805)	(3.722)	(4.319)
N	895	895	895	895	895	895
R^2	.926	.974	.944	.992	.946	.994
Panel D: High income countries						
AGVC	5.351***	−37.379***	24.74***	8.286***	−33.785***	25.47***
Participation (%)	(.996)	(3.871)	(4.066)	(1.66)	(3.824)	(3.896)
N	892	892	892	892	892	892
R^2	.949	.964	.969	.974	.968	.978
Country & Year FE	yes	yes	yes	yes	yes	yes
Covariates	yes	yes	yes	yes	yes	yes

Note: The World Bank defines four income categories based on GNI per capita in US\$ in year 2010: low income (≤ 1,005); lower middle income (1,006–3,975); upper middle income (3,976–12,275); high income (> 12,275). GDP and employment shares data are sourced from the World Development Indicator database. All regression specifications include country fixed effects and year fixed effects. Country-level characteristics include population bins (by age, by gender, rural and urban population ratio), agricultural production conditions (arable land, agricultural land, total land area, food production index, livestock production index, land under cereal production, total cereal production, total fisheries production), and economic characteristics (GDP, GDP growth, inflation GDP deflator, trade proportion [%], exports of goods and services, self-employment total). Trade policy controls include the number of 5 types of trade agreements and a binary variable for each trade agreement (RTA, CU, FTA, PSA, EIA). A full list of variables included in the regression can be found in the table 2A.2. Standard errors clustered at the country level are in parentheses. *** $p < 0.01$; ** $p < 0.05$, * $p < 0.1$

agricultural production if their goal is to transform their economies by reallocating resources across sectors. In debates about Brexit, the redesign of the North American Free Trade Agreement, and the recent trade war between the US and China, trade policies aimed at protecting domestic agriculture from agricultural imports have featured prominently. This perspective seems to reflect a tacit expectation that GVC linkages alter the conventional calculus of trade protection (Blanchard, Bown, and Johnson 2017). The results suggest that trade liberalization through agricultural GVCs can lead to structural transformation in the same way that a country can reallocate its economic resources into non-agricultural sectors, which has been seen as a main driver of economic growth.

Second, although it may be tempting for governments to foster participation in GVCs with an eye toward structural transformation, policy makers should be cautious when trying to open up their agricultural markets. The results here suggest that a country is able to transition its economy out of agriculture when the country participates in GVCs by producing intermediate inputs related to manufacturing and services but not in the agriculture sector. Given that many poor developing countries have a competitive advantage in agriculture rather than manufacturing or service, they may be tempted to consider participating in agricultural GVCs by allocating more agricultural resources to intermediate production for export. Although doing so might result in higher overall GDP or employment, it is unlikely to transform an economy into one primarily based on manufacturing and services. Trade policies that promote manufacturing or services related to domestic activities in intermediate agricultural production can promote this transformation.

Appendix

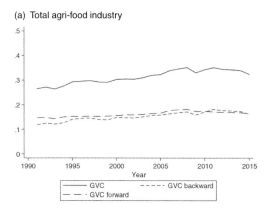

(a) Total agri-food industry

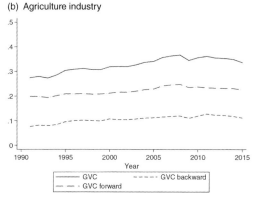

(b) Agriculture industry

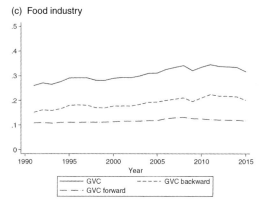

(c) Food industry

Figure 2A.1   Average GVC participation trends, 1991–2015 (%, N= 155 countries)

Note: Data are sourced from the UNCTAD-Eora Global Value Chain (GVC) database. GVC is measured by the GVC share of a country's gross exports following Koopman, Wang, and Wei (2014). Downstream participation is measured by the foreign value added (FVA); upstream participation is measured by the domestic value added (DVX). *"Total"* includes both agricultural industry and food industry by calculating

$$TotalAGVCparticipation = \frac{DVX_{agr} + DVX_{food} + FVA_{agr} + FVA_{food}}{GrossExport_{agr} + GrossExport_{food}}$$

Table 2A.1 Summary statistics: agri-food GVC participation by income level, 1991–2015

	N	Mean	S.D.	Min	Max	p25	Median	p75
Panel 1.1: Low income								
Total								
AGVC participation (%)	558	30.73	8.856	9.088	60.07	25.425	29.905	35.48
Downstream participation (%, FVA)	558	8.404	4.663	.082	32.049	5.307	7.701	10.102
Upstream participation (%, DVX)	558	22.326	8.998	4.476	48.711	17.056	21.162	27.438
Agricultural Industry								
AGVC participation (%)	558	31.304	9.726	8.506	61.866	25.298	30.632	38.423
Downstream participation (%, FVA)	558	6.123	4.041	.078	30.592	3.846	5.051	7.227
Upstream participation (%, DVX)	558	25.181	9.968	4.396	52.384	18.407	23.525	32.157
Food Industry								
AGVC participation (%)	558	30.165	8.872	13.051	57.649	23.183	29.529	35.915
Downstream participation (%, FVA)	558	14.004	6.667	.133	44.47	10.03	12.541	17.232
Upstream participation (%, DVX)	558	16.161	7.637	3.512	41.82	11.063	14.732	20.688
Panel 1.2: Lower-middle income								
Total								
AGVC participation (%)	855	29.5	7.706	13.302	53.724	23.974	29.222	33.786
Downstream participation (%, FVA)	855	11.821	7.062	2.394	45.829	6.779	9.828	15.618
Upstream participation (%, DVX)	855	17.679	7.262	4.532	40.024	11.852	17.036	21.714
Agricultural Industry								
AGVC participation (%)	855	30.784	8.545	12.769	54.559	24.141	31.641	35.852
Downstream participation (%, FVA)	855	7.535	4.56	1.507	38.494	4.967	6.185	9.09
Upstream participation (%, DVX)	855	23.248	8.048	8.198	42.729	16.142	23.51	28.532
Food Industry								
AGVC participation (%)	855	28.05	7.883	13.68	55.956	22.504	26.495	32.549
Downstream participation (%, FVA)	855	15.634	7.977	3.98	50.742	9.781	13.384	20.616
Upstream participation (%, DVX)	855	12.416	5.7	3.338	28.888	7.249	11.811	16.434

Panel 1.3: Upper-middle income
Total

AGVC participation (%)	895	29.221	9.203	11.909	66.022	22.398	27.895	34.54
Downstream participation (%, FVA)	895	15.414	8.539	2.899	45.995	8.916	12.623	21.373
Upstream participation (%, DVX)	895	13.807	6.206	3.928	53.649	9.817	12.475	16.88
Agricultural Industry								
AGVC participation (%)	895	31.012	9.538	9.729	74.923	24.559	30.554	36.461
Downstream participation (%, FVA)	895	11.24	5.932	2.272	30.299	5.975	10.587	14.904
Upstream participation (%, DVX)	895	19.772	7.832	4.149	67.814	15.481	19.849	24.181
Food Industry								
AGVC participation (%)	895	28.544	10.081	9.693	64.449	20.808	26.984	34.84
Downstream participation (%, FVA)	895	18.825	9.809	3.285	58.482	11.248	15.884	25.097
Upstream participation (%, DVX)	895	9.719	4.749	2.394	40.936	6.498	9.325	11.707

Panel 1.4: High income
Total

AGVC participation (%)	892	37.127	10.997	13.791	85.507	29.5	36.641	42.849
Downstream participation (%, FVA)	892	24.166	10.698	5.775	76.929	16.933	23.067	28.339
Upstream participation (%, DVX)	892	12.961	4.329	3.578	27.556	10.319	12.875	15.873
Agricultural Industry								
AGVC participation (%)	892	38.928	12.006	13.052	71.916	28.13	39.857	46.555
Downstream participation (%, FVA)	892	16.818	8.758	3.518	63.581	10.795	15.79	20.434
Upstream participation (%, DVX)	892	22.11	7.018	4.389	35.518	16.994	23.576	27.029
Food Industry								
AGVC participation (%)	892	36.49	11.098	13.876	87.333	29.127	35.699	41.627
Downstream participation (%, FVA)	892	26.561	11.299	6.458	80.974	18.664	25.213	31.643
Upstream participation (%, DVX)	892	9.929	3.803	3.088	25.705	7.545	9.621	11.732

Note: Data are sourced from the UNCTAD-Eora Global Value Chain (GVC) database. GVC is measured by the GVC share of a country's gross exports following Koopman, Wang, and Wei (2014). Downstream participation is measured by the foreign value added (FVA); upstream participation is measured by the domestic value added (DVX). The World Bank defines four income categories based on GNI per capita in US$ in year 2010: low income (≤ 1,005); lower middle income (1,006–3,975); upper middle income (3,976–12,275); high income (> 12,275).

Table 2A.2   List of control variables

	Obs.	Data Source
Population ages 65 and above total	9600	World Development Indicator Database
Population ages 0–14 total	9600	World Development Indicator Database
Population ages 15–64 total	9600	World Development Indicator Database
Population female	9600	World Development Indicator Database
Rural population	9600	World Development Indicator Database
Urban population	9600	World Development Indicator Database
Arable land (hectares)	9600	World Development Indicator Database
Agricultural land (sq.km)	9600	World Development Indicator Database
Land area (sq. km)	9600	World Development Indicator Database
Food production index (2004–2006=100)	9600	World Development Indicator Database
Livestock production index (2004–2006=100)	9600	World Development Indicator Database
Land under cereal production (hectares)	9600	World Development Indicator Database
Cereal production (metric tons)	9600	World Development Indicator Database
Total fisheries production (metric tons)	9600	World Development Indicator Database
Capture fisheries production (metric tons)	9600	World Development Indicator Database
GDP growth (annual %)	9600	World Development Indicator Database
Inflation GDP deflator (annual %	9600	World Development Indicator Database
GDP (constant 2010 US$)	9600	World Development Indicator Database
Trade (% of GDP)	9600	World Development Indicator Database
Exports of goods and services (% of GDP)	9600	World Development Indicator Database
Self-employed total (% of total employment)	9600	World Development Indicator Database
Number of Regional Trade Agreements (RTA)	9600	Mario Larch's RTA Database
Number of Customs Unions (CU)	9600	Mario Larch's RTA Database
Number of Free Trade Agreements (FTA)	9600	Mario Larch's RTA Database
Number of Partial Scope Agreements (PSA)	9600	Mario Larch's RTA Database
Number of Economic Integration Agreements (EIA)	9600	Mario Larch's RTA Database
Regional Trade Agreements (RTA)(dummy)	9600	Mario Larch's RTA Database
Customs Unions (CU)(dummy)	9600	Mario Larch's RTA Database
Free Trade Agreements (FTA)(dummy)	9600	Mario Larch's RTA Database
Partial Scope Agreements (PSA)(dummy)	9600	Mario Larch's RTA Database
Economic Integration Agreements (dummy)	9600	Mario Larch's RTA Database

References

Abadie, Alberto, Susan Athey, Guido W. Imbens, and Jeffrey Wooldridge. 2017. "When Should You Adjust Standard Errors For Clustering?" NBER Working Paper #24003. Cambridge, MA: National Bureau of Economic Research.

Alvarez-Cuadrado, Francisco, and Markus Poschke. 2011. "Structural Change Out of Agriculture: Labor Push versus Labor Pull." *American Economic Journal: Macroeconomics* 3 (3): 127–58.

Antràs, P. 2016. *Global Production: Firms, Contracts, and Trade Structure.* Princeton University Press.

Antràs, Pol, Alonso De Gortari, and Oleg Itskhoki. 2017. "Globalization, Inequality and Welfare." *Journal of International Economics* 108: 387–412.

Antràs, Pol, and Davin Chor. 2018. "On the Measurement of Upstreamness and Downstreamness in Global Value Chains." NBER Working Paper #24185. Cambridge, MA: National Bureau of Economic Research.

Balié, Jean, Davide Del Prete, Emiliano Magrini, Pierluigi Montalbano, and Silvia Nenci. 2019a. "Does Trade Policy Impact Food and Agriculture Global Value Chain Participation of Sub-Saharan African Countries?" *American Journal of Agricultural Economics* 101 (3): 773–89.

Balié, Jean, Davide Del Prete, Emiliano Magrini, Pierluigi Montalbano, and Silvia Nenci. 2019b. "Food and Agriculture Global Value Chains: New Evidence from Sub-Saharan Africa." In *Governance for Structural Transformation in Africa*, edited by Adam Elhiraika, Gamal Ibrahim, William Davis.. Springer

Barrett, C., Thomas Reardon, Johan Swinnen, and David Zilberman. 2019. "Structural Transformation and Economic Development: Insights from the Agri-Food Value Chain Revolution." Mimeo, Cornell University.

Bellemare, Marc F. 2012. "As You Sow, So Shall You Reap: The Welfare Impacts of Contract Farming." *World Development* 40 (7): 1418–1434.

Belotti, Federico, Alessandro Borin, and Michele Mancini. 2020. *icio: Economic Analysis with Inter-Country Input-Output Tables in Stata.* The World Bank.

Blanchard, Emily J., Chad P. Bown, and Robert C. Johnson. 2017. "Global Value Chains and Trade Policy." *Dartmouth College and Peterson Institute for International Economics* 2.

Borin, Alessandro, and Michele Mancini. 2019. *Measuring What Matters in Global Value Chains and Value-Added Trade.* The World Bank.

Bustos, Paula, Bruno Caprettini, and Jacopo Ponticelli. 2016. "Agricultural Productivity and Structural Transformation: Evidence From Brazil." *American Economic Review* 106 (6): 1320–65.

Cattaneo, Olivier, Gary Gereffi, Sébastien Miroudot, and Daria Taglioni. 2013. *Joining, Upgrading and Being Competitive in Global Value Chains: A Strategic Framework.* The World Bank.

Dasgupta, Sukti, and Ajit Singh. 2007. "Manufacturing, Services and Premature Deindustrialization in Developing Countries: A Kaldorian Analysis." In *Advancing Development*, edited by George Mavrotas and Anthony Shorrocks. Springer.

Devarajan, Shantayanan. 2013. "Africa's Statistical Tragedy." *Review of Income and Wealth* 59: S9–S15.

De Vries, Gaaitzen, Marcel Timmer, and Klaas De Vries. 2015. "Structural Transformation in Africa: Static Gains, Dynamic Losses." *The Journal of Development Studies* 51 (6): 674–88.

Diao, Xinshen, Margaret McMillan, and Dani Rodrik. 2019. "The Recent Growth Boom in Developing Economies: A Structural-Change Perspective." In *The Palgrave Handbook of Development Economics*, 281–334. Springer.

Duarte, Margarida, and Diego Restuccia. 2010. "The Role of the Structural Transformation in Aggregate Productivity." *The Quarterly Journal of Economics* 125 (1): 129–73.

Egger, Peter, and Mario Larch. 2008. "Interdependent Preferential Trade Agreement Memberships: An Empirical Analysis." *Journal of International Economics* 76 (2): 384–99.

Feyaerts, Hendrik, Goedele Van den Broeck, and Miet Maertens. 2020. "Global and Local Food Value Chains in Africa: A Review." *Agricultural Economics* 51 (1): 143–57.

Gereffi, Gary, and Karina Fernandez-Stark. 2011. "Global value chain analysis:

A Primer." Center on Globalization, Governance & Competitiveness (CGGC), Duke University, North Carolina.

Herrendorf, Berthold, Richard Rogerson, and Akos Valentinyi. 2014. "Growth and Structural Transformation." In *Handbook of Economic Growth*, Vol. 2, 855–941. Elsevier.

Hnatkovska, Viktoria, Amartya Lahiri, and Carlos A. Végh. 2016. "The Exchange Rate Response to Monetary Policy Innovations." *American Economic Journal: Macroeconomics* 8 (2): 137–81.

Hummels, David, Jun Ishii, and Kei-Mu Yi. 2001. "The Nature and Growth of Vertical Specialization in World Trade." *Journal of international Economics* 54 (1): 75–96.

Inomata, Satoshi. 2017. "Analytical Frameworks for Global Value Chains: An Overview." In *Global Value Chain Development Report*. WTO report paper.

Jerven, Morten. 2013. *Poor Numbers: How We Are Misled by African Development Statistics and What To Do About It.* Cornell University Press.

Jerven, Morten, and Deborah Johnston. 2015. "Statistical Tragedy in Africa? Evaluating the Data Base for African Economic Development." *The Journal of Development Studies* 51 (2): 111–15.

Johnson, Robert C. 2018. "Measuring Global Value Chains." *Annual Review of Economics* 10: 207–36.

Johnson, Robert C., and Guillermo Noguera. 2012. "Proximity and Production Fragmentation." *American Economic Review* 102 (3): 407–11.

Koopman, Robert, Zhi Wang, and Shang-Jin Wei. 2014. "Tracing Value-Added and Double Counting in Gross Exports." *American Economic Review* 104 (2): 459–94.

Kuznets, Simon, and John Thomas Murphy. 1966. *Modern Economic Growth: Rate, Structure, and Spread*, Vol. 2, New Haven: Yale University Press.

Landefeld, J. Steven, Eugene P. Seskin, and Barbara M. Fraumeni. 2008. "Taking the Pulse of the Economy: Measuring GDP." *Journal of Economic Perspectives* 22 (2): 193–216.

Los, Bart, and Marcel P. Timmer. 2018. "Measuring Bilateral Exports of Value Added: A Unified Framework." NBER Working Paper # 24896. Cambridge, MA:National Bureau of Economic Research.

Mergenthaler, Marcus, Katinka Weinberger, and Matin Qaim. 2009. "The Food System Transformation in Developing Countries: A Disaggregate Demand Analysis for Fruits and Vegetables in Vietnam." *Food Policy* 34 (5): 426–36.

Michaels, Guy, Ferdinand Rauch, and Stephen J. Redding. 2012. "Urbanization and Structural Transformation." *The Quarterly Journal of Economics* 127 (2): 535–86.

Minten, Bart, Lalaina Randrianarison, and Johan F. M. Swinnen. 2009. "Global Retail Chains and Poor Farmers: Evidence from Madagascar." *World Development* 37 (11): 1728–1741.

Montalbano, Pierluigi, Rebecca Pietrelli, and Luca Salvatici. 2018. "Participation in the Market Chain and Food Security: The Case of the Ugandan Maize Farmers." *Food Policy* 76: 81–98.

Newfarmer, Richard, John Page, and Finn Tarp. 2019. *Industries without Smokestacks: Industrialization in Africa Reconsidered.* Oxford University Press.

Ravallion, Martin. 2001. "Growth, Inequality and Poverty: Looking Beyond Averages." *World Development* 29 (11): 1803–1815.

Reardon, Thomas, and C. Peter Timmer. 2007. "Transformation of Markets for Agricultural Output in Developing Countries since 1950: How Has Thinking Changed?" *Handbook of Agricultural Economics* 3: 2807–2855.

Reardon, Thomas, Christopher B. Barrett, Julio A. Berdegué, and Johan F. M. Swinnen. 2009. "Agrifood Industry Transformation and Small Farmers in Developing Countries." *World Development* 37 (11): 1717–1727.

Rodrik, Dani. 2016. "Premature Deindustrialization." *Journal of Economic Growth* 21 (1): 1–33.

Rogerson, Richard. 2008. "Structural Transformation and the Deterioration of European Labor Market Outcomes." *Journal of Political Economy* 116 (2): 235–59.

Sexton, Richard J. 2013. "Market Power, Misconceptions, and Modern Agricultural Markets." *American Journal of Agricultural Economics* 95 (2): 209–19.

Sheldon, Ian M., Daniel C. K. Chow, and William McGuire. 2018. "Trade Liberalization and Constraints on Moves to Protectionism: Multilateralism vs. Regionalism." *American Journal of Agricultural Economics* 100 (5): 1375–1390.

Syrquin, Moshe. 1988. "Patterns of Structural Change." *Handbook of Development Economics* 1: 203–73.

Timmer, C. Peter. 2009. A world without agriculture: The structural transformation in historical perspective. Washington, DC: Aei Press.

Wang, Zhi, Shang-Jin Wei, Xinding Yu, and Kunfu Zhu. 2017. "Measures of Participation in Global Value Chains and Global Business Cycles." NBER Working Paper #23222. Cambridge, MA: National Bureau of Economic Research.

3

Exchange Rate Volatility and Global Food Supply Chains

Sandro Steinbach

3.1 Introduction

Most countries have moved from a fixed exchange rate system to a floating or soft-pegged regime since the disintegration of the Bretton Woods system in the 1970s (Clark et al. 2004). The fixed system's dismissal allowed monetary policy makers to pursue independent monetary policy and ensure free capital movement. Simultaneously, the move to a floating exchange rate system implies a significant increase in exposure to foreign market forces. Studies have shown that high variability of foreign exchange correlates with a rise in uncertainty regarding the terms of trade (McKenzie 1999). Not surprisingly, the consequences of exchange volatility remain a primary source of concern for monetary policy makers worldwide but are of particular relevance in countries with relatively low financial development levels. Therefore, many developing countries use soft-pegged exchange regimes to reduce their exposure to foreign exchange risk.[1] Still, there is no consensus

Sandro Steinbach is an associate professor in the Department of Agribusiness and Applied Economics at North Dakota State University. He directs the Center for Agricultural Policy and Trade Studies and is a Challey Institute Scholar.

I thank participants of the NBER "Risk in Agricultural Supply Chains" Virtual Conference in May 2021 for comments on an earlier version of this paper. I also acknowledge Dongin Kim for his excellent research assistance. This work is supported by the Agriculture and Food Research Initiative (Award Number 2019–67023–29343) from the National Institute of Food and Agriculture. Any opinions, findings, conclusions, or recommendations expressed in this publication are those of the authors and do not necessarily reflect the view of the US Department of Agriculture or the National Bureau of Economic Research. For acknowledgments, sources of research support, and disclosure of the author's material financial relationships, if any, please see https://www.nber.org/books-and-chapters/risks-agricultural-supply-chains/exchange-rate-volatility-and-global-food-supply-chains.

1. I use the terms *exchange rate risk* and *exchange rate volatility* interchangeably throughout the paper. Exchange rate volatility is a primary measure of currency exchange risk (Viaene and de Vries 1992).

about the impact of exchange volatility on economic outcomes and how they vary for different industries along the food supply chains. The implications for international trade are poorly understood, and the related empirical literature is mostly inconclusive (Auboin and Ruta 2013).

The theoretical literature has developed several explanations for a causal relationship between exchange rate volatility and international trade. The conventional wisdom is that an increase in exchange rate uncertainty causes an increase in revenue uncertainty, which will hamper the exchange of goods and services across international borders. This uncertainty is the result of risk aversion and irreversible investment in productive capital (Ethier 1973; Demers 1991). Market imperfections can lead to imperfect and costly hedging, a primary source of exchange risk avoidance that is of particular relevance in less developed countries. Therefore, it is likely that international trade correlates negatively with exchange rate volatility due to risk aversion of economic agents (Mundell 2000). The work of Johnson (1969) challenges this view, since he argues that arbitrage between spot and forward markets and speculation would tend to keep the cost of forward exchange cover within reasonable bound in a flexible exchange rate system. Due to these characteristics of financial markets, neither appreciation nor depreciation would harm trade badly. Still, it would benefit economic agents, since policy makers would no longer need to pursue otherwise irrational and difficult policy objectives for the sake of improving the balance of payments. Franke (1991) showed that an increase in exchange rate volatility could have a positive effect on trade. He argues that a multinational monopolist with a trading strategy that factors in exchange rate uncertainty may increase international trade due to growing exchange rate volatility. As pointed out by Grauwe (1988), exchange rate volatility can have a negative or positive effect on trade flows, depending on the shape of the expected marginal utility of income function specific to different sectors of the economy.

The substantial uncertainty regarding the impact of exchange rate risk is echoed in the empirical literature on international trade (for an extensive review, see Auboin and Ruta 2013). Most earlier studies provide evidence for an adverse effect of exchange rate volatility on manufacturing trade (Thursby and Thursby 1987; Koray and Lastrapes 1989; Rose 2000). The empirical evidence for the agricultural and food industry is mostly in line with the assertion for manufacturing trade (Pick 1990; Cho, Sheldon, and McCorriston 2002; Kandilov 2008). Tenreyro (2007) challenged this view by arguing that the negative and significant effect estimates are the result of endogeneity and heteroskedasticity issues neglected so far. She outlined an identification strategy that addresses both identification issues and accounts for reverse causality. Her findings indicate that an increase in short-run exchange rate volatility does not affect international trade. These findings find support in the work of Klaassen (2004), who shows that the maximal effect of exchange rate volatility on international trade occurs with a delay of one year. Therefore, long-term (about one year) risk for trade flows is constant over time, with only short-term deviations from average presenting a risk for global supply chains. Broda and Romalis (2011) introduced a structural estimation approach to account for reverse causality. They argue that the insignificant estimates in Tenreyro (2007) result from aggregation bias and that exchange rate volatility depresses trade mainly for differentiated products. It is reasonable to assume that an agent's reaction to short-run uncertainty differs from the response to long-run uncertainty, which is a possible explanation for the largely insignificant estimates presented in Tenreyro (2007). The lack of consensus about the impact of exchange volatility in light of increasingly integrated global food supply chains represents a significant challenge for understanding better the functioning of agricultural and food markets.

This paper provides three distinct contributions to the ongoing academic debate on the impact of exchange rate volatility on global food supply chains. First, I add to the ongoing discussion by testing for a causal relationship at the product level. I consider 781 agricultural and food products in my analysis and categorize these products according to the liberal product classification of Rauch (1999) into homogenous, reference-priced, and differentiated products and Regmi et al's (2005) classification into aquaculture, bulk, horticulture, semi-processed, and processed products. Second, I study the effect of both short-run and long-run exchange rate volatility. Agents may react differently to these sources of uncertainty. I extracted daily exchange rate data for 25,122 currency pairs and 22 years from the Thomson Reuters database to calculate the volatility measures. The exchange rate measures are assigned to bilateral export data for 159 countries covering 2001 to 2017. I divert from the literature and use daily instead of end-month exchange rate data to calculate the short-run and long-run exchange rate volatility measures following the methods outlined in Rose (2000) and Tenreyro (2007). The end-month volatility measures are likely biased, as they do not accurately represent the distribution of exchange rates within a month. Third, my identification strategy simultaneously addresses the following identification issues: Endogeneity, heteroskedasticity, zero trade flows, sampling, and reverse causality. Using a Poisson count data regression, I account for high-dimensional fixed effects, heteroskedasticity, and zero trade flows (Silva and Tenreyro 2006; Correia, Guimarães, and Zylkin 2020). The multilateral trade resistance terms that may cause an endogeneity issue are accounted for with time-varying fixed effects for importers and exporters (Anderson and van Wincoop 2003). I also include standard gravity control variables such as distance, economic integration agreements, contiguity, and others in my baseline and consider country-pair fixed effects in my preferred regression specification. The sampling issue is addressed by analyzing trade flows for all available country pairs. Lastly, since I conduct my analysis at the product level, I can deal with the reverse causation, since agents operating in these markets do not influence the exchange rate regime (Tenreyro 2007; Broda and Romalis 2011).

I estimate the gravity model at the product level and summarize the parameter estimates according to product and industry characteristics for short-run and long-run volatility measures. The results are analyzed using both mean and trade-weighted effect estimates, providing considerable evidence for a heterogeneous exchange rate volatility effect on global food supply chains. My elasticity estimates indicate that the short-run effects are smaller than the long-run for the overall volatility impact. More specifically, I find that bulk products are positively affected by short-run exchange rate volatility, whereas aquaculture products are negatively impacted by short-run and long-run exchange rate volatility. I observe similar results for horticulture products, which indicates an adverse effect of exchange rate volatility. These findings imply that the impact of exchange rate volatility can vary significantly depending on the product and industry characteristics. The results also indicate that products produced by industries with high upstreamness have positive trade effects, while lower downstreamness of an industry correlated with larger trade effects. I find that export prices correlate positively with trade effects for long-run but not for short-run volatility. The findings do not indicate any relevant correlation between trade effects of exchange rate volatility and both product sophistication and product complexity. I also find no evidence of differences in the trade effects according to the economic development stage of trading partners. Several robustness checks are deployed to explain why my results divert from earlier work. These estimations confirm that gravity model misspecification, aggregation bias, exchange rate measurement errors, and treatment misspecification are the primary causes for significant and negative estimates in these earlier studies (see, for example, Rose 2000, Tenreyro 2007). I conclude that both short-run and long-run exchange rate volatility have limited trade effects, but the average trade effects hide significant heterogeneity between agricultural and food products. There is substantial heterogeneity between different products along the global food supply chain. These estimates enhance the understanding of the implications of exchange rate volatility, which is a primary source of concern for monetary policy makers worldwide.

The remainder of this paper is organized as follows. Section 3.2 presents the empirical model, explains data sources, and details my estimation strategy. Section 3.3 summarizes the regression results, discusses heterogeneity in the trade effect estimates, and explains sources of estimation bias in earlier work. Section 3.4 concludes with a review of my findings and sorts them into the broader literature.

3.2   Identification Strategy

I rely on a sectoral gravity-type regression specification to estimate the impact of exchange rate volatility on global food supply chains (Hallak 2010;

Costinot, Donaldson, and Komunjer 2012; Anderson and Yotov 2016). The baseline regression model accounts for multilateral trade resistance terms with country-time specific fixed effects for importers and exporters (Anderson and van Wincoop 2003). The sectoral gravity model is specified in its general form as follows:

(1) $$X_{ij,t}^{s} = \exp(e_{i,t}^{s} - \theta \log \tau_{ij,t}^{s} + m_{j,t}^{s}) \eta_{ij,t},$$

where $X_{ij,t}^{s}$ stands for bilateral export flows of product s from country i to country j in year t. The time-variant multilateral resistance terms for exporters are denoted by $e_{i,t}^{s}$ and for importers by $m_{j,t}^{s}$. The trade cost function is denoted by $\tau_{ij,t}^{s}$ (symmetric and of the iceberg form) and includes measures of exchange rate volatility and common gravity-type control variables. I measure nominal exchange rate variability ($\delta_{ij,t}$) by the standard deviation (σ) of the first difference of the logarithmized bilateral exchange rate ($e_{ij,k}$) as follows:

(2) $$\delta_{ij,t} = \sigma[\ln(e_{ij,k}) - \ln(e_{ij,k-1})].$$

I extracted exchange rate data for 25,122 currency pairs and 22 years from the Thomson Reuters database. The exchange rate volatility measures were calculated based on daily exchange rate data for 159 countries and the period from 1996 to 2017 (Thomson Reuters 2019). Table 3A.1 provides the list of sample countries. I divert from the literature and use daily exchange rate data to calculate the short-run and long-run exchange rate volatility measures. This decision is informed by concerns about spurious breaks in the exchange rate volatility measures (Rose 2000; Tenreyro 2007). These measures are likely biased as they do not represent the distribution of exchange rates within a month accurately. I define short-run exchange rate volatility α_{δ}^{S} according to Tenreyro (2007) based on the preceding year and long-run exchange rate volatility α_{δ}^{L} according to Rose (2000) based on the five preceding years.

The trade cost function $\tau_{ij,t}^{s}$ includes additional control variables that vary at the country-pair level over time. The covariates in my regression model are the log of weighted distance, common legacy, economic integration, WTO membership, shared border, and common language. I also include the log of GDP and the log of the population in a partial model that only includes importer, exporter, and time fixed effects and serves as a comparison to the literature (see, e.g., Tenreyro 2007). I obtained data on GDP and population from the World Development Indicators database (World Bank 2021). The GDP variable is measured in the current US$. I also constructed a variable for multilateral economic integration with membership information from the World Trade Organization (WTO 2021). The bilateral economic integration variable was obtained from the Economic Integration Agreement Dataset (Bergstrand 2016). This data set indexes the amount of trade openness on a scale from 0 to 6, where 0 stands for no economic integration and 6 for an economic union. The remaining gravity control variables are from the GeoDist Database by Mayer and Zignago (2011). I extracted information on geographical distance, common legacy, shared border, and common language from this database. My preferred model specification accounts for multilateral trade resistance terms with country-time specific fixed effects for importers and exporters, controls for time-invariant trade costs with country-pair fixed effects, and includes time-variant covariates to control for trade cost changes over time. The descriptive statistics of all regressors are provided in table 3A.2.

I denote the outcome variable in my preferred regression specification by $X_{ij,t}$. The variable represents the non-negative integer count of bilateral trade flows at the product level. The trade data were obtained from the Comtrade Database and cover the period from 2001 to 2017 (United Nations 2021). I use the reconciled export flows published in BACI (CEPII 2021). I consider 781 food products in my analysis and categorize these products according to the liberal trade product classification of Rauch (1999) into homogenous (202), reference-priced (303), and differentiated products (231). I also use Regmi et al's (2005) classification of agricultural sectors to classify the food products into aquaculture (104), bulk (63), horticulture (238), semi-processed (121), and processed products (255). Although I could transform the outcome variable and then estimate the relationship using a linear regression model, I believe that this approach is inappropriate for the data because the outcome variable is a count. A linear regression model is incapable of identifying the relationship of primary interest because the model does not ensure positivity of the predicted values for the count outcome (Wooldridge 1999). Moreover, the discrete nature of the count outcome makes it difficult to find a transformation with a conditional mean that is linear in parameters. This issue is further exaggerated in the presence of heteroskedasticity as the transformed errors correlate with the covariates. Such correlation can result in an inconsistent identification of the treatment effect. Even if the transformation of the conditional mean is correctly specified, it would be impossible to obtain an unbiased measure of the relationship. Therefore, I model the relationship between the outcome and the trade cost variables directly. I ensure the positivity of the covariates by employing a nonlinear regression model which uses an exponential form equation.

I use the Poisson pseudo-maximum likelihood (PML) estimator to identify the relationship between the treatment variable and the count outcome (Gong and Samaniego 1981; Gourieroux, Monfort, and Trognon 1984).[2]

---

2. Although I could also rely on the standard Poisson regression model to estimate the relationship, this estimator has two properties that could complicate the identification of the exchange rate volatility treatment effect. First, this regression is known to suffer from convergence problems which can result in spurious estimation results. Second, it is sensitive to numerical difficulties, which is a particular issue for regressions with high-dimensional fixed effects and highly disaggregated data (Silva and Tenreyro 2010). Therefore, I use the PML estimator as it allows me to circumvent these cavities of the standard Poisson regression.

The estimator is unbiased and consistent in the presence of heteroskedasticity. Even if the conditional variance is not proportional to the conditional mean, the estimator is still consistent (Wooldridge 1999; Cameron and Trivedi 2013). Note that because the estimator does not make any specific assumption on the dispersion of the fitted values, I do not have to test for this aspect of the data. A further advantage of the Poisson PML estimator is that the scale of the dependent variable has no effect on the parameter estimates, which is a particular concern for the Negative Binomial PML estimator. As long as the conditional mean is correctly specified, the Poisson PML estimator yields parameter estimates that have a similar magnitude to the estimates of both the Gaussian and Negative Binomial PML estimators. I account for high-dimensional fixed effects using the approach outlined in Correia, Guimarães, and Zylkin (2020). Lastly, I suspect the presence of residual correlation at the country-pair level. Therefore, I address the potential heteroskedasticity in the error term using a robust variance estimator that accounts for clustering at the country-pair level (Cameron and Miller 2015).

3.3 Results

3.3.1 Baseline Results

Table 3.1 summarizes the baseline regression results for agricultural and food products (columns 2–3) and compares these estimates to all other

Table 3.1   **Parameter estimates for baseline model**

	Agriculture and food		All other products	
	α_δ^S	α_δ^L	α_δ^S	α_δ^L
Sign of parameter estimates				
Positive estimates	51.54	52.27	51.50	53.89
Negative estimates	48.46	47.73	48.50	46.11
Significance of parameter estimates				
Significant at 1% level	15.90	13.33	12.83	14.34
Significant at 5% level	24.87	29.60	24.12	26.86
Significant at 10% level	34.36	37.87	33.25	35.52
Magnitude of parameter estimates				
Mean estimate	0.008	0.115	0.002	−0.068
Median estimate	−0.050	−0.105	−0.033	−0.167
% percentile estimate	−0.800	−1.554	−0.659	−1.343
% percentile estimate	0.767	1.631	0.623	1.147

Note: The table summarizes the parameter estimates of the short-run and long-run exchange rate volatility. Columns 2–5 summarize the estimates for α_δ^S and α_δ^L. The arithmetic mean effects are presented for agricultural and food products in columns 2–3 and all other products in columns 4–5.

products (columns 4–5). I indicate the parameter estimates for short-run volatility with α_8^S and the ones for long-run volatility with α_8^L. The table presents summary statistics for the sign, significance, and magnitude of parameter estimates. All estimations incorporate dyadic importer-exporter fixed effects and control for multilateral resistance terms with importer-year and exporter-year fixed effects. I also include time-variant covariates potentially correlated with the volatility measures.

The sign of the parameter estimates for short-run and long-run volatility indicate an almost equal distribution of positive and negative volatility effects: 51.54 percent of short-run and 52.27 percent of long-run volatility estimates have a positive sign. The distribution is similar for all other products. In terms of the significance of parameter estimates, I find that 34.36 percent of short-run and 37.87 percent of long-run volatility parameter estimates are significant at the 10 percent confidence level. The distribution for all other products looks similar to that for agricultural and food products. The magnitude of parameter estimates indicates a mean positive effect that is larger for the long-run than for the short-run exchange rate volatility. The mean is 0.008 for short-run and 0.115 for long-run volatility estimates. The estimates for all other products show a different picture. The mean estimate of long-run volatility is negative, and the short-run volatility estimate is similar to that for agricultural and food products. Note that the median estimates are negative for short-run and long-run volatility. The results indicate that the long-run volatility effect is more pronounced than the short-run volatility effect. The wide distribution of volatility estimates is striking. I find a wider spread for the long-run than for the short-run elasticity estimates for agricultural and food products and all other products.

Table 3.2 provides a summary of the baseline regression results according to different agricultural and food products and Rauch's product classification. The table compares mean and trade-weighted effects for short-run α_8^S and long-run volatility α_8^L based on the preferred model specification.[3] I distinguish between aquaculture, bulk, horticulture, semi-processed, and processed products. The product distribution at the HS-6 level indicates that most products are either processed or horticulture products. Bulk products have the lowest share. I find that apart from bulk products, all mean and trade-weighted short-run volatility estimates have a negative sign. The largest volatility effects are found for processed and semi-processed agricultural and food products. The short-run volatility estimates for bulk products are positive, with a parameter estimate of 0.095 for the mean and 0.075 for the trade-weighted effects. The picture is different for long-run volatility estimates, where I find that several product groups (aquaculture, horticulture, and semi-processed products) record a positive volatility effect. This effect is

---

3. I weigh the parameter estimates by the total export value of the specific HS-6 product for 2001 to 2017.

Table 3.2   **Trade effects for baseline model**

	#	Mean effect		Trade-weighted effect	
		α_6^S	α_6^L	α_6^S	α_6^L
Agriculture and food products					
Aquaculture	101	−0.038	0.037	−0.031	0.040
Bulk	58	0.095	−0.021	0.075	−0.005
Horticulture	208	−0.016	0.054	−0.010	0.038
Semi-processed	120	−0.043	0.056	−0.038	0.045
Processed	250	−0.041	−0.026	−0.035	−0.024
Product differentiation					
Homogenous	222	−0.055	0.029	−0.043	0.023
Reference-priced	314	0.001	0.036	−0.001	0.031
Differentiated	186	−0.004	−0.002	−0.003	−0.005

Note: The table summarizes the parameter estimates of the exchange rate volatility measures by product category. The upper part of the table presents the trade effects according to Regmi's (2005) classification of agricultural and food products, while the lower part summarizes the trade effects according to Rauch's (1999) goods classification. Column 2 shows the number of parameters used for calculation in each category. Columns 3–6 summarize the estimates for α_6^S and α_6^L. The arithmetic mean effects are presented in columns 3–4 and trade-weighted effects in columns 5–6.

present for mean and trade-weighted effects. I find that bulk and processed product exports are negatively affected by exchange rate volatility, but this effect is comparably small for mean and trade-weighted estimates. According to Rauch's product classification, the parameter estimates indicate adverse short-run volatility effects for homogenous products and positive long-run volatility effects for homogenous and reference-priced products. They do not show short-run and long-run volatility effects for differentiated products. The mean and trade-weighted effects are similar in magnitude and have the same parameter signs.

Figure 3.1 illustrates the ranked distribution of trade effects for a one standard deviation change in short-run and long-run exchange rate volatility for agricultural and food products. Subfigure (a) presents the estimates for the short-run and subfigure (b) the ones for the long-run volatility. The dashed lines indicate pooled estimates. The trade effects are calculated by the formula $\beta^* = sd_x / sd_y * \hat{\beta}$. The pooled estimates for the preferred regression specification indicate no evidence for a significant impact of short-run and long-run exchange rate volatility on agricultural and food exports. The disaggregated trade effects at the HS-6 product level indicate a different picture. I find for short-run and long-run exchange rate volatility strong evidence for heterogeneity between different products. This heterogeneity effect is more pronounced for the long-run than for short-run volatility, with the trade effects ranging between –2.95 and 3.64 per one standard deviation change in exchange rate volatility.

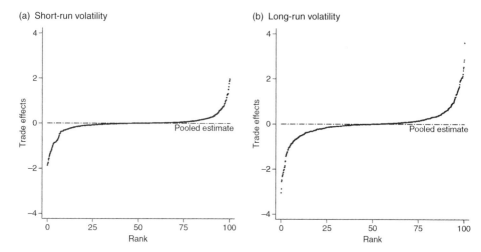

Figure 3.1 Ranked trade effects of exchange rate volatility

Note: The figure shows the ranked trade effects of a one standard deviation change in short-run and long-run exchange rate volatility for agricultural and food products. The trade effects are calculated by the formula $\beta^* = sd_x / sd_y * \hat{\beta}$.

3.3.2 Product and Industry Characteristics

3.3.2.1 Supply Chain

Figure 3.2 shows the link between supply chain characteristics and trade effects of exchange rate volatility. I measure trade effects according to one standard deviation change in short-run and long-run exchange rate volatility and indicate piecewise cubic spline interpolations with dashed lines. Subfigures (a) and (b) shows the results for upstreamness and subfigures (c) and (d) the ones for downstreamness. Upstreamness measures the distance between the production stage and final demand (Antràs et al. 2012).[4] Upstreamness is measured based on a production function:

$$(3) \qquad y(s) = c(s) + \sum_t d(s,t)c(t) + \sum_t \sum_u d(s,t)d(s,u)c(t) + \ldots,$$

where $c(s)$ represents the final consumption of good s and $d(s, t)$ represents the amount of input s needed to produce good t. This definition allows us to derive upstreamness (U) as follows:

$$(4) \qquad U(s) = 1 + \sum_{t=1}^{N} \frac{d(s,t)y(t)}{y(s)} U(t),$$

4. I convert NAICS classification into HS-92 classification using conversion tables provided by the United Nations.

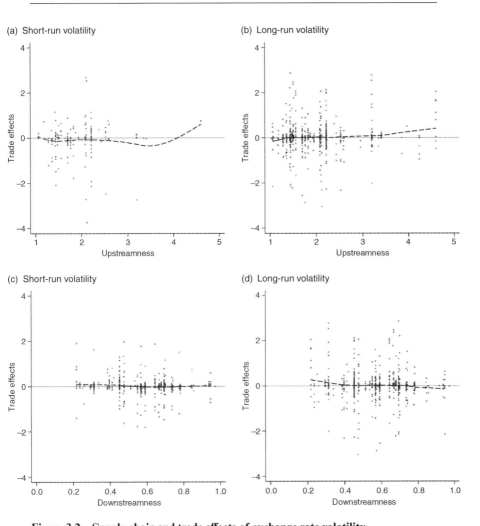

Figure 3.2   Supply chain and trade effects of exchange rate volatility

Note: The figure shows the relationship between supply chain position and trade effects of exchange rate volatility. The supply chain length is measured by upstreamness and downstreamness. The trade effects are expressed as one standard deviation change in short-run and long-run exchange rate volatility for agricultural and food products. The dashed lines indicate piecewise cubic spline interpolations.

where $[d(s, t)y(t)] / y(s)$ is the share of s purchased by t. If the upstreamness measure is equal to one, then the entire output is directly consumed. The larger the upstreamness measure, the more upstream the industry is. The piecewise cubic spline interpolations indicate a weak positive relationship between upstreamness and the trade effects of exchange rate volatility. The effects are more pronounced for the long-run than for the

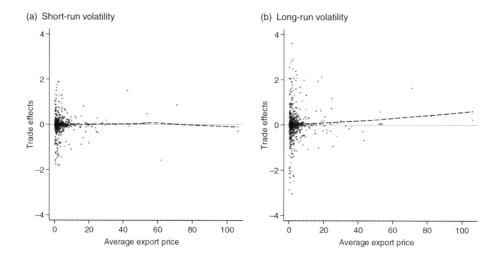

(a) Short-run volatility   (b) Long-run volatility

Figure 3.3   Export prices and trade effects of exchange rate volatility
Note: The figure shows the relationship between average export prices and trade effects of exchange rate volatility. The average export price is defined as the total value of exports divided by the total quantity of exports overall years within the sample. The trade effects are calculated by the formula $\beta^* = sd_x / sd_y * \hat{\beta}$.

short-run volatility measures. The results indicate that the upstreamness of the supply chain has a minor impact on the magnitude of the exchange rate volatility effects. I also use the downstreamness measure to investigate supply chain effects (Antràs and Chor 2013). The downstreamness measure is a weighted index of the average position in the value chain at which an industry's output is used, with the weights given by the ratio of the use of that industry's output in that position relative to the total production of that industry. Antràs and Chor (2013) calculate the downstreamness measure from 2002 US input-output tables. The piecewise cubic spline interpolations indicate a weak negative association between downstreamness and the trade effects of exchange rate volatility. These effects are more pronounced for the long-run than for the short-run volatility measure. The results indicate that an industry's position in the supply chain has no impact on the magnitude of the exchange rate volatility effects.

3.3.2.2   Export Prices

Figure 3.3 shows the relationship between the average export price of agricultural and food products and the trade effects of short-run and long-run exchange rate volatility. The average export price is calculated as the unit value at the HS-6 product level, and the trade-weighted average unit value is used to illustrate the relationship. The presented trade effects are measured according to one standard deviation change in short-run and long-run exchange rate volatility. I indicate piecewise cubic spline interpolations with dashed lines. The results show no significant relationship between export prices and trade effects of short-run exchange rate volatility for agricultural and food products. I find evidence for a positive association between the average export price and the trade effects of long-run exchange rate volatility. The higher the unit value, the more likely it is that exchange rate volatility has a positive trade effect. However, the statistical evidence for such a relationship remains weak, being driven by few products with positive trade effects.

3.3.2.3   Product Sophistication

To measure the impact of product sophistication on the link between exchange rate volatility and agricultural and food trade, I implement the framework outlined by Hausmann, Hwang, and Rodrik (2007) and calculate a product-level sophistication index. The rationale underlying the sophistication index is that products exported by highly developed countries will have characteristics that allow high-wage producers to compete globally. These characteristics include technology as an essential determinant, but they are also related to other factors such as marketing, logistics and proximity, fragmentability, information and familiarity, natural resources, infrastructure, and value chain organization (Lall, Weiss, and Zhang 2006). The index measures the level of sophistication associated with product k as follows:

$$(5) \qquad S_k = \sum_j \frac{x_{jk} / X_j}{\sum_j x_{jk} / X_j} Y_j,$$

where the numerator stands for the value-share of product k in country j's overall export basket and the denominator represents the aggregated value-shares of all countries exporting product k. The index is calculated by year, and the grand mean is used to illustrate the relationship between product sophistication and the trade effects of exchange rate volatility. I measure trade effects according to one standard deviation change in short-run and long-run exchange rate volatility and indicate piecewise cubic spline interpolations with dashed lines. The results show no relationship between product sophistication and the trade effects of short-run and long-run exchange rate volatility. Although there is a downward trend for the cubic spline estimates, the association is weak and provides insufficient evidence for a significant relationship. These estimates imply that the trade effects caused by exchange rate volatility are not affected by product sophistication.

3.3.2.4   Product Complexity

Product complexity correlates with income inequality, which is strongly associated with exchange rate volatility (Galí and Monacelli 2005). To account for the role of product complexity, I use the Product Complexity Index (PCI) developed by Hartmann et al. (2017). The PCI derives from the

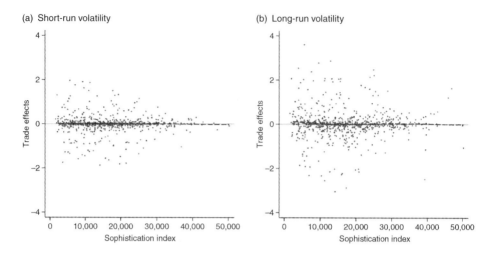

Figure 3.4   Product sophistication and trade effects of exchange rate volatility

Note: The figure shows the relationship between product sophistication and trade effects of exchange rate volatility. The product-level sophistication index is calculated using the approach outlined by Hausmann, Hwang, and Rodrik (2007). The trade effects are calculated by the formula $\beta^* = sd_x / sd_y * \hat{\beta}$.

Economic Complexity Index, which is a holistic measure of the productive capabilities of large economic systems. I relate the PCI with the trade effects of short-run and long-run exchange rate volatility in figure 3.5. The PCI ranges between −2 and 2. I measure trade effects according to one standard deviation change in exchange rate volatility and indicate piecewise cubic spline interpolations with dashed lines. The spline estimates indicate no significant relationship between exchange rate volatility and the PCI. These results imply that the product complexity does not correlate with the ability to hedge exchange rate risk.

3.3.2.5   Economic Development

The economic development stage of an economy could impact its ability to hedge exchange rate risk (CITE). I interact the short-run and long-run volatility measures with a dyadic variable for OECD membership to measure differences in the trade effects according to economic development. I estimate the directional trade effects for North-North, North-South, South-North, and South-South. The results of this analysis are illustrated in figure 3.6. I show the trade effects for agricultural and food products and use box-and-whisker plots to summarize the findings. The figures indicate no differences in the average trade effects for short-run and long-run exchange rate volatility based on the economic development stage. All average trade effects are close to zero. An interesting observation is the wider spread of trade effects for North-South and South-South trade.

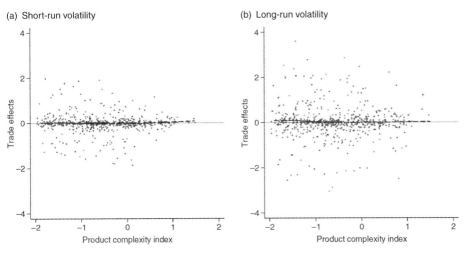

Figure 3.5   Product compexity and trade effects of exchange rate volatility

Note: The figure shows the relationship between product complexity and trade effects of exchange rate volatility. The product-level sophistication index is calculated using the approach outlined by Hartmann et al. (2017) (CITE). The trade effects are calculated by the formula $\beta^* = sd_x / sd_y * \hat{\beta}$.

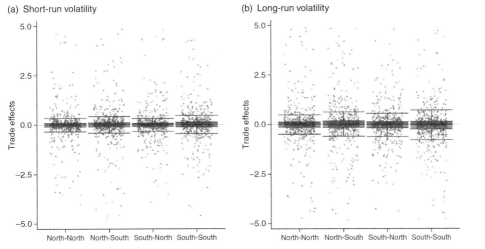

Figure 3.6   Economic development and trade effects of exchange rate volatility

Note: The figure shows the relationship between economic development and trade effects of exchange rate volatility. The directional trade effects are measures by interacting a dyadic development stage dummy with the short-run and long-run volatility measures. The trade effects are calculated by the formula $\beta^* = sd_x / sd_y * \hat{\beta}$.

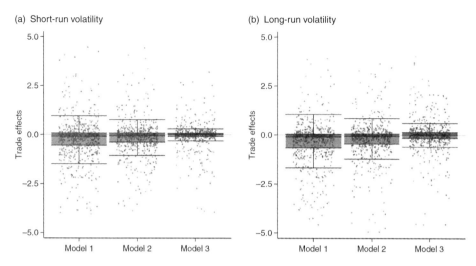

Figure 3.7   Gravity model specification and trade effects of exchange rate volatility
Note: The figure shows the impact of the gravity model specification on the trade effects of exchange rate volatility. The trade effects are calculated by the formula $\beta^* = sd_x / sd_y * \hat{\beta}$.

3.3.3   Identification Challenges

3.3.3.1   Gravity Model Specification

A potential explanation for the starkly different results in this analysis compared to earlier work relates to the gravity model specification. In addition to aggregation bias, earlier studies also suffer from model misspecification issues by either exploring the relationship using cross-sectional data only or not accounting for multilateral resistance terms and time-invariant trade cost. Figure 3.7 shows the distribution of trade effects for three model specifications. Model 1 includes time-invariant importer and exporter as well as year fixed effects. This specification suffers from the "gold medal mistake" by not accounting accurately for the multilateral resistance terms. Model 2 represents a theoretically justified gravity specification with time-varying importer and exporter fixed effects. A potential concern relates to the correlation between time-invariant trade costs and the exchange rate volatility measures. To account for this issue, Model 3 includes time-varying importer and exporter and dyadic importer-exporter fixed effects. This specification is my preferred gravity model specification as it accounts for any correlation between the volatility measures and time-invariant trade costs. To illustrate the consequences of gravity model misspecification, I use a box-and-whisker plot for the trade effects of short-run and long-run exchange rate volatility. The results provide clear evidence for an adverse effect of gravity model misspecification on the reliability of the exchange rate volatility estimates. I find strong evidence that model misspecification has an adverse impact on the exchange rate volatility estimates for agricultural and food exports, both for short-run and long-run volatility measures.

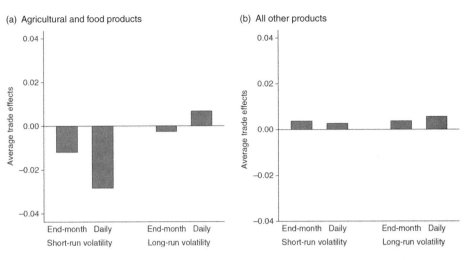

Figure 3.8   Exchange rate measure and trade effects of exchange rate volatility

Note: The figure shows the impact of the exchange rate measure on the trade effects of exchange rate volatility. The average trade effect represents the arithmetic mean of the individual trade effects calculated by the formula $\beta^* = sd_x / sd_y * \hat{\beta}$.

3.3.3.2   Exchange Rate Measure

A further issue related to earlier studies is the use of end-month instead of daily volatility measures. Figure 3A.1 shows the exchange rate quotation USD/CAD for 2010. Earlier studies solely rely on end-month quotations to calculate volatility measures. This choice can introduce substantial bias in the estimation as the end-month quotations are not representative of the experienced volatility for exchange rate time series. To illustrate the impact of this issue, I compare average trade effects for short-run and long-run volatility based on end-month and daily exchange rate quotations in figure 3.8. These estimates are based on the preferred model specification. Subfigure (a) shows the estimates for agricultural and food products and subfigure (b) the estimates for all other products. The estimates indicate a larger average trade effect for daily than for end-month exchange rate volatility measures. The short-run volatility effect is twice as large for daily than for end-month volatility, while the average trade effect turns positive for the long-run volatility measures. These results indicate that the choice of the exchange rate measure has a significant impact on the gravity estimation results.

3.3.3.3   Treatment Specification

A further concern relates to the joint inclusion of short-run and long-run volatility measures. Most earlier studies measure either the effects of short-run or long-run volatility. The Pearson correlation coefficient between both measures is 0.3382, indicating only limited multicollinearity concerns for both variables. Figure 3.9 shows the average trade effects for short-run and long-run exchange rate volatility by estimating the preferred model specifica-

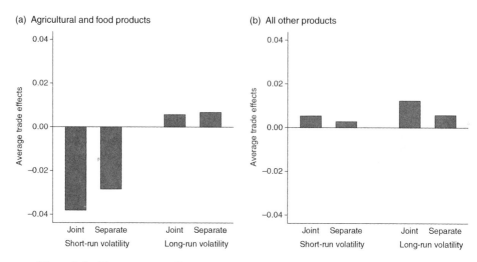

Figure 3.9   Treatment specification and trade effects of exchange rate volatility

Note: The figure shows the impact of the treatment specification on the trade effects of exchange rate volatility. I compare the joint estimation with the separate estimation for short-run and long-run volatility estimates. The average trade effect represents the arithmetic mean of the individual trade effects calculated by the formula $\beta^* = sd_x / sd_y * \hat{\beta}$.

tion with short-run and long-run volatility measures jointly and separately. The average trade effects are larger for the joint specification than for the separate specification, indicating some correlation between short-run and long-run volatility effects. These effects are small for the long-run volatility measure and more pronounced for the short-run volatility measure. The results indicate that separate or joint estimation of trade effects for short-run and long-run exchange rate volatility has a limited impact on the average trade effects.

3.3.3.4   Non-linearity

Non-linearity could have an impact on the trade effects of short-run and long-run exchange rate volatility. The rationale is that higher volatility levels associate with non-linear treatment effects. To account for these effects, I include linear and quadratic exchange rate volatility measures in the preferred regression specification. The results of this analysis are presented in figure 3.10. Subfigures (a) and (b) show the change in the rank for all agricultural and food products comparing the linear to the quadratic specification. The arrows indicate the movement in rank and trade effects. For the majority of agricultural and food products, the inclusion of quadratic exchange rate volatility measures has a limited impact on the trade effects. This observation applies to short-run and long-run volatility effects. Subfigures (c) and (d) compare the absolute change in the trade effects for one-standard deviation change in exchange rate volatility. The figures indicate that most agricultural and food products show a minor change in trade effects. However, some

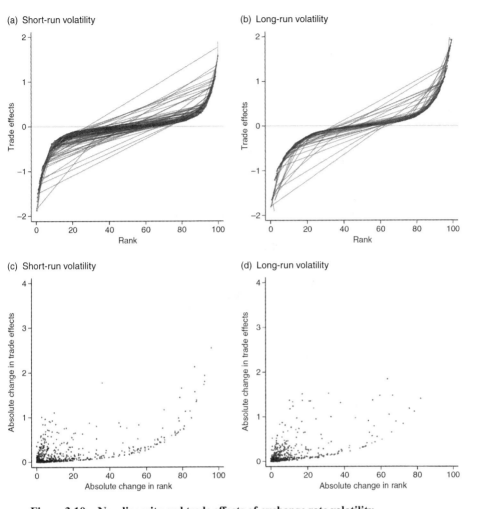

Figure 3.10   Non-linearity and trade effects of exchange rate volatility
Note: The figure shows the impact of the model specification on the trade effects of short-run and long-run exchange rate volatility. I compare the joint with the separate trade effect estimates.

product are strongly impacted by non-linearity indicated by significant rank movement and change in trade effects.

3.4   Conclusion

This paper contributes to the ongoing academic debate on the impact of exchange rate volatility on global food supply chains. I estimate a theoretically consistent sectoral gravity model to measure the effects of short-run and long-run exchange rate volatility on agricultural and food trade at the product level. Earlier studies are characterized by several sources of misspecification and measurement error that are addressed in my analysis. I consider 781 food products and categorize them according to the liberal product classification of Rauch (1999) into homogenous, reference-priced, and differentiated products. My estimates indicate significant differences between product categories and industries. I find some evidence for an adverse effect of short-run and a positive impact of long-run exchange rate volatility on global food supply chains. The results indicate that products produced by industries with high upstreamness have positive trade effects, while low downstreamness of an industry correlated with larger and positive trade effects. I also find that export prices correlate positively with trade effects for the long-run but not for short-run volatility measures. The estimates do not indicate any relevant correlation between trade effects of exchange rate volatility and both product sophistication and product complexity. I also find no evidence of differences in the trade effects according to the economic development stage. Several robustness checks are conducted to explain why my results divert from common wisdom in the international trade literature. These checks confirm that gravity model misspecification, aggregation bias, exchange rate measurement errors, and treatment misspecification are the leading causes for the significant and negative estimates in earlier studies (see, for example, Rose 2000; Tenreyro 2007). Both short-run and long-run exchange rate volatility have a limited mean impact on agricultural and food trade. There is substantial heterogeneity between different products along the global food supply chain that requires a product-level analysis to be unmasked.

Appendix

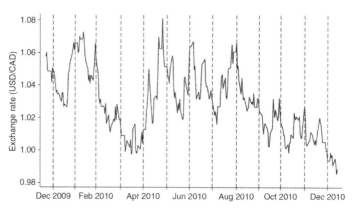

Figure 3A.1   Temporal resolution of the exchange rate data
Note: The figure shows the exchange rate quotation for the USD/CAD pair for 2010. Red vertical lines indicate end-month exchange rate quotations.

Table 3A.1 **Sample countries**

Country name	ISO code	Country name	ISO code
Angola	AGO	Djibouti	DJI
Albania	ALB	Dominica	DMA
United Arab Emirates	ARE	Denmark	DNK
Argentina	ARG	Dominican Rep.	DOM
Antigua and Barbuda	ATG	Algeria	DZA
Australia	AUS	Ecuador	ECU
Austria	AUT	Egypt	EGY
Benin	BEN	Spain	ESP
Burkina Faso	BFA	Estonia	EST
Bangladesh	BGD	Finland	FIN
Bulgaria	BGR	Fiji	FJI
Bahrain	BHR	France	FRA
Bahamas	BHS	Gabon	GAB
Belarus	BLR	United Kingdom	GBR
Belize	BLZ	Ghana	GHA
Bolivia	BOL	Guinea	GIN
Brazil	BRA	Gambia	GMB
Barbados	BRB	Guinea-Bissau	GNB
Central African Republic	CAF	Greece	GRC
Canada	CAN	Grenada	GRD
Switzerland	CHE	Guatemala	GTM
Chile	CHL	Guyana	GUY
China	CHN	China, Hong Kong SAR	HKG
Cote d'Ivoire	CIV	Honduras	HND
Cameroon	CMR	Croatia	HRV
Congo	COG	Haiti	HTI
Colombia	COL	Hungary	HUN
Comoros	COM	Indonesia	IDN
Cape Verde	CPV	India	IND
Costa Rica	CRI	Ireland	IRL
Cyprus	CYP	Iran	IRN
Czech Republic	CZE	Iceland	ISL
Germany	DEU	Israel	ISR
Italy	ITA	Pakistan	PAK
Jordan	JOR	Peru	PER
Japan	JPN	Philippines	PHL
Kazakhstan	KAZ	Poland	POL
Kenya	KEN	Portugal	PRT
Cambodia	KHM	Paraguay	PRY
Rep. of Korea	KOR	Russian Federation	RUS
Kuwait	KWT	Rwanda	RWA
Lebanon	LBN	Saudi Arabia	SAU
Liberia	LBR	Senegal	SEN
Libya	LBY	Singapore	SGP
Saint Lucia	LCA	Sierra Leone	SLE
Sri Lanka	LKA	El Salvador	SLV
Lithuania	LTU	Suriname	SUR
Latvia	LVA	Slovakia	SVK
Morocco	MAR	Slovenia	SVN

(*continued*)

Table 3A.1   **(continued)**

Country name	ISO code	Country name	ISO code
Moldova	MDA	Sweden	SWE
Madagascar	MDG	Seychelles	SYC
Mexico	MEX	Syria	SYR
Mali	MLI	Chad	TCD
Malta	MLT	Togo	TGO
Mozambique	MOZ	Thailand	THA
Mauritania	MRT	Tonga	TON
Mauritius	MUS	Trinidad and Tobago	TTO
Malawi	MWI	Tunisia	TUN
Malaysia	MYS	Turkey	TUR
Niger	NER	Tanzania	TZA
Nigeria	NGA	Uganda	UGA
Nicaragua	NIC	Ukraine	UKR
Netherlands	NLD	Uruguay	URY
Norway	NOR	USA	USA
Nepal	NPL	Saint Vincent and Grenadines	VCT
New Zealand	NZL	Venezuela	VEN
Oman	OMN	Vietnam	VNM
Vanuatu	VUT	South Africa	ZAF
Yemen	YEM		

Note: The table reports the list of sample countries. I report the country name and ISO code.

Table 3A.2   **Descriptive statistics**

Variables	Mean	Standard deviation			Trend
		Overall	Between	Within	
Log of weighted distance	8.76	0.80	0.00	0.80	0.00
Log of market size	26.31	1.78	0.19	1.77	0.10
Log of income difference	9.25	1.39	0.08	1.39	0.05
Economic integration	0.61	1.25	0.15	1.24	0.11
WTO membership	0.63	0.48	0.17	0.46	−0.05
Common colonizer	0.01	0.11	0.00	0.11	0.00
Shared border	0.02	0.12	0.00	0.12	0.00
Common language	0.16	0.36	0.00	0.36	0.00
Common legacy	0.01	0.10	0.00	0.10	0.00

Note: The table presents the descriptive statistics. The calculation are based on data by country-pair for 2001 to 2017.

References

Anderson, J., and Y. Yotov. 2016. "Terms of Trade and Global Efficiency Effects of Free Trade Agreements, 1990–2002." *Journal of International Economics* 99: 279–98.

Anderson, J. E., and E. van Wincoop. 2003. "Gravity with Gravitas: A Solution to the Border Puzzle." *American Economic Review* 93: 170–92.

Antràs, P., and D. Chor. 2013. "Organizing the Global Value Chain." *Econometrica* 81: 2127–2204.

Antràs, P., D. Chor, T. Fally, and R. Hillberry. 2012. "Measuring the Upstreamness of Production and Trade Flows." *American Economic Review* 102: 412–16.

Auboin, M., and M. Ruta. 2013. "The Relationship between Exchange Rates and International Trade: A Literature Review." *World Trade Review* 12: 577–605.

Bergstrand, J. H. 2016. *Economic Integration Agreement Dataset*. https://kellogg.nd.edu/faculty/fellows/bergstrand.

Broda, C., and J. Romalis. 2011. "Identifying the Relationship Between Trade and Exchange Rate Volatility." In *Commodity Prices and Markets*, NBER-East Asia Seminar on Economics, Volume 20, edited by Takatoshi Ito and Andrew K. Rose, 79–110. Chicago, IL: University of Chicago Press.

Cameron, C., and D. Miller. 2015. "A Practitioner's Guide to Cluster-Robust Inference." *Journal of Human Resources* 50: 317–72.

Cameron, C., and P. Trivedi. 2013. *Regression Analysis of Count Data*. Cambridge: Cambridge University Press.

CEPII. 2021. *BACI*. http://www.cepii.fr/CEPII.

Cho, G., I. M. Sheldon, and S. McCorriston. 2002. "Exchange Rate Uncertainty and Agricultural Trade." *American Journal of Agricultural Economics* 84: 931–42.

Clark, P., S. J. Wei, N. Tamirisa, A. Sadikov, and L. Zeng. 2004. *A New Look at Exchange Rate Volatility and Trade Flows*. Occasional Papers. USA: International Monetary Fund.

Correia, S., P. Guimarães, and T. Zylkin. 2020. "Fast Poisson Estimation with High-Dimensional Fixed Effects." *The Stata Journal* 20: 95–115.

Costinot, A., D. Donaldson, and I. Komunjer. 2012. "What Goods Do Countries Trade? A Quantitative Exploration of Ricardo's Ideas." *Review of Economic Studies* 79: 581–608.

Demers, M. 1991. "Investment under Uncertainty, Irreversibility and the Arrival of Information Over Time." *Review of Economic Studies* 58: 333–50.

Ethier, W. 1973. "International Trade and the Forward Exchange Market." *American Economic Review* 63: 494–503.

Franke, G. 1991. "Exchange Rate Volatility and International Trading Strategy." *Journal of International Money and Finance* 10: 292–307.

Galí, Jordi, and T. Monacelli. 2005. "Monetary Policy and Exchange Rate Volatility in a Small Open Economy." *The Review of Economic Studies* 72: 707–34.

Gong, G., and F. J. Samaniego. 1981. "Pseudo Maximum Likelihood Estimation: Theory and Applications." *Annals of Statistics* 9: 861–69.

Gourieroux, C., A. Monfort, and A. Trognon. 1984. "Pseudo Maximum Likelihood Methods: Applications to Poisson Models." *Econometrica* 52: 701–20.

Grauwe, P. D. 1988. "Exchange Rate Variability and the Slowdown in Growth of International Trade." *IMF Staff Papers* 35: 63–84.

Hallak, J. C. 2010. "A Product-Quality View of the Linder Hypothesis." *Review of Economics and Statistics* 92: 453–66.

Hartmann, D., M. R. Guevara, C. Jara-Figueroa, M. Aristarán, and C. A. Hidalgo.

2017. "Linking Economic Complexity, Institutions, and Income Inequality." *World Development* 93: 75–93.

Hausmann, R., J. Hwang, and D. Rodrik. 2007. "What You Export Matters." *Journal of Economic Growth* 12: 1–25.

Johnson, H. G. 1969. "The Case for Flexible Exchange Rates." In *Federal Reserve Bank of St. Louis Review*. St. Louis: MI, 12–24.

Kandilov, I. T. 2008. "The Effects of Exchange Rate Volatility on Agricultural Trade." *American Journal of Agricultural Economics* 90: 1028–1043.

Klaassen, F. 2004. "Why Is It So Difficult to Find an Effect of Exchange Rate Risk on Trade?" *Journal of International Money and Finance* 23: 817–39.

Koray, F., and W. D. Lastrapes. 1989. "Real Exchange Rate Volatility and U.S. Bilateral Trade: A Var Approach." *The Review of Economics and Statistics* 71: 708–12.

Lall, S., J. Weiss, and J. Zhang. 2006. "The 'Sophistication' of Exports: A New Trade Measure." *World Development* 34: 222–37.

Mayer, T., and S. Zignago. 2011. "Notes on CEPII's Distances Measures: The Geo-Dist Database." In *CEPII Working Paper 2011–25*.

McKenzie, M. D. 1999. "The Impact of Exchange Rate Volatility on International Trade Flows." *Journal of Economic Surveys* 13: 71–106.

Mundell, R. 2000. "Currency Areas, Exchange Rate Systems and International Monetary Reform." *Journal of Applied Economics* 3: 217–56.

Pick, D. H. 1990. "Exchange Rate Risk and U.S. Agricultural Trade Flows." *American Journal of Agricultural Economics* 72: 694–700.

Rauch, J. E. 1999. "Networks versus Markets in International Trade." *Journal of International Economics* 48: 7–35.

Regmi, A., M. J. Gehlhar, J. Wainio, T. L. Vollrath, P. V. Johnston, and N. Kathuria. 2005. "Market Access For High-Value Foods." Agricultural economic reports No. 33999, United States Department of Agriculture, Economic Research Service.

Rose, A. K. 2000. "One Money, One Market: The Effect of Common Currencies on Trade." *Economic Policy* 15: 08–45.

Silva, J. M. C. S., and S. Tenreyro. 2006. "The Log of Gravity." *The Review of Economics and Statistics* 88: 641–58.

Silva, J. M. C. S., and S. Tenreyro. 2010. "On the Existence of the Maximum Likelihood Estimates in Poisson Regression." *Economics Letters* 107: 310–12.

Tenreyro, S. 2007. "On the Trade Impact of Nominal Exchange Rate Volatility." *Journal of Development Economics* 82: 485–508.

Thomson Reuters. 2019. *Datastream*. https://infobase.thomsonreuters.com.

Thursby, J. G., and M. C. Thursby. 1987. "Bilateral Trade Flows, the Linder Hypothesis, and Exchange Risk." *The Review of Economics and Statistics* 69: 488–95.

United Nations. 2021. *UN Comtrade Database*. https://comtrade.un.org.

Viaene, J. M., and C. G. de Vries. 1992. "International Trade and Exchange Rate Volatility." *European Economic Review* 36: 1311–1321.

Wooldridge, J. 1999. *Handbook of Applied Econometrics Volume II: Quasi-Likelihood Methods for Count Data*. Oxford: Blackwell Publishing Inc.

World Bank. 2021. *World Development Indicators Database*. http://data.worldbank.org/data-catalog/world-development-indicators.

WTO. 2021. *Understanding the WTO*. https://www.wto.org.

4

Fertilizer and Algal Blooms
A Satellite Approach to Assessing Water Quality

Charles A. Taylor and Geoffrey Heal

4.1 Introduction

The US Environmental Protection Agency considers nutrient pollution one of the "most widespread, costly and challenging environmental problems."[1] Increasing flows of nitrogen have far exceeded the Earth's carrying capacity and have impaired ecosystem functioning (Vitousek et al. 1997; Gruber and Galloway 2008; Erisman et al. 2013), and nutrient levels far exceed the planetary boundaries of certainty (Steffen et al. 2015).

Nutrient enrichment, hypoxia, and algal blooms are interrelated environmental phenomena. They are caused by excess nitrogen and phosphorus, coming primarily from fertilizer use but also from human and industrial waste. These nutrients leach into waterways and feed the growth of phytoplankton in a process called eutrophication (Nixon 1995). Eutrophication can produce algal blooms, which are considered harmful when concentrations of algae (e.g., cyanobacteria) achieve sufficient density to create negative environmental or health effects (Smayda 1997).

Occurring in both fresh and salt water, algal blooms can be produced by excess nutrients and climactic anomalies like warmer water tempera-

Charles A. Taylor was working toward his PhD in Sustainable Development at Columbia University when this chapter was written, and is currently an S.V. Ciriacy-Wantrup postdoctoral fellow at the University of California, Berkeley.

Geoffrey Heal is a professor of economics at Columbia Business School and a research associate of the National Bureau of Economic Research.

Taylor received support from the Center for Environmental Economics and Policy (CEEP), Columbia University. For acknowledgments, sources of research support, and disclosure of the authors' material financial relationships, if any, please see https://www.nber.org/books-and -chapters/risks-agricultural-supply-chains/fertilizer-and-algal-blooms-satellite-approach -assessing-water-quality.

1. Source: www.epa.gov/nutrientpollution/issue, accessed December 9, 2020.

tures (Paerl and Huisman 2008; Michalak et al. 2013; Ho, Michalak, and Pahlevan 2019). Algal blooms are often followed by hypoxic aquatic conditions, defined by dissolved oxygen levels below two ml per liter, as dead phytoplankton sink to the seafloor and are decomposed by bacteria. Sustained low oxygen levels, in turn, can result in aquatic dead zones.

Algal blooms have increased in frequency and intensity over the decades (Anderson 1989; Hallegraeff 1993; Hudnell 2008; Huisman et al. 2018; Ho, Michalak, and Pahlevan 2019). The quantity and extent of dead zones have also increased across the globe (Diaz and Rosenberg 2008). Dead zones are now considered a major threat to the health of aquatic ecosystems (Diaz and Rosenberg 2008; Doney 2010). While natural processes like upwelling of nutrient-rich ocean water contribute to eutrophication, anthropogenic nutrient loading is increasingly the driver of algal blooms and hypoxic events.

Fertilizer use is mostly exempt from federal regulation under the Clean Water Act despite being the major source of water quality impairment in the US (Olmstead 2010), and individual states have been hesitant to regulate agricultural inputs (Kling 2013). While regulation of agriculture is politically difficult to implement, several other challenges also inhibit efficient regulation of this market.

First, the economic impacts of hypoxia and algal blooms and the related external cost of fertilizer are difficult to quantify (Rabotyagov et al. 2014; Barbier 2012). This is partly due to the inherent challenges of estimating the costs of nonpoint pollution (Shortle and Horan 2001, 2013), in which it is difficult to link accumulated downstream pollution to specific upstream sources. In an analysis of contributors to the dead zone in the Gulf of Mexico, David, Drinkwater, and McIsaac (2010) found that the highest nitrogen yields occurred in the tile-drained Corn Belt of Minnesota, Iowa, Illinois, Indiana, and Ohio—areas 1,500 km upstream from the pollution culmination point at the mouth of the Mississippi River.

A second challenge to rigorous estimation of the social cost of fertilizer is the lack of temporally consistent and spatially relevant data on water quality (Brooks et al. 2016) that can be linked to economic outcomes. Water quality studies rely on data from *in situ* samples of water bodies, which are limited in temporal and spatial extent and face challenges related to inconsistent sampling practices and lack of coordination between scientific and governmental entities (Monitoring Water Quality 1995).[2] Past studies of the impact of algal blooms have been limited to specific geographies or relatively short time frames. To overcome this problem, we construct a measure of county-level algal bloom intensity that is derived from over three decades of Landsat satellite imagery, as well as a spatially weighted measure of fertilizer use that is linked to watersheds.

---

2. The availability of standardized historic water quality data has improved following the launch of the Water Quality Portal by USGS, EPA, among others (Read et al. 2017).

4.2   Data

Algal blooms: We construct a county-level measure of algal bloom intensity derived from over three decades of Landsat satellite imagery and processed using computing power available through Google Earth Engine.[3] Several satellite products have been used to detect and monitor algal blooms, including the European Space Agency's Medium Resolution Imaging Spectrometer (MERIS) product (Clark et al. 2017) and a Moderate Resolution Imaging Spectroradiometer (MODIS) product for ocean color, which measures chlorophyll levels at 500 m resolution in the ocean and large inland lakes. Each satellite product has its own trade-offs around duration, revisit time, resolution, and geographic extent. We opt for Landsat given its longer time series and the higher spatial resolution at 30 m, which allows us to better capture small inland water bodies and rivers.

We build on the approach of Ho, Michalak, and Pahlevan (2019) to analyzing global lakes. We use Landsat Thematic Mapper top-of-atmosphere (TOA), combining Landsat 5 (1984–2000) and Landsat 7 (2000–present). The bloom algorithm is based on the near-infrared (NIR) band with an atmospheric correction for shortwave radiation (SWIR): B4 − 1.03*B5 (Wang and Shi 2007). In matching Landsat 5 with Landsat 7, we subtract the satellite bias based on the difference in county-level bloom values during the years in which the products overlapped.

We filter out all images with over 25 percent cloud cover. Unlike Ho et al. (2017), we do not filter out pixels beyond a certain hue threshold. We then take the temporal average of the bloom measure across all the 16-day revisit periods for each pixel during the peak bloom time in late summer (July to September). Next, we take the US county-level mean over a 30 m water mask from the National Land Cover Dataset (NLCD) for the maximum water extent from 2001 to 2016. US state boundaries extend three nautical miles from the coast, and this area is included in each state's county calculations of bloom intensity. We thus include both saline coastal waters and inland fresh water. We exclude counties lacking significant water features (less than 5 km^2 of surface water), dropping about 25 percent of US counties. However, the results are robust to their inclusion.

It is worth noting that our calculated index is not a direct measure of concentrations of either chlorophyll or any specific algal species; rather, it measures relative greenness in the upper layer of the water column. Many studies over the years have used Landsat to identify algal blooms (Tyler et al. 2006; Duan et al. 2007; Tebbs, Remedios, and Harper 2013). This specific algorithm has been validated on the ground in Lake Erie (Ho et al. 2017) and globally through tests of how the index reflects the spatial gradients of chlorophyll-a levels within lakes (Ho, Michalak, and Pahlevan 2019).

---

3. Google Earth Engine, https://earthengine.google.com.

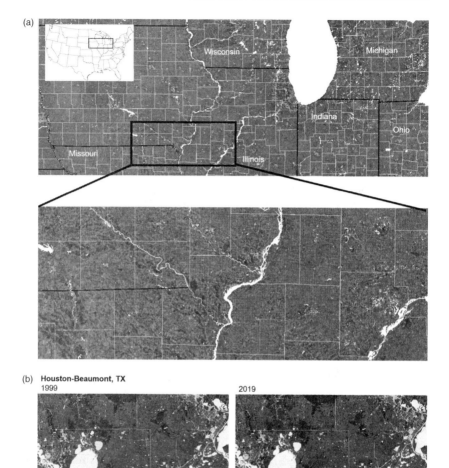

Figure 4.1   Panel A shows late summer bloom index averaged over 20 years from 1999 to 2019 in the US Corn Belt, then with a close-up of the boundary region of Iowa, Illinois and Missouri, where the Des Moines River meets the Mississippi. Panel B shows the late summer algal bloom index at two discrete points in time (1999 and 2019) in the Houston-Beaumont region.

The construction of our bloom index can be visualized in panel A of figure 4.1, along with how the bloom index changes over time in panel B.

Fertilizer: We employ the US Geological Survey (USGS)'s annual county-level estimates of nitrogen and phosphorus use from 1987 to 2012 (Brakebill and Gronberg 2017), which was recently updated for the year 2017 (Falcone 2021). Data are based on fertilizer product sales compiled by the Association of American Plant Food Control Officials (AAPFCO), and thus exclude organic fertilizers like manure. We normalize fertilizer values by the

County flow direction of selected counties

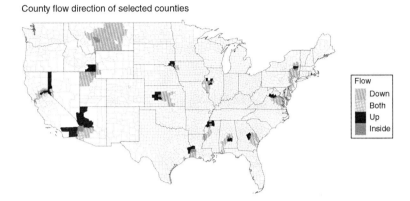

Figure 4.2 **Watershed classification of counties based on their relative location within the USGS NHD hydrologic unit code HUC 4 watershed boundary. Thirteen randomly selected counties are shown in gray. Areas with diagonal lines represent counties that are at least partly within the same HUC 4 and downstream from the gray county, as determined by their overlap with finer resolution HUC 12 watersheds. Likewise, black counties are upstream from gray counties. Finally, the areas with dashed lines, "Both," include counties that have land area that is both upstream and downstream from gray counties.**

land area in a given county. We further calculate the sum of fertilizer use in upstream counties within a given watershed (HUC 4) from a county. The upstream-downstream relationship for a random subset of counties can be visualized in figure 4.2. Our main measure is farm fertilizer use, but results hold including non-farm fertilizer use as well.

The upstream-downstream analysis is based on USGS watershed boundaries of hydrologic unit code HUC 4 and HUC 12 to assign water flow relationships between counties using flow relationships from the National Hydrography Dataset (NHD) (Buto and Anderson 2020).

County-level climate data come from NOAA's Climate Divisional Database (nCLIMDIV) of monthly temperature and precipitation levels. Annual estimates of hypoxic extent in the northern Gulf of Mexico spanning 1985 to 2019 come from Nancy Rabalais, LUMCON, and R. Eugene Turner, LSU.[4] County-level data on agricultural yields come from the US Department of Agriculture's historical census and National Agricultural Statistics Service (NASS).

4.2.1 Validation of Satellite Algal Bloom Measure

To provide evidence that our algal bloom measure is both accurate and representative nationally, we compare our Landsat algal measure to a recent

4. Source: https://www.epa.gov/ms-htf/northern-gulf-mexico-hypoxic-zone.

Table 4.1   Relationship between measures of Landsat algal bloom and Sentinel-3 chlorophyll

	Dependent variable: Sentinel-3 Chlorophyll			
	(1)	(2)	(3)	(4)
Landsat bloom	195.47***	146.44***	151.57***	100.24***
	(30.90)	(23.99)	(18.38)	(31.51)
Climate controls		X	X	X
Spatial FE			Division	County
Observations	9,109	9,109	9,109	9,109
R^2	0.19	0.23	0.34	0.64

Note: Linear regression. Dependent variable is Sentinel-3 OLCI band 11 (Chl fluorescence baseline, red edge transition). Predictor is Landsat algal bloom intensity measure used in this paper. Both measures aggregated at county-level from July to September over areas with water. Time series from 2017 to 2020 when both satellite products available. Counties with less than 5 km^2 of water dropped from analysis. Standard errors clustered at the state level. * $p < 0.1$; ** $p < 0.05$; *** $p < 0.01$

satellite product for chlorophyll-a, an indicator of algal activity. We make the comparison at the county-year level, using a similar construction by averaging values over water area in a county and across July to September. Since late 2016, the Sentinel-3 Ocean and Land Color Instrument has provided chlorophyll measures at 300 m resolution with a two-day revisit time. We use the band at 709.75 nm for chlorophyll fluorescence baseline, red edge transition. While MODIS has an Ocean Colour SMI Chlorophyll-a product going back to 2000, we do not use this measure due to its even lower resolution and geographic restriction to primarily oceanic and coastal regions. Table 4.1 shows the results of regressing Sentinel chlorophyll on our Landsat algal bloom measure at the county-year level. We find a strong positive relationship as expected, which persists with controlling for climate and various spatial fixed effects.

Figure 4A.1 shows a scatterplot of these two measures of water quality at the county-year level from 2017 to 2020, splitting counties into quartile by water area. We note a positive relationship, which improves with amount of water in an area. The weak relationship in the first quartile motivates the fact that we drop counties in the first quartile (less than 5 km^2 water area) from our general analyses. Figure 4A.2 shows a similar scatterplot but facets across regions to test the generalizabilty across the US. We find a generally positive relationship between our Landsat measure of bloom intensity and Sentinel chlorophyll at the county-year level in all places except the Mountain region. It is worth noting that this region is the driest part of the US with the lowest proportions of water area by counties.

Altogether, we take the persistent correlation we see between our Landsat algal bloom measure and Sentinel chlorophyll at the county level to mean

Table 4.2   **Bloom algorithm and *in situ* measurements of chlorophyll-a**

	(1)	(2)	(3)	(4)	(5)	(6)	(7)
	Dependent variable: Chlorophyll-a concentration (ug/L)						
Bloom	0.066***	0.063***					
	(0.010)	(0.008)					
Bloom:Estuary			0.031***	0.031***	0.024***	0.024***	0.027***
			(0.010)	(0.009)	(0.007)	(0.007)	(0.005)
Bloom:Lake			0.065***	0.072***	0.065***	0.064***	0.039***
			(0.008)	(0.009)	(0.008)	(0.009)	(0.008)
Bloom:Stream			0.042***	0.044***	0.043***	0.044***	0.024***
			(0.011)	(0.010)	(0.008)	(0.007)	(0.005)
RGB controls	No	Yes	Yes	Yes	Yes	Yes	Yes
Month FE	No	No	No	Yes	Yes	Yes	Yes
Geo FE	No	No	No	No	Grid	County	Site
Observations	137,246	137,246	137,246	137,246	137,246	137,246	137,246
R^2	0.070	0.165	0.171	0.182	0.305	0.355	0.629

Note: Linear regression. Dependent variable is *in situ* chlorophyll-a concentration from on-the-ground sampling. Bloom is the computed Landsat algal bloom measure. Observations filtered to exclude images with less than 50 percent water in surrounding pixels and more than 25 percent cloud cover. Outliers beyond the 99.9th percentile dropped. RGB includes controls for Landsat's red, green, and blue radiance bands. Standard errors clustered at the HUC 4 watershed level. * $p < 0.1$; ** $p < 0.05$; *** $p < 0.01$.

that both are measuring broadly similar phenomena. A perfect correlation would not be expected, given that these two measures aggregate millions of images over an entire county's water area from independent satellite products with different spatial resolutions and revisit times to create one annual value per county.

For further validation, we compare our Landsat measure of algal bloom intensity to *in situ* measurements of chlorophyll at the individual site level—instead of aggregating over time and space. To do so, we employ the Aquasat data set, which matches over 600,000 *in situ* water quality measures (including total suspended sediment, dissolved organic carbon, chlorophyll-a, and Secchi disk depth) with spectral reflectance from Landsat 5, 7, and 8 collected within one day of the sample over 1984 to 2019 (Ross et al. 2019). We calculate an image-specific algal bloom measure using the same algorithm used in our paper (Wang and Shi 2007).

Results are shown in table 4.2. At the site level, we see a consistently positive relationship between sampled chlorophyll-a concentration and our site-specific Landsat algal bloom measure, holding across the three main water type classifications in the Aquasat data set (estuary, lake, and stream).

4.2.2   Satellite-Derived Bloom Intensity Trends

Figure 4.3 showcases the temporal and spatial patterns of the constructed bloom index across US counties. As expected, bloom intensity is higher

(a) Summer algal bloom average

(b) Summer algal bloom change, 1985–2019

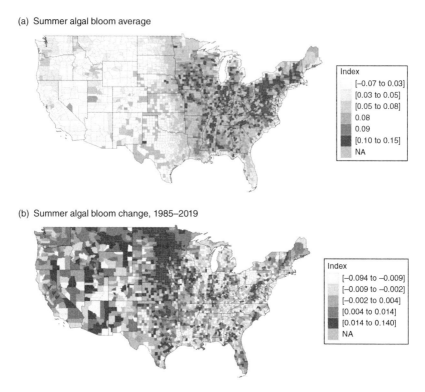

Figure 4.3   Panel A plots the county-level late summer bloom index averaged over the entire sample time period from 1984 to 2020. Panel B plots long-term change from 1985 to 2019 using three-year averages around the endpoints (i.e., 1984–1986 for 1985). Gray counties lack enough surface water for a reading.

in agricultural regions. There is significant geographic variation in where bloom intensity increased and decreased, although there seems to be a general upward trend in the upper Great Plains and along the 100th meridian.

Figure 4.4 graphs average annual bloom intensity by US region from 1984 to 2020. Trends appear flat or decreasing in most locations. Decreasing bloom intensity in the US Southeast (South Atlantic) signifying potential water quality improvement may be attributable to a reduction in cropland area in that region. Algal blooms have intensified in the upper Midwest (West North Central) beginning in the mid-2000s. This may be linked to Corn Belt cropland expansion and intensification driven by ethanol demand in response to the Energy Policy Act of 2005, as noted by others (Metaxoglou and Smith 2021). We see that four of the five largest ethanol producers in the US are included in the West North Central division (Iowa, Nebraska, South Dakota, Minnesota).

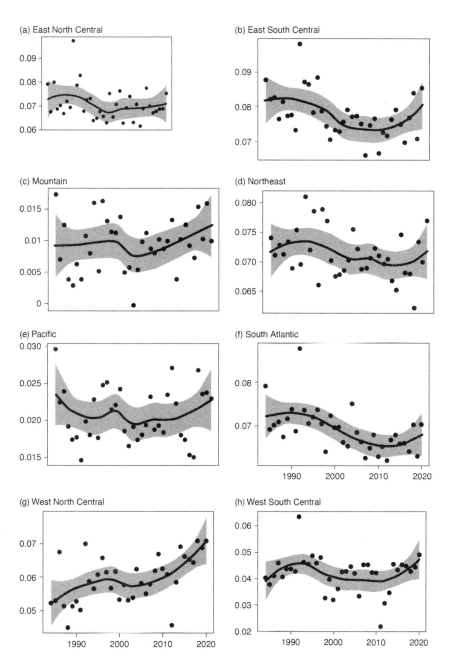

Figure 4.4   Trends in late summer algal bloom intensity from 1984 to 2020 by US Census division. "Northeast" includes New England and the Middle Atlantic. Legend map in panel (i) below.

(i) Legend map

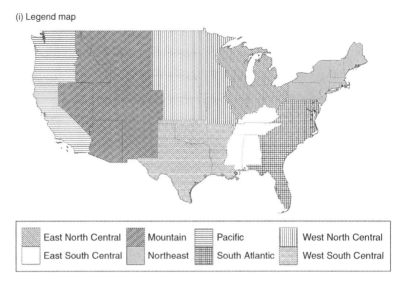

East North Central	Mountain	Pacific	West North Central
East South Central	Northeast	South Atlantic	West South Central

Figure 4.4   (continued)

Notwithstanding some anomalies in recent years, the overall improvement in water quality that we see aligns with Topp et al. (2021), who use a similar approach to ours that links Landsat to *in situ* measures of water quality to model water clarity over 14,000 lakes in the US. They find a marked improvement in water quality over time. Our findings also align with Keiser and Shapiro (2019), who note a reduction in water pollution through 2001 using *in situ* data.

4.3   Empirical Strategy

We employ several empirical approaches: a panel approach of county-year observations to assess annual variation; a five-year panel to assess intermediate variation; and a long-difference cross-sectional approach to assess longer-term effects. We apply these approaches to estimate the impact of fertilizer on algal blooms.

Panel

(1) $$bloom_{it} = \beta_1 fert_{itw} + \beta_2 W_{it} + state_{s(i)} + \alpha_i + \gamma_t + \varepsilon_{it}.$$

Long-difference

(2) $$\Delta bloom_i = \beta_1 \Delta fert_i + \beta_2 \Delta W_i + state_{s(i)} + \varepsilon_i.$$

In the panel model, the outcome variable, *bloom*, is the satellite-derived measure of late summer algal bloom intensity in county i and year t. *fert* is tons of nitrogen fertilizer in county i and year t, or alternatively the sum of fertilizer use in counties upstream of county i but within its watershed w. Fertilizer values are normalized by dividing by county land area. W is a vector of climate controls including mean summer *temp* and *precip*.

County-level fixed effects α are used to demean the observations and allow for interannual comparisons, as well as year-level fixed effects γ to account for national-level variation (i.e., commodity prices). State-specific annual time trends *state* are also included to account for differential state-level policy. Standard errors are clustered at the state level s.

In the long-difference, the outcome variable, $\Delta bloom$, is the change in our satellite-derived measure of late summer algal bloom intensity between 1987 and 2017, each period calculated as a three-year average (i.e., period 1987 is the average of 1986 to 1988) to reduce the likelihood of anomalous years influencing outcomes. Similarly, $\Delta fert$ and ΔW represent the change in each variable at the county level over that same time period. We also employ state-level fixed effects, *state*, to isolate within-state variation. Standard errors are again clustered at the state level. Note we restrict our analysis to the continental US. To ensure a clear satellite signal for water quality, we drop counties with less than 5 km^2 of water cover (one-quarter of US counties), as well as counties with no cropland. However, results are robust to the inclusion of such counties.

For robustness, we also estimate "intermediate" effects with a panel of five-year intervals using three-year rolling-window moving averages calculated over our annual panel data set. This allows us to account for a multi-year process. For example, it can take several years for fertilizer to leach into downstream waterways (Rabotyagov et al. 2014), and likewise, fertilizer use over a multi-year period may result in elevated bloom intensity over the course of several years. For this intermediate analysis, we utilize the five-year panel of county-level fertilizer data developed by Falcone (2021).

4.4 Results

4.4.1 Drivers of Fertilizer Use

Nitrogen fertilizer consumption in 2015 in the US was 13 million tons,[5] and world nitrogen demand was 119 million tons in 2019 (FAO 2018). Nitrogen usage has steadily increased over the last couple of decades, aided by the Haber-Bosch process and low-cost energy (Glibert 2020), while the use of phosphate and potash-based fertilizers has flattened or declined, as shown

---

5. Fertilizer Use and Price: www.ers.usda.gov/data-products/fertilizer-use-and-price.

(a) Historical US fertilizer use by type   (b) Annual growth rate

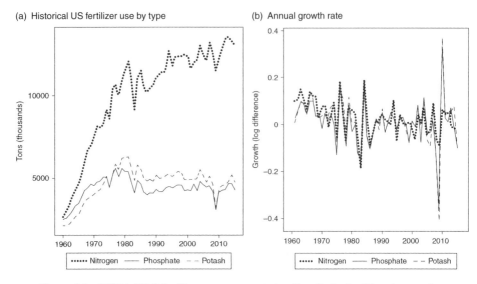

Figure 4.5   USDA ERS fertilizer use aggregated nationally by fertilizer type and year

in figure 4.5. However, phosphates are also an important driver of algal blooms. Figure 4A.3 plots the relationship between nitrogen and phosphate use at the county level. Again, we see a very high correlation.

We first analyze the drivers of fertilizer use at the county level. For an individual farmer, the yield-response curve for fertilizer use is well-known. As described earlier, nitrogen fertilizer accounts for a large cost component of commercial farm operations (~10 percent of production value). There is a strong incentive to apply an amount that optimizes yield response relative to the marginal cost of fertilizer. Since fertilizer and crops have transparent commodity pricing, we are not concerned about pricing differentials across location driving changes in input use.

At the county level we expect fertilizer use to be driven by changes in land use. In table 4.3, we regress county-level nitrogen use on several potential land use variables: total harvested acres of the four major crops in the US (corn, soy, wheat, cotton), the ratio of corn-to-soy acres, and acres of land enrolled under the USDA Conservation Reserve Program (CRP). Cropland area is strongly related to nitrogen use. We would expect that places that increased corn production relative to soy production would increase their nitrogen fertilizer use given that soybeans are nitrogen-fixing leguminous plants that require less nitrogen compared to corn. Finally, we see a negative relationship with CRP enrollment, which makes sense given that this program entails taking land out of active farm production.

Overall, these results reassure us that fertilizer use is responding to the

Table 4.3   **Drivers of farm nitrogen use**

	Dependent variable: Nitrogen use (1,000 tons)			
	(1)	(2)	(3)	(4)
Crop area	0.009***	0.012***	0.009***	0.012***
	(0.003)	(0.003)	(0.003)	(0.003)
Corn-soy ratio		0.929***		0.920***
		(0.252)		(0.248)
CRP acres			−0.008***	−0.010**
			(0.003)	(0.004)
County FE	X	X	X	X
Year FE	X	X	X	X
State-Yr trends	X	X	X	X
Observations	83,094	51,538	82,804	51,458
R^2	0.954	0.956	0.954	0.956

Note: Linear regression. Dependent variable is aggregate farm-level nitrogen use (1,000s of tons) at the county level. Crop area is the total harvested acres of corn, soy, wheat, and cotton. Corn-soy ratio is the amount of corn acres divided by the sum of corn and soybean acres. CRP acres is the amount of acres under the USDA Conservation Reserve Program. Time series to 1987 to 2012 and 2017. Sample size varies based on extent of counties with both corn and soy production and CRP data. Standard errors clustered at the state level. * $p < 0.1$; ** $p < 0.05$; *** $p < 0.01$.

individual and aggregate-level factors that one would expect and that our nitrogen use data are capturing meaningful variation across counties and over time.

4.4.2 Fertilizer on Blooms

We next test the relationship between nitrogen use and algal bloom intensity at the county level, as captured by a satellite measure of late summer water greenness. In table 4.4 we separately test for the effects of nitrogen use in the county and the sum of nitrogen use over upstream counties within the county's watershed. We further control for weather conditions and county and year fixed effects, as well as state-year trends, as described earlier.

Figure 4.6 plots the coefficients for the annual panel, the five-year panel, and the long difference cross-section over thirty years from 1987 to 2017. We see that algal bloom intensity responds to nitrogen use across short-term, medium-term, and long-term horizons.

There are valid concerns about the extent to which weather is a potential confounder given its influence on farm-level decisions (e.g., reducing fertilizer use in response to adverse weather) as well as bloom intensity directly through phytoplankton biological processes. While we cannot completely untangle this relationship, in figure 4A.4 we run the analyses from figure 4.6 but omit the controls for growing season precipitation and temperature. The resulting coefficients are quite similar.

Table 4.4 Late summer algal bloom intensity and fertilizer use per km^2

	Dependent variable: Algal boom intensity			
	(1)	(2)	(3)	(4)
Nitrogen, in county	1.409***	0.589*		
	(0.440)	(0.320)		
Nitrogen, upstream			1.576***	0.529
			(0.448)	(0.471)
County FE	X	X	X	X
Year FE	X	X	X	X
State-Yr trend		X		X
Controls	Weather	Weather	Weather	Weather
SE cluster	State	State	State	State
Observations	61,020	61,020	54,221	54,221
R^2	0.856	0.858	0.858	0.860

Note: Linear regression. Dependent variable is county-level average bloom intensity from July to September in areas with water. Nitrogen is 1,000s of tons of farm-level use per km^2 land area of either county or counties upstream within the HUC 4 watershed. Time series to 1987 to 2012 and 2017. Counties with less than 5 km^2 of water dropped from analysis. Standard errors clustered at the state level. * $p < 0.1$; ** $p < 0.05$; *** $p < 0.01$.

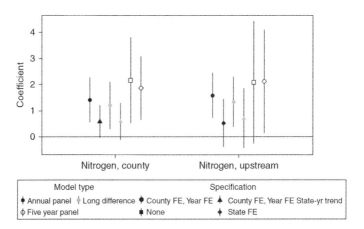

Figure 4.6 **Effect of nitrogen use on late summer algal bloom intensity. Coefficient plot. Lines with black shapes include the same specification as table 4.4. Lines with gray shapes include observations every five years from 1987 to 2017, using average values in the year prior through the year after each point. Lines with white shapes are the results of the cross-sectional long difference from 1987 to 2017, similarly using three-year average values around the endpoints. All models control for average weather conditions. Counties with less than 5 km^2 of water dropped from analysis. Standard errors clustered at the state level. Error bars are at the 95 percent confidence range.**

Table 4.5   **Mississippi River basin annual nitrogen use and Gulf hypoxia extent**

	Dependent variable:					
	Hypoxia (sq km)			Log Hypoxia (sq km)		
	(1)	(2)	(3)	(4)	(5)	(6)
Nitrogen	4.386**	3.702*	4.633*			
	(2.087)	(1.960)	(2.409)			
Log Nitrogen				6.571**	5.448**	5.709*
				(2.902)	(2.577)	(3.241)
Weather upstream		X	X		X	X
Weather coastal			X			X
Observations	26	26	26	26	26	26
R^2	0.155	0.375	0.398	0.176	0.455	0.456
Adjusted R^2	0.120	0.290	0.247	0.142	0.380	0.320
F Statistic	4.417**	4.407**	2.641*	5.128**	6.117***	3.356**

Note: Linear regression. Dependent variable is Gulf of Mexico summer hypoxic extent as defined by the estimated area where bottom-water dissolved oxygen is below 2 mg/L. Nitrogen is measured in 1,000s of tons for farm use, inverse weighted by distance from the mouth of the Mississippi River and summed across all counties in the Mississippi River basin. Weather controls include average temperature and precipitation from January to June of the given year for all counties in the Mississippi River basin (upstream) and counties along the coast of the Gulf of Mexico (coastal). Time period from 1985 to 2019. * $p < 0.1$; ** $p < 0.05$; *** $p < 0.01$.

4.5   Gulf of Mexico Effect

This paper has focused on the within-county impact of fertilizer on algal blooms in that same county. While we account for nutrient pollution from the fertilizer deployed upstream from the county, we do not explicitly assess downstream impacts. A proportion of all fertilizer applied across the entire Mississippi River basin (3.2 million km², or about 40 percent of the continental US including the entire Midwestern Corn Belt) reaches the Gulf of Mexico via the Mississippi River (and the nearby Atchafalaya River). This upstream nutrient pollution creates hypoxic conditions in the Gulf of Mexico (Rabotyagov et al. 2014). Figure 4A.5 shows the correlation between upstream nitrogen and phosphate use and the size of the Gulf of Mexico hypoxic zone. We see the strong correlation between nitrogen and phosphate fertilizer use, as well as a positive but weaker correlation with hypoxic zone extent.

In table 4.5 we estimate the impact of upstream nutrients on the extent of the hypoxic zone. We take the inverse distance-weighted average of fertilizer use across all counties in the Mississippi River basin. Since weather also affects hypoxia via its impact on water flow and phytoplankton activity, we flexibly control for precipitation and temperature across the Mississippi River basin and along the coast. We find a somewhat weak but persistently positive relationship between nitrogen use and hypoxic extent: a 1,000 ton increase in upstream nitrogen adds 4 km^2 to the hypoxic zone in the Gulf. The average hypoxic zone during this time period was 14,000 km^2. In log form, we see that a 1 percent increase in nitrogen is associated with about a 6 percent increase in hypoxic extent in km^2. We also show the results for phosphates, another important limiting factor in phytoplankton growth (Turner and Rabalais 2013), in table 4A.1.

4.6   Discussion

Estimating the economic cost of fertilizer via water quality is difficult due to the fact that farm pollution is largely exempt under the Clean Water Act, as well as the lack of annual panel on water quality linked to an administrative level. To this end, we create such a data set using a satellite algorithm to approximate algal bloom intensity at the US county level from 1984 to 2020.

We find that fertilizer is a major driver of water quality impairment at an annual and longer-term timescale. Impacts are apparent both locally and downstream from the fertilizer use, extending to the Gulf of Mexico.

We find significant geographic variation in where blooms occur, and where bloom intensity has increased and decreased over time. On average bloom levels have been relatively flat with the exception of an upward trend in the upper Great Plains and along the 100th meridian starting in the mid-2000s. This finding may be linked to Corn Belt cropland expansion and intensification driven by ethanol demand in response to the Energy Policy Act of 2005.

We hope that this new satellite product of water quality can be tested, refined, and utilized in research on other policy-relevant questions, including the valuation of wetlands and other ecosystem services—and assessing the benefits of land use programs such as the USDA's Conservation Reserve Program and Wetlands Reserve Program. For example, wetland protection and restoration may significantly reduce downstream nutrient pollution (Mitsch et al. 2005) while providing co-benefits like flood mitigation (Taylor and Druckenmiller 2021).

Further, given the global nature of remote sensing data, we hope this product can be utilized in an international context where water quality impairment and algal blooms are increasing challenges.

Appendix

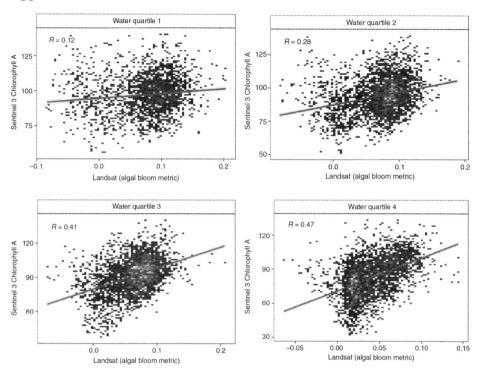

Figure 4A.1   Scatterplot of water quality at the county-year level for Landsat algal bloom measure (x-axis) and Sentinel chlorophyll measure (y-axis) from 2017 to 2020. Outliers outside the 99.9th percentile dropped for clarity. Panels split counties into quartile by water area (1 is least water; 4 is most water). Lighter areas show higher density of points.

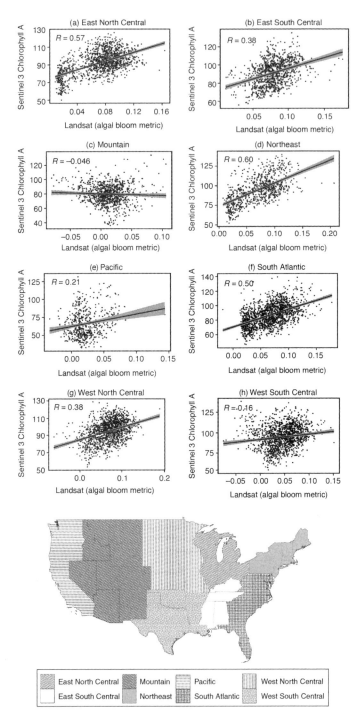

Figure 4A.2 **Scatterplot of water quality at the county-year level for Landsat algal bloom measure (x-axis) and Sentinel chlorophyll measure (y-axis) from 2017 to 2020. Outliers outside the 99.9th percentile dropped for clarity, as well as counties with less than 5 km² water area. Panels split counties into US census regions corresponding to the bottom map.**

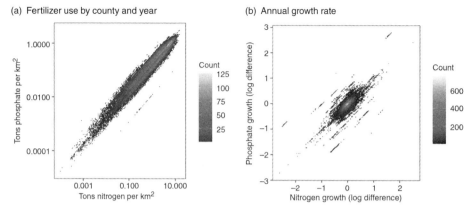

Figure 4A.3 Scatterplot of USGS county-level farm nitrogen and phosphate use per km². Left panel shows annual levels, right panel shows annual change in term of growth rate.

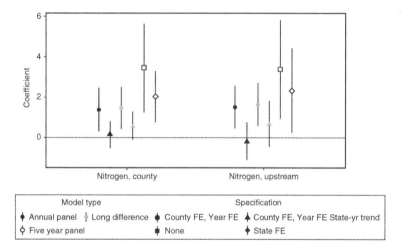

Figure 4A.4 Effect of nitrogen use on late summer algal bloom intensity, no climate controls. Coefficient plot. Same as figure 4.6 except does not include weather controls. Lines with black shapes include the same specification as table 4.4. Lines with gray shapes include observations every five years from 1987 to 2017, using average values in the year prior through the year after each point. Lines with white shapes are the results of the cross-sectional long difference from 1987 to 2017, similarly using three-year average values around the endpoints. All models control for average weather conditions. Counties with less than 5 km² of water dropped from analysis. Standard errors clustered at the state level. Error bars are at the 95 percent confidence range.

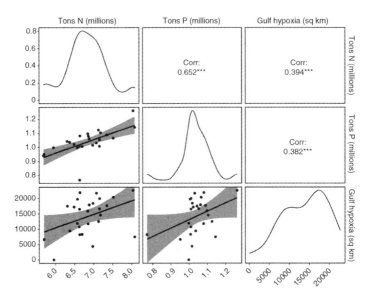

Figure 4A.5 Scatterplots with line of best fit for weighted upstream basin fertilizer use of nitrogen (N) and phosphate (P) in millions of tons and Gulf of Mexico hypoxic zone extent in km². Diagonal line is kernel density plots showing distribution of annual values.

Table 4A.1   Mississippi River basin annual phosphate use and Gulf hypoxia extent

	Dependent variable:					
	Hypoxia (sq km)			Log Hypoxia (sq km)		
	(1)	(2)	(3)	(4)	(5)	(6)
Phosphate	27.314*	26.447**	26.622*			
	(13.499)	(12.068)	(13.379)			
Log Phosphate				3.159	3.207	3.239
				(2.908)	(2.487)	(2.671)
Weather upstream		X	X		X	X
Weather coastal			X			X
Observations	26	26	26	26	26	26
R^2	0.146	0.404	0.404	0.047	0.390	0.415
Adjusted R^2	0.110	0.323	0.255	0.007	0.307	0.269
F Statistic	4.094*	4.975***	2.714**	1.180	4.691**	2.836**

Note: Linear regression. Dependent variable is Gulf of Mexico summer hypoxic extent as defined by the estimated area where bottom-water dissolved oxygen is below 2 mg/L. Phosphate is measured in 1,000s of tons for farm use, inverse weighted by distance from the mouth of the Mississippi River and summed across all counties in the Mississippi River basin. Weather controls include average temperature and precipitation from January to June of the given year for all counties in the Mississippi River basin (upstream) and counties along the coast of the Gulf of Mexico (coastal). Time period from 1985 to 2019. * $p < 0.1$; ** $p < 0.05$; *** $p < 0.01$

References

Anderson, Donald M. 1989. "Toxic Algal Blooms and Red Tides: A Global Perspective." *Red Tides: Biology, Environmental Science and Toxicology*: 11–16.

Barbier, Edward B. 2012. "Progress and Challenges in Valuing Coastal and Marine Ecosystem Services." *Review of Environmental Economics and Policy* 6 (1): 1–19.

Brakebill, J. W., and J. M. Gronberg. 2017. "County-level Estimates of Nitrogen and Phosphorus from Commercial Fertilizer for the Conterminous United States, 1987–2012." US Geological Survey, United States.

Brooks, Bryan W., James M. Lazorchak, Meredith D. A. Howard, Mari-Vaughn V. Johnson, Steve L. Morton, Dawn A. K. Perkins, Euan D. Reavie, Geoffrey I. Scott, Stephanie A. Smith, and Jeffery A. Steevens. 2016. "Are Harmful Algal Blooms Becoming the Greatest Inland Water Quality Threat to Public Health and Aquatic Ecosystems?" *Environmental Toxicology and Chemistry* 35 (1): 6–13.

Buto, Susan G., and Rebecca D. Anderson. 2020. *NHDPlus High Resolution (NHDPlus HR)—A Hydrography Framework for the Nation*. Technical report. US Geological Survey.

Clark, John M., Blake A. Schaeffer, John A. Darling, Erin A. Urquhart, John M. Johnston, Amber R. Ignatius, Mark H. Myer, Keith A. Loftin, P. Jeremy Werdell, and Richard P. Stumpf. 2017. "Satellite Monitoring of Cyanobacterial Harmful Algal Bloom Frequency in Recreational Waters and Drinking Water Sources." *Ecological Indicators* 80: 84–95.

David, Mark B., Laurie E. Drinkwater, and Gregory F. McIsaac. 2010. "Sources of Nitrate Yields in the Mississippi River Basin." *Journal of Environmental Quality* 39 (5): 1657–1667.

Diaz, Robert J., and Rutger Rosenberg. 2008. "Spreading Dead Zones and Consequences for Marine Ecosystems." *Science* 321 (5891): 926–29.

Doney, Scott C. 2010. "The Growing Human Footprint on Coastal and Open-Ocean Biogeochemistry." *Science* 328 (5985): 1512–1516.

Duan, Hongtao, Yuanzhi Zhang, Bai Zhang, Kaishan Song, and Zongming Wang. 2007. "Assessment of Chlorophyll-a Concentration and Trophic State for Lake Chagan Using Landsat TM and Field Spectral Data." *Environmental Monitoring and Assessment* 129 (1–3): 295–308.

Erisman, Jan Willem, James N. Galloway, Sybil Seitzinger, Albert Bleeker, Nancy B. Dise, A. M. Roxana Petrescu, Allison M. Leach, and Wim de Vries. 2013. "Consequences of Human Modification of the Global Nitrogen Cycle." *Philosophical Transactions of the Royal Society B: Biological Sciences* 368 (1621): 20130116.

Falcone, James A. 2021. *Estimates of County-Level Nitrogen and Phosphorus from Fertilizer and Manure from 1950 through 2017 in the Conterminous United States*. Technical report. US Geological Survey.

FAO. 2018. World Fertilizer Trends and Outlook to 2018.

Glibert, Patricia M. 2020. "Harmful Algae at the Complex Nexus of Eutrophication and Climate Change." *Harmful Algae* 91:101583.

Gruber, Nicolas, and James N. Galloway. 2008. "An Earth-System Perspective of the Global Nitrogen Cycle." *Nature* 451 (7176): 293–96.

Hallegraeff, Gustaaf M. 1993. "A Review of Harmful Algal Blooms and Their Apparent Global Increase." *Phycologia* 32 (2): 79–99.

Ho, Jeff C., Anna M. Michalak, and Nima Pahlevan. 2019. "Widespread Global Increase in Intense Lake Phytoplankton Blooms since the 1980s." *Nature* 574 (7780): 667–70.

Ho, Jeff C., Richard P. Stumpf, Thomas B. Bridgeman, and Anna M. Michalak. 2017.

"Using Landsat to Extend the Historical Record of Lacustrine Phytoplankton Blooms: A Lake Erie Case Study." *Remote Sensing of Environment* 191: 273–85.

Hudnell, H. Kenneth. 2008. *Cyanobacterial Harmful Algal Blooms: State of the Science and Research Needs.* Vol. 619. Springer Science & Business Media.

Huisman, Jef, Geoffrey A. Codd, Hans W. Paerl, Bas W. Ibelings, Jolanda M. H. Verspagen, and Petra M. Visser. 2018. "Cyanobacterial Blooms." *Nature Reviews Microbiology* 16 (8): 471–83.

Keiser, David A., and Joseph S. Shapiro. 2019. "Consequences of the Clean Water Act and the Demand for Water Quality." *The Quarterly Journal of Economics* 134 (1): 349–96.

Kling, Catherine L. 2013. "State Level Efforts to Regulate Agricultural Sources of Water Quality Impairment." *Choices* 28 (316–2016–7675).

Metaxoglou, Konstantinos, and Aaron Smith. 2021. "Nutrient Pollution and U.S. Agriculture." Working Paper.

Michalak, Anna M., Eric J. Anderson, Dmitry Beletsky, Steven Boland, Nathan S. Bosch, Thomas B. Bridgeman, Justin D. Chaffin, Kyunghwa Cho, Rem Confesor, Irem Daloglu, et al. 2013. "Record-Setting Algal Bloom in Lake Erie Caused by Agricultural and Meteorological Trends Consistent with Expected Future Conditions." *Proceedings of the National Academy of Sciences* 110 (16): 6448–6452.

Mitsch, William J., John W. Day, Li Zhang, and Robert R. Lane. 2005. "Nitrate-Nitrogen Retention in Wetlands in the Mississippi River Basin." *Ecological Engineering* 24 (4): 267–78.

Monitoring Water Quality, Intergovernmental Task Force on. 1995. *The Strategy for Improving Water-Quality Monitoring in the United States.* USGS Water Information Coordination Program.

Nixon, Scott W. 1995. "Coastal Marine Eutrophication: A Definition, Social Causes, and Future Concerns." *Ophelia* 41 (1): 199–219.

Olmstead, Sheila M. 2010. "The Economics of Water Quality." *Review of Environmental Economics and Policy* 4 (1): 44–62.

Paerl, Hans W., and Jef Huisman. 2008. "Blooms Like It Hot." *Science* 320 (5872): 57–58.

Rabotyagov, Sergey S., Catherine L. Kling, Philip W. Gassman, Nancy N. Rabalais, and Robert Eugene Turner. 2014. "The Economics of Dead Zones: Causes, Impacts, Policy Challenges, and a Model of the Gulf of Mexico Hypoxic Zone." *Review of Environmental Economics and Policy* 8 (1): 58–79.

Read, Emily K., Lindsay Carr, Laura De Cicco, Hilary A. Dugan, Paul C. Hanson, Julia A. Hart, James Kreft, Jordan S. Read, and Luke A. Winslow. 2017. "Water Quality Data for National-Scale Aquatic Research: The Water Quality Portal." *Water Resources Research* 53 (2): 1735–1745.

Ross, Matthew R. V., Simon N. Topp, Alison P. Appling, Xiao Yang, Catherine Kuhn, David Butman, Marc Simard, and Tamlin M. Pavelsky. 2019. "AquaSat: A Data Set to Enable Remote Sensing of Water Quality for Inland Waters." *Water Resources Research* 55 (11): 10012–10025.

Shortle, James, and Richard D. Horan. 2001. "The economics of Nonpoint Pollution Control." *Journal of Economic Surveys* 15 (3): 255–89.

———. 2013. "Policy Instruments for Water Quality Protection." *Annual Review of Resource Economics* 5 (1): 111–38.

Smayda, Theodore J. 1997. "What Is a Bloom? A Commentary." *Limnology and Oceanography* 42 (5, part2): 1132–136.

Steffen, Will, Katherine Richardson, Johan Rockström, Sarah E. Cornell, Ingo Fetzer, Elena M. Bennett, Reinette Biggs, Stephen R. Carpenter, Wim De Vries,

Cynthia A. De Wit, et al. 2015. "Planetary Boundaries: Guiding Human Development on a Changing Planet." *Science* 347 (6223).

Taylor, Charles A., and Hannah Druckenmiller. 2021. "Wetlands, Flooding, and the Clean Water Act." Working Paper.

Tebbs, E. J., J. J. Remedios, and D. M. Harper. 2013. "Remote Sensing of Chlorophyll-A as a Measure of Cyanobacterial Biomass in Lake Bogoria, A Hypertrophic, Saline–Alkaline, Flamingo Lake, Using Landsat ETM+." *Remote Sensing of Environment* 135: 92–106.

Topp, Simon N., Tamlin M. Pavelsky, Emily H. Stanley, Xiao Yang, Claire G. Griffin, and Matthew R. V. Ross. 2021. "Multi-decadal Improvement in US Lake Water Clarity." *Environmental Research Letters* 16 (5): 055025.

Turner, R. Eugene, and Nancy N. Rabalais. 2013. "Nitrogen and Phosphorus Phytoplankton Growth Limitation in the Northern Gulf of Mexico." *Aquatic Microbial Ecology* 68 (2): 159–69.

Tyler, A. N., E. Svab, T. Preston, M. Présing, and W. A. Kovács. 2006. "Remote Sensing of the Water Quality of Shallow Lakes: A Mixture Modelling Approach to Quantifying Phytoplankton in Water Characterized by High-Suspended Sediment." *International Journal of Remote Sensing* 27 (8): 1521–1537.

Vitousek, Peter M., John D. Aber, Robert W. Howarth, Gene E. Likens, Pamela A. Matson, David W. Schindler, William H. Schlesinger, and David G. Tilman. 1997. "Human Alteration of the Global Nitrogen Cycle: Sources and Consequences." *Ecological Applications* 7 (3): 737–50.

Wang, Menghua, and Wei Shi. 2007. "The NIR-SWIR Combined Atmospheric Correction Approach for MODIS Ocean Color Data Processing." *Optics Express* 15 (24): 15722–15733.

Demand Shocks and Supply Chain Resilience
An Agent-Based Modeling Approach and Application to the Potato Supply Chain

Liang Lu, Ruby Nguyen, Md Mamunur Rahman, and Jason Winfree

5.1 Introduction

The COVID-19 pandemic caused a shock to consumer demand for food, which then caused demand shocks throughout the food supply chain. The pandemic and the need for social distancing caused a sharp decrease in dining demand at restaurants, hotels, and schools. As consumers quickly switched from dining out to cooking at home, surpluses and shortages arose. One emerging issue was that the supply chain was not flexible enough to fully accommodate consumers. Many food inputs were wasted because they were already in the supply chain and were slotted for production in segments that had a sharp decline in consumer demand.

Figure 5.1 shows the rapid and massive shift away from dining out in 2020 in the US. Reservations in restaurants vanished in March and still did not fully recover one year later. Conversely, figure 5.2 shows the large spike in grocery sales in the US. There was a very large shock in March 2020, and sales have continued to be higher than pre-COVID-19 levels. While

Liang Lu is an assistant professor in the Department of Agricultural Economics and Rural Sociology at the University of Idaho.

Ruby Nguyen is the lead of System Dynamics and Modeling Group, within the Systems Science and Engineering Department, at Idaho National Laboratory.

Md Mamunur Rahman is a postdoctoral research fellow in Idaho National Laboratory's Systems Science and Engineering department.

Jason Winfree is a professor in the Department of Agricultural Economics and Rural Sociology at the University of Idaho.

Funding for this research project was provided, in part, by the Idaho Agricultural Experiment Station, LDRD grant from Idaho National Lab, and the USDA-NIFA. For acknowledgments, sources of research support, and disclosure of the authors' material financial relationships, if any, please see https://www.nber.org/books-and-chapters/risks-agricultural-supply-chains/demand-shocks-and-supply-chain-resilience-agent-based-modelling-approach-and-application-potato.

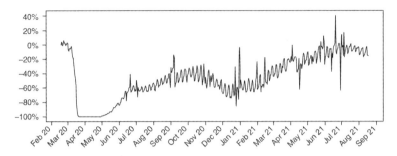

Figure 5.1   Change in seated diners from online, phone, and walk-in reservations in the US from 2019 to 2020

Note: Data are from https://www.opentable.com/state-of-industry. Only states or metropolitan areas with at least 50 restaurants in the OpenTable network were included.

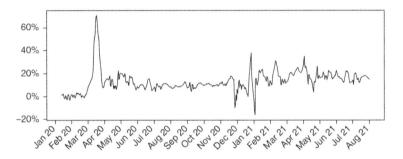

Figure 5.2   Change in grocery sales in the US from 2019 to 2020

Note: Data are from Affinity Solutions and represent "seasonally adjusted credit/debit card spending relative to January 4–31 2020 in grocery and food store (GRF) MCCs, 7 day moving average."

there was a large shift from dining out to eating at home, the decline in restaurant sales and the increase in eating at home did not create a uniform change across all types of foods sold at restaurants or grocery stores. For example, many restaurants were still able to continue to serve consumers via a drive-in or delivery service, but this still represented a shift in the types of food being consumed at restaurants. Consumers who ate at home flocked toward "comfort foods" such as frozen pizza, macaroni and cheese, and liquor (Chaudhuri 2020). This dramatic shift in food demand caused volatility for food prices and large amounts of wasted food, including milk, eggs, onion, cabbage, beans, potatoes, cucumbers, squash, and other food inputs (Yaffe-Bellany and Corkery 2020; Ebrahimji 2020; Jeffery and Newburger 2020). This food waste led to uncertainty in the food supply chain and concerns over increasing global food insecurity (Yeung 2020).

Given the relatively constant aggregate food consumption, demand for many types of food sharply increased. Even in dairy, after much of the milk was initially wasted, prices sharply increased once demand started to rebound (Ellis 2020). Other commodities such as wheat and liquor saw higher than usual demand. In many instances, the change in the demand for inputs depended upon the viability of certain types of production. For example, restaurants sometimes buy eggs in liquid form, but consumers don't buy liquid eggs from the grocery store. As a result, liquid egg prices dropped and regular egg prices increased at grocery stores (Linnekin 2020). Similarly, since chicken wings are generally consumed in restaurants, demand for wings decreased while demand for other parts of the chicken increased (Repko and Lucas 2020). These examples present efficiency problems when the food supply chain is disrupted.

The existing literature has looked extensively at the economics of supply chain design and supply chain management, yet conceptual modeling and analysis of supply chain resilience and how various players along a supply chain respond to demand shocks are lacking. To fill the research gap, the goal of this article is to provide an agent-based modeling framework that models a shock to consumer demand and estimates welfare implications for various agents along the supply chain. We also discuss solutions that could focus on mitigating shocks and bring consistency to food demand. Specifically, we apply this framework to illustrate the case of potato supply chain in Idaho. Idaho is one of the leading potato-producing states in the US. In 2019, Idaho produced around 131 million hundredweight (cwt) of potatoes, which accounted for 30.8 percent of the total production of the US (USDA 2020). Involved stakeholders include farmers, shippers, potato processing companies, and retailers. In this study, we carefully examine the roles of different actors in the supply chain, their activities, and their connections with one another. In addition, we explore which stakeholders of the supply chain are affected the most when the market faces a sudden demand disruption.

5.2   Literature Review

Broadly speaking, this paper relates to four strands of literature: (1) consumer behavior; (2) supply chain design uncertainty; (3) COVID-19 economic impact; and (4) agent-based modeling of food supply chains. The first strand of literature is consumer behavior with regards to food. Prior to COVID-19, there were many instances over the last few decades of both gradual and abrupt shifts in consumer demand for food. Consumer preferences have changed gradually due to a myriad of food-related factors, including organic, GMOs, local, and many others. There have also been rapid changes in demand due to the Alar scare, E.coli outbreaks, and other food safety concerns. However, the COVID-19 pandemic created a very large and quick shift in eating habits and therefore had a dramatic impact on the food supply. Hobbs (2020) discusses consumer behavior during COVID-19 and argues that it may have a long-term impact on food supply chains. For example, these disruptions may create concerns about traditional food supply chains and gravitate toward local food supply chains. While externalities around non-local food supply chains are typically centered on environmental or transportation costs (Winfree and Watson 2017), it could be the case that supply disruptions are also an externality. Disruptions in traditional supply chains could also hasten the use of online food sales (Chang and Meyerhoefer 2020). There may be a long-term shift in consumer preferences that influences the food supply chain.

Understanding consumer behavior alone may not capture the full picture, as some of the food supply distortions were not consumer demand driven. For example, meat shortages during early months of COVID-19 were largely caused by virus concerns in meatpacking plants (Repko and Lucas 2020). However, this exacerbated supply chain problems caused by changes in consumer demand. This created a clear benefit for the supply chain to increase its flexibility. For example, for some processing plants, it was simply too costly to produce goods for grocery stores instead of restaurants (Yaffe-Bellany and Corkery 2020). Also, the disruptions eliminated many vertical relationships, making it too difficult for some upstream producers to find downstream buyers. For example, many local food systems and "farm to table" supply chains were devastated (Stevenson 2020).

The second strand of literature focuses on understanding the economics of supply chain design under uncertainty. For example, Du et al. (2016) examined how the efficiency of a supply chain might be impacted by quantity decisions as well as contracting/integration decisions. This research showed that optimal decisions often depend on the level of uncertainty. Zilberman, Lu, and Reardon (2019) found that the design of the supply chain can also factor into the innovation or efficiency of the food supply. Also, Fang and Shou (2015) examined the relationship between supply chain uncertainty under various degrees of market competition. Yet, this line of research does not focus on the modeling of optimal decision making regarding the flexibility in the food supply chain, which has been increasingly rigid in recent years, in part, because of the specificity of inputs. With the increases in varieties of various commodities, various inputs have become more unique, which in turn may increase the benefit of contracting and vertical relationships. The increasing heterogeneity in consumer preferences, as well as market power effects, has created many incentives for producers to engage in supply chains that resemble silos instead of markets with many buyers and sellers. For example, the rise in the "buy local" movement in recent years has increased the segmentation of supply chains.

The third strand of literature focuses on understanding the economic impact of COVID-19 and rapidly emerging mitigation strategies. The COVID-19 pandemic has shown the consequences of having an inflexible supply chain. Contracts and growing commodities for very specific types of consumption create a supply chain that may not be able to move as swiftly as necessary. However, there are ways to increase supply chain flexibility. In some instances, certain varieties of inputs are more flexible. Also, some types of food packaging could be changed so that they could be more versatile with either restaurants or grocery stores. There may also be solutions to entail either mitigating changes in consumer demand or making the final products more versatile (e.g., restaurant delivery). Gray (2020) looks at logistical issues created by COVID-19 on the food supply. Other studies have concentrated on specific industries, from more fragmented sectors such as fruits and vegetables (Richards and Rickard 2020), to relatively more concentrated meat sector (McEwan et al. 2020), from early struggles of hog farms in China (Zhang 2020) to the recent innovations in e-commerce and other resilience innovations (Reardon and Swinnen 2020). Our conceptual framework allows for a hedonic demand analysis on the potential market for such innovations. Lusk (2020) provided a comprehensive overview of the economic impact of COVID-19 through 16 topics such as the impact of COVID-19 on US food supply chain, international trade, retail, rural health care, etc. Reardon, Bellmare, and Zilberman (2020) analyzed the impact of COVID-19 on food supply chains in developing countries. They found that COVID-19 may have large impacts, in terms of higher prices and shortages, for small- and medium-sized businesses in urban markets in these developing countries.

The fourth strand of research is on supply chain agent-based modeling. Craven and Krejci (2017) studied a regional food supply chain of Iowa using an agent-based modeling (ABM) approach. Food hubs play an important role in regional food supply chains, and failures of food hubs might result in serious disruption in the entire regional food system. In this research, they studied the effectiveness of different policies to prevent failures of regional food hubs to ensure an uninterrupted supply chain. In a different study, Rahman et al. (2021) studied the impact of supply chain disruptions due to the COVID-19 pandemic on an Australian face mask manufacturing company. They developed an agent-based simulation model and scrutinized how recovery strategies such as building extra production capacities and maintaining an additional emergency supply of critical inventories could help mitigate demand, supply, and financial shocks. In another study, Van Voorn, Hengeveld, and Verhagen (2020) developed an agent-based model to investigate the resiliency and efficiency of a food supply chain. They investigated different network structures and concluded that an efficient supply chain network is vulnerable to supply chain shocks, while an inefficient or less efficient supply chain network is more resilient to supply chain shocks. However, none of these studies considered the market dynamics such as the dependency of a product price on supply and demand, price elasticity of demand, and alternative products for demand substitution during supply chain disruptions.

This paper makes two contributions to the literature. First, our model helps explain why food waste and shortages may occur with dramatic shifts in consumer demand and what may be done to solve this issue. In particular, supply chains may be able to become more versatile to handle such shifts in demand. Second, this paper provides a new angle on evaluating the various mitigation strategies and policy responses to COVID-19.

5.3   Methodology

In this study, we followed the agent-based modeling (ABM) approach (Railsback and Grimm 2019), a powerful simulation paradigm that has gained significant attention among researchers from various disciplines in recent years. The modeling approach is extremely flexible in nature and allows modelers to design a complex system with capabilities to capture time dynamics, causal dependencies, and stochasticity. ABM is a bottom-up approach where agents are the building blocks of the simulation model. The overall system behavior emerges from the micro-level agent-agent and agent-environment interactions. The agents are autonomous in nature; they assess the situation and determine their course of actions by their predefined behavior rules. We used AnyLogic 8.7 professional edition (AnyLogic 2021), a multimethod Java programming language–based simulation software, to develop our potato supply chain model. In the following sections, we give a detailed description of model agents, key market mechanisms, key physical processes, data sources, values of the simulation parameters used in the model, and how we designed different experiments to answer our research questions.

5.3.1   Description of the Agents

We modeled a multi-echelon potato supply chain with five types of agents—farmers, shippers, processors, retailers, and logistics companies. Figure 5.3a illustrates the connection and information flow among the agents, and figure 5.3b shows the flow of fresh and processed potatoes in the supply chain. We modeled eight farmers, two shippers, two processors, three retailers, and two logistics companies in our simulation. Detail descriptions of the agents are provided below.

5.3.1.1   *Farmers*

The farmer agents grow potatoes commercially from seed potatoes in their farmland. They harvest potatoes using self-propelled mechanical harvesters and complete post-harvest activities such as cleaning, sorting, and curing. The potatoes are then stored in warehouses known as cellars. In Idaho, farmers usually get 20 metric tons of yield per acre (USDA 2020). There are many varieties of potatoes—Russet Burbank, Norland, Huckleberry, Yukon Gem, and Milva, to name a few (Idaho Potato Commission 2021). For simplicity, we considered only the Russet Burbank, the most popular

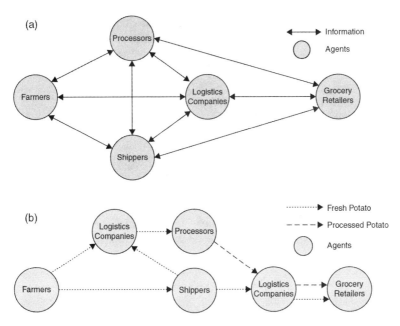

Figure 5.3 **(a) Flow of information among different agents; (b) flow of fresh and processed potato products at different stages of supply chain.**

variety, which accounts for approximately 70 percent of the total potato production in Idaho (Muthusamy et al. 2008). There are two types of farmers in our model—with contract and without contract. The farmers with contracts have an existing written agreement with processors to sell fresh potatoes at a predefined price and the current market price does not have any effect on their decision-making process. These farmers usually possess big farmland areas compared to farmers without a contract. On the other hand, farmers without a contract can sell their potatoes in the open market to any interested buyers at the market price.

The supply of fresh potatoes in the open market depends on the amount non-contract farmers are willing to sell. Since potato is an annual crop, farmers can harvest potatoes only once a year. In our model, farmers harvest new potatoes during August and the supply chain will not have any new inventory in the middle of the season. At a profitable price, if farmers offer all the inventory on hand to the market for sale, it could potentially lead to a zero supply situation in the middle of a season. To mimic a practical supply chain, we employed the following algorithm into the farmer agents' behavior to make sure the daily supply of potatoes in the open market is responsive to the seasonal demand pattern and avoids zero supply situations in the middle of the season.

Step 1: Check the farmer agents' on-hand available inventory.

Step 2: Check the current date of the simulation.

Step 3: Sum up the monthly seasonal factors of the demand and divide the on-hand inventory by the summation to obtain the deseasonalized supply.

Step 4: Multiply the seasonal factor of the current month with the deseasonalized supply to reflect the seasonal pattern. Farmers will offer this amount for sale in the open market.

In our simulation model, we also incorporated a potato disposal mechanism. If the market price does not meet the expectations of the non-contract farmers, they hold the potatoes and wait for the market price to rise. In some years, the overall production of potatoes is so high that it creates an oversupply situation even after covering the yearly market demand. In this circumstance, the farmers closely monitor the market. If the price is consistently too low for 30 days to cover the holding cost of the potatoes in cold storage, especially in the last quarter before harvesting new potatoes, farmers take actions to dispose of the surplus potatoes to avoid incurring additional storage costs.

5.3.1.2   Shippers

In our potato supply chain model, the shipper agents purchase potatoes from farmers, store them in their warehouses known as fresh sheds, and wholesale to the processors and retailers. Usually, shippers keep three to five days of inventory on hand to fulfill the orders they receive. In our model, the shippers follow the periodic review inventory control policy, which means that they place a new order after a fixed period to replenish their inventory of fresh potatoes. On average, a shipper places two new orders in a week to purchase fresh potatoes from the farmers. The shippers have their in-house vehicles to transport potatoes from farmer's warehouses to their own. However, to deliver orders to the processors and retailers, they rely on the services provided by third-party logistics companies.

5.3.1.3   Processors

The processor agents purchase fresh potatoes from farmers and shippers. Around 80 percent of the potatoes come from the farmers under contract at an agreed price. The rest of the 20 percent comes from the shippers at market price. In our model, the processors follow a continuous review inventory control policy, which means that they monitor their inventory levels continuously and place a new order when the inventory level drops below the reordering point (ROP). They process fresh potatoes to produce different types of processed products. In our simulation model, for simplicity, we considered only one type of processed product, which is frozen French fries. Processors sell frozen French fries to retailers. Processors depend on third-party logistics companies for the inbound and outbound transportation of their inventories.

5.3.1.4   *Retailers*

The retailer agents sell fresh and processed potatoes to the end consumers. In our model, the demand for fresh potatoes is seasonal; for example, the retailers experience high demand for fresh potatoes during November and December because of holidays such as Thanksgiving and Christmas. On the other hand, the demand for processed potatoes remains almost constant year-round. The retailers follow a continuous inventory review policy to replenish their inventories.

5.3.1.5   *Logistics Companies*

The logistics company agents own semi-trucks and offer services to transport inventories between facilities. The retailers, processors, and shippers contact logistics companies near the pickup locations and send necessary information regarding order quantity, pickup, and drop-off location. The vehicles in our simulation model follow the actual road network and corresponding road speeds to travel from one facility to another. Our model utilizes the GIS capability of AnyLogic software, where road network and road speed data are fed into our model from the Open Street Map (OSM) server (Luxen and Vetter 2011).

5.3.2   Market Mechanism

5.3.2.1   *Product Pricing*

In our supply chain simulation model, there are two types of products—fresh potatoes and frozen French fries. From the discussion with potato processors, the price of processed potato products remains unchanged throughout the year. Therefore, we assumed that only the price of fresh potatoes will change over time and the price of French fries will remain constant during our simulation period.

The price of fresh potatoes changes, based on demand, supply, and previous period price following equation (1) (Nguyen et al. 2021):

$$(1) \qquad P_t = P_{t-1} \times \left(\frac{Q_t^s}{Q_t^d} \right)^{1/\varepsilon},$$

where

P_t: price of the product at time t
P_{t-1}: price of the product at time $t - 1$
Q_t^s: supply of the product at time t
Q_t^d: demand of the product at time t
ε: demand elasticity of the product

In our model, shippers are in the middle of the supply chain who can aggregate demand and supply to determine market balance. As a result, prices are simulated at the shipper's level to reflect wholesale prices. The fresh potato demand to shippers comes from retailers and potato processors. On the other hand, the supply of fresh potatoes in the open market comes only from farmers without contracts, since farmers with contracts do not sell potatoes in the open market. To calculate the open market daily fresh potato price, we used the demand elasticity value as -0.58 (Andreyeva, Long, and Brownell 2010). Daily supply is aggregated from all non-contract farmers, and daily demand is aggregated from both retailers and processors.

5.3.2.2   Price Lag

We incorporated a price lag mechanism in our simulation to minimize the volatility of fresh potato prices. The current price of fresh potatoes will increase only if the demand is consistently higher than supply at least for one week. On the other hand, the current fresh potato price will drop only if the supply is consistently higher than demand at least for one week. Consequently, when the price of potatoes changes, the new price sustains at least for one week before it changes to a new value. Moreover, we set a maximum and minimum price of fresh potatoes by analyzing the fresh potato price history, which allows the price to fluctuate within a predefined range, instead of unrealistic high and low values.

5.3.2.3   Demand Substitution

When the availability of a product at retailers is low, customers may switch to alternative available products. In our case, customers can switch between fresh potato and frozen French fries if any of the items undergo a stockout situation. Consumers' preference is given by a constant elasticity of substitution utility function: $U(x_1, x_2) = (x_1^\alpha + x_2^\beta)^\rho$.

We utilized equations (2) and (3) to calculate the amount of shifted demands.

$$(2) \qquad x_1 = \frac{M}{p_1\left(1 + \left(\frac{\alpha}{\beta}\right)^{1/(\rho-1)}\left(\frac{p_2}{p_1}\right)^{1/(\rho-1)}\right)},$$

$$(3) \qquad x_2 = \frac{M}{p_2\left(1 + \left(\frac{\beta}{\alpha}\right)^{1/(\rho-1)}\left(\frac{p_1}{p_2}\right)^{1/(\rho-1)}\right)},$$

where

x_1: substituted quantity of product 1
x_2: substituted quantity of product 2
M: income of the customers

p_1: unit price of fresh potato
p_2: unit price of frozen French fries
α: share parameter of product 1
β: share parameter of product 2
ρ: substitution parameter

The ratio of x1 and x2:

(4)
$$\frac{x_1}{x_2} = \frac{p_2\left(1 + \left(\frac{\beta}{\alpha}\right)^{1/(\rho-1)}\left(\frac{p_1}{p_2}\right)^{1/(\rho-1)}\right)}{p_1\left(1 + \left(\frac{\alpha}{\beta}\right)^{1/(\rho-1)}\left(\frac{p_2}{p_1}\right)^{1/(\rho-1)}\right)}.$$

Amount of shifted demand from frozen French fries to the fresh potatoes:

$$x_{frozen\_to\_fresh} = Unmet\ demand\ of\ frozen\ product \times \frac{x_1}{x_2}.$$

Amount of shifted demand from frozen French fries to the fresh potatoes:

$$x_{fresh\_to\_frozen} = Unmet\ demand\ of\ fresh\ potato \times \frac{x_2}{x_1}.$$

We used $\alpha = 0.5$, $\beta = 1$, $\rho = 0.5$, and the values of unmet demand for fresh potatoes and frozen French fries are obtained every day from our simulation model. We choose a value of ρ between 0 and 1 to reflect the imperfect substitution nature of fresh and frozen potatoes. We choose the share parameters α and β according to the household expenditure on these products (Smallwood and Blaylock 1984).

The substitution of fresh potatoes for frozen French fries has a ripple effect. When frozen product demand is high due to substitution, processors have to procure more fresh potatoes as input materials. This increased demand will be met by both contracted farmers and the shippers.

5.3.2.4   Price Elasticity of Demand

In our supply chain model, we calculated the adjusted demand only for fresh potatoes. Since the price of frozen French fries does not change over time, demand adjustment is not required for this product. We calculated the adjusted demand of fresh potatoes by comparing present and expected prices with the demand elasticity using equation (5) (Nguyen et al. 2021):

(5)
$$Q_t^d = Q_t^{base} \times \left(\frac{P_t}{P_{t-1}}\right)^\varepsilon,$$

where

Q_t^d: adjusted demand of the product at time t
Q_t^{base}: base demand of the product at time t

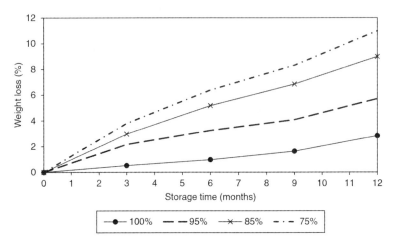

Figure 5.4   Impact of relative humidity on potato weight loss
Source: (Olsen and Kleinkopf 2020).

P_t: price of the product at time t
P_{t-1}: price of the product at time $t - 1$
ε: demand elasticity of the product

5.3.2.5   *Potato Weight Loss and Humidity*

There is a significant impact of relative humidity on potato weight loss. Figure 5.4 shows the impact of relative humidity and storage time on potato weight loss. From the plot, it can be observed that the weight potatoes lose is proportional to the storage duration and inversely proportional to relative humidity. As per the figure, potatoes can lose more than 10 percent of their weight at 75 percent relative humidity in one year. Therefore, it is recommended to maintain relative humidity over 95 percent of cold storage facilities to avoid unsought weight loss (Olsen and Kleinkopf 2020). In our simulation, we modeled relative humidity as a parameter and calculated weight loss of fresh potatoes farmers and shippers store in their storage facilities, assuming 95 percent relative humidity. The humidity level can be easily changed in our model by simply changing the parameter value.

5.3.3   Data Source and Simulation Parameters

We conducted several meetings with different stakeholders of potato supply chains primarily located in Idaho. From the discussions, we got better insights on the overall potato supply chain and associated activities at different stages. We received information on different processes and decision-making rules of the stakeholders, such as inventory replenishment, inventory storage, placement of new orders, preparation of received orders, and transportation of inventories among facilities. We also learned about percent of contracted farmers and risk hedging strategies under disruption. Additional data, such as farmlands average production per acre, breakdown of consumptions of potatoes by sectors, demand elasticity of potato products, and fresh potato price history, are collected from USDA annual report (USDA 2020) and some other sources (Idaho Potato Commission 2021; National Potato Council 2021; Stark, Thornton, and Nolte 2020).

For the development of the potato supply chain simulation model, we used AnyLogic 8.7 professional edition (AnyLogic 2021), a multimethod Java programming language–based simulation software. We utilized the GIS capability of the software to model the actual movements of the transportation vehicles in the actual road network. We simulated the potato supply chain for two years, August 1, 2020 to July 31, 2022. The first year served as the simulation warm-up period, the time a simulation model requires to reach a steady state before representing the actual system. As a result, only the statistics for the second year were presented in the result section. Table 5.1 presents a list of simulation parameters and the corresponding values we used in our model.

5.3.4   Design of Experiments

In addition to the baseline model, we designed the following scenarios to investigate how our supply chain model responds to sudden demand changes. To implement these scenarios, we created experimental models where we employed demand shock events that were triggered during the target months as described below to reflect the desired demand changes.

After the simulation we do several welfare calculations. We measure the aggregate welfare changes before and after the demand shock throughout the year for various agents. Using the demand function and demand elasticity reported in table 5.1, we calculate the welfare changes for consumers. We measure the producer welfare changes by calculating the revenue change at retail level. It should be noted that this welfare change includes the profit change not only for retailers but also for farmers. Since the pricing mechanism is not explicitly modeled here, we only report the aggregate welfare change. Finally, we measure the welfare changes for the logistics company by tracking the aggregate quantity of potatoes being delivered.

5.3.4.1   *Sudden Demand Rise Scenario*

Under this scenario, we are interested to see how the performance metrics of the supply chain get impacted due to a sudden demand rise. The motivation for the demand rise scenario is from the COVID-19 pandemic, when consumers cannot go to restaurants and consequent demand for fresh potatoes at grocery stores increases tremendously. For this purpose, in our simulation model, the daily base seasonal demand is raised to five times of its original value for an entire month. We are also interested in investigating

Table 5.1   Values of different parameters used in the simulation

Parameter Names	Values	Units	Source
Number of farmer agents	6	-	Assumption
Number of shipper agents	2	-	Assumption
Number of processor agents	2	-	Assumption
Number of logistics company agents	2	-	Assumption
Number of retailer agents	3	-	Assumption
Average yield of the farmlands	20	Metric tons/acre	(USDA 2020)
Number of farmers with contract	2	-	Assumption
Number of farmers without contract	4	-	Assumption
Farmland area of a farmer agent with contract	35–60	Acres	Assumption
Farmland area of a farmer agent without contract	150–80	Acres	Assumption
Warehouse capacity of a shipper agent	300–350	Metric tons	Assumption
Warehouse capacity of a processor agent	400–500	Metric tons	Assumption
Warehouse capacity of a retailer agent	50–60	Metric tons	Assumption
Daily production capacity of a processor agent	25	-	Assumption
Yearly consumer demand of fresh potatoes by consumers	2400–2700	Metric tons	Assumption
Yearly consumer demand of French fries by consumers	3300–3750	Metric tons	Assumption
Number of in-house vehicles of a shipper agent	3–4	-	Assumption
Number of vehicles owned by a logistics company agent	10–15	-	Assumption
Demand elasticity of fresh potatoes	−0.58	-	(Andreyeva et al. 2010)
Relative humidity of storage facilities	95	%	(Olsen and Kleinkopf 2020)

the effect of the timing of the disruption. For this purpose, we introduced this sudden demand at two different months of the season—September and June, separately. We defined the demand shock in September as an early demand shock scenario, since it happens just after one month of harvesting potatoes by farmers in August. On the other hand, we defined the demand shock in June as a late demand shock scenario, since this happens at the end part of the season just one month before farmers begin harvesting for the next season. The rest of the simulation parameter values are kept unchanged.

5.3.4.2   Sudden Demand Drop Scenario

In symmetry to the demand rise scenarios, we also designed demand drop scenarios. Under these scenarios, we want to investigate how the performance metrics of the supply chain get affected due to a sudden demand decline at different times in a season. For this purpose, similar to the demand rise scenarios, the daily base seasonal demand is reduced to one-fifth of its original value during the months September and June, separately. As we discussed in the previous section, we defined demand shocks in September and June as early and late demand shocks, respectively.

5.4. Results

5.4.1   Base Case

Figure 5.5 presents the time plot of our target variables associated with fresh potatoes for the baseline scenario from the shippers' perspective. Part (a) of the figure illustrates the breakdowns of the fresh potato demand shippers experience over time. As mentioned earlier, the fresh potato demand for

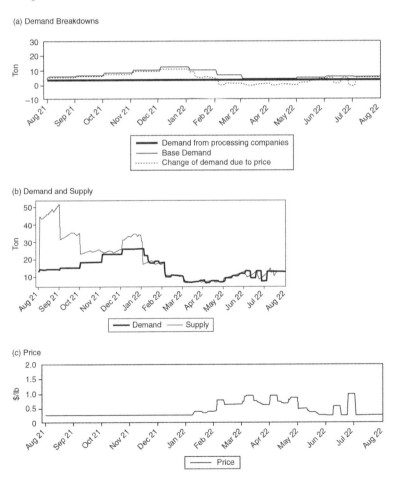

Figure 5.5   Baseline scenario

shippers comes from retailers and potato processors. Demand from retailers is directly linked to consumers' buying behavior. We modeled two important buying behaviors of the end consumers—seasonal pattern and the price elasticity of demand. In this plot, the thin solid line represents the base demand which reflects the consumers' monthly seasonal pattern. The dotted line shows the change of demand due to price elasticity. Finally, the thick line shows the demand for fresh potatoes by the potato processing companies.

Part (b) of figure 5.5 displays the values of fresh potato demand and supply over time. The demand line is the summation of the three demand components shown in part (a) of this figure. The thin solid line displays the supply of fresh potatoes in the open market from where shippers can buy fresh potatoes at market price. The overall supply of fresh potatoes in the open market depends on the amount of potatoes farmers without contracts are willing to sell from their existing inventory at a given market price.

Part (c) of figure 5.5 portrays how the price of fresh potatoes in the open market changes over time based on demand and supply. As discussed in section 5.2.2, we calculated the daily price of fresh potatoes in the open market utilizing equation (1).

5.4.2   Demand Rise Scenario

Figures 5.6 and 5.7 exhibit the time plots of our target variables associated with fresh potatoes for the sudden demand rise scenario. Part (a) of the figures shows the sudden upsurge of base demand, where impacted months are highlighted by gray shading. We also observe that demand for fresh potatoes from the processing companies increases as well. As per figure 5.10a, there is a demand shift from fresh potatoes to frozen French fries under the sudden demand rise scenarios. To keep pace with this extra demand for frozen French fries, the processors place extra orders for fresh potatoes in the open market. According to part (c) of the plots, the price of fresh potatoes increases sharply to the maximum price as soon as the price lag period of seven days is over. On the other hand, because of this high price of fresh potatoes, there is a decline in fresh potato demand as shown by the dotted lines in part (a) of the figures.

By adding the three demand components shown in part (a), we get the resultant demand, which is shown by the thick line in part (b) of the figures. The amount of supply is shown by the thin solid lines in the plots.

Since potatoes can be harvested only once in a given year, no new inventory is added to the supply chain in our model before the next year's harvesting season no matter how large the demand. If an additional amount of potatoes is consumed in one month, it will have an impact on the supply and hence on the price during the later months of the year until next year's harvesting season. This phenomenon can be marked if we carefully compare the price curves between baseline and demand rise scenarios. The impact

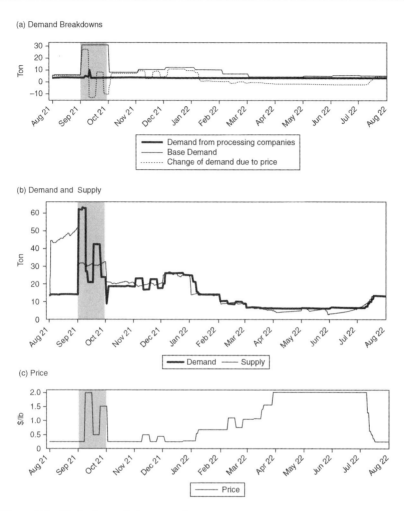

(a) Demand Breakdowns

Demand from processing companies
Base Demand
Change of demand due to price

(b) Demand and Supply

Demand   Supply

(c) Price

Price

Figure 5.6   Early demand rise scenario

of demand disruption on price is not limited to the gray-shaded periods only—the impact is long lasting. It should be noted that the timing of the demand disruption is also very significant. The impact of early demand rise on fresh potato average yearly price is far worse than the late demand rise scenario. For example, according to figure 5.10c, early demand rise resulted in a 139 percent price hike compared to the baseline scenario, while the late demand rise scenario is responsible for a 56 percent price hike only. The early demand rise scenario is also responsible for an additional 10 tons of demand shift from fresh potatoes to frozen French fries (figure 5.10a), compared to the late demand rise scenario.

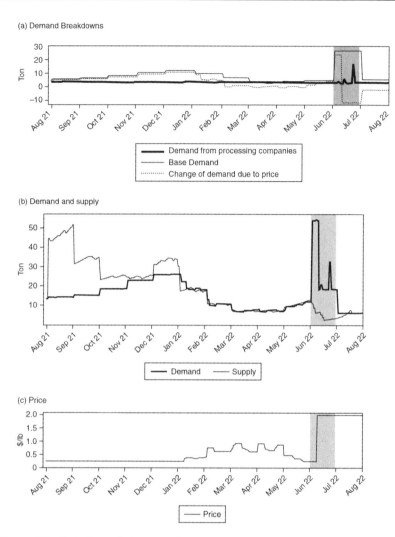

Figure 5.7   Late demand rise scenario

5.4.3   Demand Fall Scenario

Figures 5.8 and 5.9 depict the time plots of our target variables associated with fresh potatoes for the sudden demand drop scenarios. Part (a) of the figures shows the sudden fall of demand during September 2021 and June 2022 marked by gray shading. Since there is no change in demand for frozen French fries, the demand for fresh potatoes by the processing companies remains the same as the baseline scenario.

Since supply is more than demand, the price of fresh potatoes during the demand fall periods remains minimum. Similar to the demand rise scenarios,

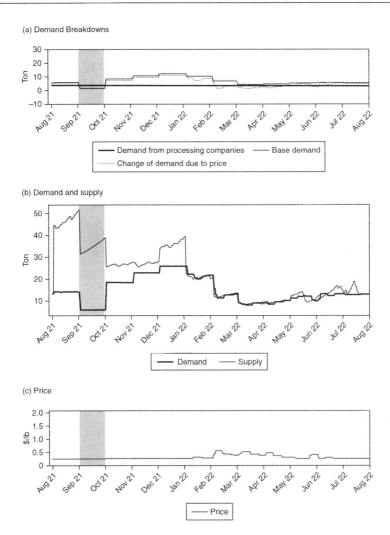

(a) Demand Breakdowns

— Demand from processing companies   — Base demand
········· Change of demand due to price

(b) Demand and supply

— Demand   — Supply

(c) Price

— Price

Figure 5.8   Early demand fall scenario

the impact of demand fall is not confined to the disruption periods only. For the early demand fall scenario, even after the disruption period, the fresh potato price is comparatively low for the remaining time of the season. Compared to the baseline scenario, the average yearly price of fresh potatoes is 29 percent and 5 percent lower for the early and late demand fall scenarios, respectively. Moreover, the timing of the demand disruption severely impacts the amount of potatoes disposed of by the farmers. As we see in figure 5.10b, farmers dispose of 145.9 tons of potatoes in the case of late demand fall scenario, as opposed to 11.7 tons of potatoes in the case of early

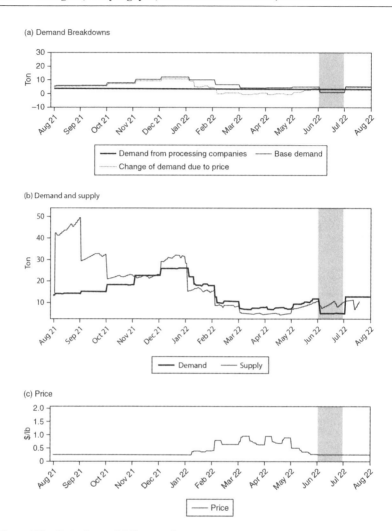

Figure 5.9   Late demand fall scenario

demand fall scenario. For the early demand fall scenario, the supply chain gets a long period to absorb the surplus inventory and hence the amount of disposed potatoes is little. On the contrary, for the late demand fall scenario, the supply chain could not absorb the surplus supply of potatoes within a short period. Therefore, the farmers had no choice but to dispose of unsold potatoes before the new harvesting season starts.

5.4.4   Welfare Implications

In this subsection, we calculate the welfare implications for the various agents along the supply chain. Table 5.2 summarizes the welfare changes

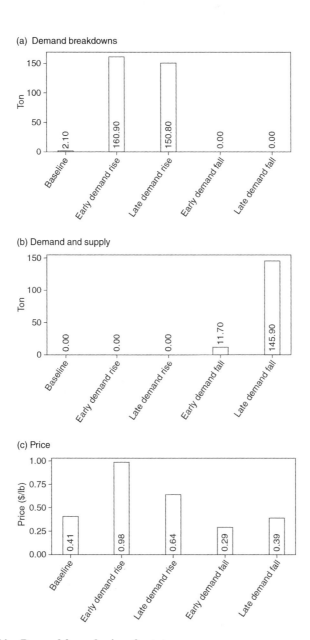

Figure 5.10   Demand for and price of potatoes

Table 5.2   Welfare changes for agents along the supply chain

Scenarios	Consumer surplus change	Producer revenue change	Logistics company change	Disposed potato amount
High demand early	$4,786	$1,397	−1,289	0
Low demand early	−$802	−$171	710	11.7
High demand late	$2,990	$250	−388	0
Low demand late	−$290	−$82	16	145.9

Note: 1. Logistics company change is measured by the total metric tons of potatoes delivered. 2. Consumer surplus change calculation uses the −0.58 demand elasticity in table 5.1.

for consumers, producers/retailers, and logistics companies under several demand change scenarios.

We draw several implications from table 5.2. First, the welfare implications for agents along the supply chain are heterogeneous. After the demand shock, consumer and producer welfare changes are in the same direction as the demand shocks. It should be noted that the welfare changes do not include the social welfare from other sectors such as food services where the demand may be shifting from. Meanwhile, logistics companies deliver fewer potatoes, and no potatoes are disposed of when there is a positive shock to demand. When demand shrinks, logistics companies deliver more potatoes, and some potatoes are disposed of. Second, timing of the demand shock matters. In fact, when the shock comes early in the production season, there would be lasting impact without intervention. Third, policy implications for reducing food waste and mitigating welfare loss can be vastly different.

5.5   Discussion

This model is meant to illustrate the effects of large shocks to consumer demand that influence the food supply chain. This model illustrates a scenario where shocks can create food waste due to separated supply chains, but at the same time, producer welfare can go up. This seems to be consistent with the empirical findings of 2020. In the state of Idaho, many potato and dairy inputs were wasted, but overall farm receipts increased (Carlson 2021). Qualitatively, this shows us the possible incentives for policy makers. Under reasonable assumptions, siloed supply chains may increase expected profits. However, it will also increase risk for producers, since it increases the variability in prices and increases the probability of wasted inputs. Siloed supply chains might also be beneficial for some consumers if siloing is associated with product differentiation and more consumer choice.

However, if food waste has associated externalities, then there may be an incentive to create more versatility in the food supply chain or reduce the size of demand shocks.

There are a few ways policy makers might be able to mitigate the effects of large demand shocks. Most obviously, policy restrictions on eating habits should take into account the strain on the supply chain. More long-term solutions may be standardized packaging or alleviating restrictions on food sales. Policy makers should consider the empirical estimates of these various costs and benefits. In some situations, there may be a need for intervention.

Similarly to increasing supply chain versatility, reducing demand shocks may decrease profitability for firms. Since prices are bounded at zero, losses are also bounded and therefore the effects of larger shocks are asymmetrical. However, this might change if different distributional assumptions are made about the shocks. Nonetheless, firms may want siloed supply chains with large demand shocks.

5.5.1   Mitigation Strategies and Policy Implications

While versatility may be the goal of a policy maker, how to increase the versatility of these inputs is not obvious. Although it may be difficult to overhaul upstream inputs, some versatility strategies were implemented in markets. For example, some food service distributors started supplying grocery stores. Similarly, ghost kitchens picked up some of the slack caused by supply chain disruptions. Also, online food sales and food banks helped maintain some of the food supply. If these avenues are flexible, there may be an incentive to increase the size of these types of food sales. However, recent disruptions may also warrant changes further up the supply chain by implementing such policies as more uniform packaging.

It is important to note that more flexible markets may also reduce market power. The trend in food is to have differentiated food (organic, GMO, local, etc.), so while a more uniform food supply may reduce food waste if there are large shocks to consumer demand, it may also decrease profits. Nonetheless, it may be beneficial for policy makers to give incentives for a more versatile food supply chain.

5.5.2   Reducing Demand Shocks

Aside from creating versatility in the supply chain, there are strategies to reduce shocks in demand. The most straightforward strategies might be to limit changes in regulations and restrictions. During the COVID-19 lockdowns, there were clear reasons to reduce restaurant services. However, virus considerations may need to be balanced with food shortage considerations if the shocks are severe.

Examples may entail limiting capacity instead of eliminating all services, making restrictions more geographically specific, or encouraging alternatives such as drive-throughs. Also, a lack of grocery licenses prevented some restaurants from selling directly to consumers, which would have helped mitigate shifts in consumer demand (Linnekin 2020). Of course, it can be difficult to weigh both the costs and benefits of these policies, especially when they are initiated very quickly. However, to the extent that food shortages may be a concern, an alternative to creating input versatility would be to reduce demand variability.

5.6 Conclusion

This paper provides a framework to illustrate how demand shock may impact the food supply chain, prices, and food waste/shortages. Producing inputs that have versatility in the supply chain can stabilize prices and reduce food waste. However, it is not clear that producers would prefer siloed supply chains depending upon the differences between prices, quantities, and costs. The recent COVID-19 pandemic has illustrated the possibility of quick, large shocks to consumer demand for virtually all types of food.

While food differentiation may alleviate some types of risk in the food supply, it can also increase risks if consumers start to rely on certain types of food. The current food supply chain seems to become more and more fractured with various food types, such as organic food, GMOs, local supply chains, and various other attributes. This is in addition to the critical distinction of wholesale versus retail food. Given the obvious necessity of eating and therefore the somewhat stable aggregated demand for all types of food, a sudden shock to a segment of the food supply can cause an enormous strain on other segments of the food supply. Therefore, this model could potentially be used for various distinctions throughout the supply chain.

There are various mechanisms that can be used to try to remedy a lack of versatility. Subsidization of versatility may alleviate food waste. Also, technology may be able to more quickly adapt inputs to various outputs. Alternatively, creating more consistency in food demand and mitigating demand shocks may also be helpful. While the food supply may be very resilient in adjusting to long-term changes in demand (Baldos and Hertel 2016), it seems less clear in the short run. Decisions about the food supply chain should take into account these various costs and benefits.

References

Andreyeva, T., M. W. Long, and K. D. Brownell. 2010. "The Impact of Food Prices on Consumption: A Systematic Review of Research on the Price Elasticity of Demand for Food." *American Journal of Public Health* 100 (2): 216–22.
AnyLogic. 2021. AnyLogic: Simulation Modeling Software Tools & Solutions for Business. https://www.anylogic.com/.
Baldos, U. L. C., and T. W. Hertel. 2016. "Debunking the 'New Normal': Why World Food Prices Are Expected to Resume Their Long Run Downward Trend." *Global Food Security* 8: 27–38.
Bellemare, M. F., M. Çakir, H. H. Peterson, L. Novak, and J. Rudi. 2017. "On the

Measurement of Food Waste." *American Journal of Agricultural Economics* 99 (5): 1148–158.

Carlson, B. 2021. "Idaho Net Farm Income Surges to Record High." *Capital Press*, Jan. 8.

Chang, H.-H., and C. Meyerhoefer. 2020. "COVID-19 and the Demand for Online Food Shopping Services: Empirical Evidence from Taiwan." NBER Working Paper 27427. Cambridge, MA: National Bureau of Economic Research.

Chaudhuri, S. 2020. "Comfort Foods Make a Comeback in the Coronavirus Age." *The Wall Street Journal*, April 24.

Craven, Teri J., and Caroline C. Krejci. 2017. "An Agent-Based Model of Regional Food Supply Chain Disintermediation." *Proceedings of the Agent-Directed Simulation Symposium*, pp. 1–10.

Du, X., L. Lu, T. Reardon, and D. Zilberman. 2016. "Economics of Agricultural Supply Chain Design: A Portfolio Selection Approach." *American Journal of Agricultural Economics* 98 (5): 1377–1388.

Ebrahimji, A. 2020. "An Idaho Farm Is Giving Away 2 Million Potatoes Because Coronavirus Has Hurt Demand." *CNN*, April 16.

Ellis, S. 2020. "Idaho Dairy Industry Encouraged By Higher Prices." *Idaho State Business Journal*, July 6.

Fang, Y., and B. Shou. 2015. "Managing Supply Uncertainty under Supply Chain Cournot Competition." *European Journal of Operational Research* 243 (1): 156–76.

Gray, Richard S. 2020. "Agriculture, transportation, and the COVID-19 crisis." Canadian Journal of Agricultural Economics/Revue canadienne d'agroeconomie 68 (2): 239–243.

Hamilton, S. F., and T. J. Richards. 2019. "Food Policy and Household Food Waste." *American Journal of Agricultural Economics* 101 (2): 600–614.

Hobbs, J. E. 2020. "Food Supply Chains during the COVID-19 Pandemic." *Canadian Journal of Agricultural Economics/Revue canadienne d'agroéconomie* 68 (2): 171–176.

Idaho Potato Commission. 2021. About Idaho Potatoes. https://idahopotato.com.

Jeffery, A., and E. Newburger. 2020. "Wasted Milk, Euthanized Livestock: Photos Show How Coronavirus Has Devastated US Agriculture." *CNBC*, May 2.

Linnekin, B. 2020. "Food Issues That Should've Been Front and Center in the 2020 Presidential Election." *Reason*, October 31.

Lusk, Jayson. 2020. "Economic impacts of covid-19 on food and agricultural markets." CAST Commentary Council for Agricultural Science and Technology: 1–44.

Luxen, D., and C. Vetter. 2011. "Real-Time Routing with OpenStreetMap Data." Proceedings of the 19th ACM SIGSPATIAL International Conference on Advances in Geographic Information Systems, 513–16.

McEwan, Ken, Lynn Marchand, Max Shang, and Delia Bucknell. 2020. "Potential implications of COVID-19 on the Canadian pork industry." Canadian Journal of Agricultural Economics/Revue canadienne d'agroeconomie 68 (2): 201–206.

Muthusamy, Kalamani, Christopher S. McIntosh, Yuliya Bolotova, and Paul E. Patterson. 2008. "Price volatility of Idaho fresh potatoes: 1987–2007." American Journal of Potato Research 85 (6): 438–444.

National Potato Council. 2021. *Potato Facts*. https://www.nationalpotatocouncil.org/.

Nguyen, R. T., R. G. Eggert, M. H. Severson, and C. G. Anderson. 2021. "Global Electrification of Vehicles and Intertwined Material Supply Chains of Cobalt, Copper and Nickel." *Resources, Conservation and Recycling* 167: 105198.

Olsen, N., and G. Kleinkopf. (2020). "Storage Management." In Potato Production

Systems, edited by J. Stark, M. Thornton, P. Nolte. Cham, Switzerland: Springer. https://doi.org/10.1007/978-3-030-39157-7_17.

Rahman, Towfique, Firouzeh Taghikhah, Sanjoy Kumar Paul, Nagesh Shukla, and Renu Agarwal. 2021. "An Agent-Based Model for Supply Chain Recovery in the Wake of the COVID-19 Pandemic." *Computers & Industrial Engineering* 158: 107401.

Railsback, S. F., and V. Grimm. 2019. *Agent-Based and Individual-Based Modeling: A Practical Introduction.* Princeton University Press.

Reardon, Thomas, Marc F. Bellemare, and David Zilberman. 2020. "How COVID-19 may disrupt food supply chains in developing countries." Chapter 17 in: COVID-19 and global food security. International Food Policy Research Institute (IFPRI): 78-80.

Reardon, Thomas, and Johan Swinnen. 2020. "COVID-19 and resilience innovations in food supply chains." Chapter 30 in: COVID-19 and global food security. International Food Policy Research Institute (IFPRI): 132–36.

Repko, M., and A. Lucas. 2020. "The Meat Supply Chain Is Broken. Here's Why Shortages Are Likely To Last during the Coronavirus Pandemic." *CNBC*, May 7.

Richards, Timothy J., and Bradley Rickard. 2020. "COVID-19 impact on fruit and vegetable markets." Canadian Journal of Agricultural Economics/Revue canadienne d'agroeconomie 68 (2): 189–194.

Smallwood, D. M., and J. R. Blaylock. 1984. "Household expenditures for fruits, vegetables, and potatoes." Technical bulletin 1690-United States Dept. of Agriculture Economic Research Service (USA).

Stark, Jeffrey C., Mike Thornton, and Phillip Nolte, eds. 2020. Potato Production Systems. Cham, Switzerland: Springer.

Stevenson, K. 2020. "The Farm-to-Table Connection Comes Undone." New York Times, April 9.

USDA. 2020. *Potatoes 2019 Summary.* https://www.nass.usda.gov/.

Van Voorn, George, Geerten Hengeveld, and Jan Verhagen. 2020. "An Agent Based Model Representation to Assess Resilience and Efficiency of Food Supply Chains." *PLOS One* 15 (11): e0242323.

Winfree, J., and P. Watson. 2017. "The Welfare Economics of 'Buy Local.'" *American Journal of Agricultural Economics* 99 (4): 971–87.

Yaffe-Bellany, D., and M. Corkery. 2020. "Dumped Milk, Smashed Eggs, Plowed Vegetables: Food Waste of the Pandemic." *New York Times*, April 12.

Yeung, J. 2020. "The Coronavirus Pandemic Could Threaten Global Food Supply, UN Warns." *CNN*, April 12.

Zhang, Xiaobo, 2020. "Chinese livestock farms struggle under COVID-19 restrictions." Chapter 19 in: COVID-19 and global food security. International Food Policy Research Institute (IFPRI): 84–85.

Zilberman, D., L. Lu, and T. Reardon. 2019. "Innovation-Induced Food Supply Chain Design." *Food Policy* 83: 289–97.

6

The Performance and Future of Ag Supply Chains

A. G. Kawamura

We live during remarkable times. In the course of a living farmer's lifetime, tractors have replaced plow horses, but the memories of the "ice-man" and the "coal-man" bringing blocks of ice for the ice box and lumps of coal for home heating still remain. Some of us remember the first color TV in the neighborhood . . . the first office fax machine, the first computer, the first man on the moon. In just the last hundred years an avalanche of new technologies and new thinking continue to mark an acceleration of mankind's potentiality to evolve on our path of civilization for better and for worse. The idea of a 21st-Century Agricultural Renaissance is certainly not speculation. It is the realization that this cascade of invention is altering our theories for change. It opens the door for a Change of Theory in how mankind may embrace successful agriculture in the decades ahead.

In 1985, the United Nations rolled out their Millennial Goals, a list of aspirational objectives for the betterment of humanity that all nations could work to achieve by the turn of the century. The successful accomplishment of those modest but important goals led to the UN's 2015 *Sustainable Development Goals* (SDGs). The timeline for completion of these ambitious 17 goals was set for a rapidly approaching 2030. For those who spend their lives working in the world of policy and development, the SDGs at first

A. G. Kawamura co-owns Orange County Produce LLC, is founding co-chair of Solutions from the Land, a nonprofit organization devoted to solving global challenges through mindful and collaborative land management initiatives (https://www.solutionsfromtheland.org/), and is the former secretary of the California Department of Food and Agriculture.

For acknowledgments, sources of research support, and disclosure of the author's material financial relationships, if any, please see https://www.nber.org/books-and-chapters/risks-agricultural-supply-chains/performance-and-future-ag-supply-chains.

glance seem to be an overreach of what is possible for humans to deliver in a 15-year span of time. How will the world's nations eliminate poverty and hunger (Goals #1 & #2) by 2030? Many of the other 17 *SDG*s seemed equally daunting and unachievable when examined one by one. Indeed, that is how the 20th-century global community has approached so many of our world's greatest problems: One issue area at a time, with silo-like thinking and narrow discipline methodology driven by carefully hoarded streams of funding. Old thinking for old problems that never get solved.

When we look at the *SDG*s as a whole set of incredibly achievable challenges that require interconnected solution pathways, innovative collaboration may be needed—that is, new thinking. Like a quilt comprised of many aligned and woven components, it suddenly becomes clear that these SDGs cannot be accomplished individually, but only collectively. And the remarkable observation that has emerged for many dedicated world changers is that agriculture can play a primary role in accomplishing them. The many "Solutions from the Land" are the catalysts for a multi-benefit platform upon which the SDGs can be delivered.

> You cannot trust your judgement if your imagination is out of focus.
> —Mark Twain

When we see the world through a different lens, our vision changes. The SDGs let us imagine a world of human endeavor that has never existed and yet is within our grasp . . . and imagination. The pace of change, delayed by old thinking and old conflicts, is giving way to an accelerated kind of progress disclosed every day by the expanded sharing of knowledge and events worldwide. New tools, new thinking driven by liberated imagination can create a unique and exciting tapestry of life for every region of the planet.

What makes us believe that an Agricultural Renaissance is well underway? With eyes open, it's happening all around us in all corners of the world where food is produced, harvested, processed, prepared, cooked, and delivered. We can be frustrated with the perceived pace of change . . . but the rapidity of this transformation is staggering.

In 1994, I participated in a Western Growers trade tour to China to explore the opportunities for exporting fresh produce by ocean and air freight. What we found was a country with no existing infrastructure of cold storage, transportation, and market distribution for our perishable products. We turned around and said let's focus on Japan and Australia. The point to be made is that 17 years later, the world has certainly changed. China is soon to be the planet's biggest economy, and the opportunities for trade expansion continue to progress as old ways of getting things done give way to new alliances. Today global sourcing is on steroids as a world of almost 8 billion steps into the century with new appetites, expectations, and desires to leave the past behind.

What does a renaissance look like? In the 40 plus seasons during which I've had the privilege of stewarding my farm, the progression of our farming method has been staggering. We've gone from furrow to sprinkler to precision drip irrigation and fertigation. We've gone from molecular chemistry pest control to Integrated Pest Management (IPM) to bio-control with biological predators, repellents, and antagonists. We have fertilized and augmented our soils with chicken and dairy manure, petroleum-based NPK products, seaweed, fish and bone meal, green waste compost blends, earthworm castings, pulverized volcanic rocks delivering micro-nutrients. We are experimenting with oxygen-enriched nano-bubbles, hydroponics, aquaponics, and aeroponics in various arrays of vertical, horizontal, and platform aboveground systems . . . always looking for a new practice or methodology to add to our toolbox of crop implements, technology, and knowledge. Our hand-guided tractors are now satellite driven for precision field cultivation. We anticipate demo use of a hydrogen fuel cell tractor in the year ahead, with autonomous driverless tractors on the horizon. Our fresh produce is food-safety tracked and scanned and ID'd so that a consumer knows when, where, and even who might have harvested the product. We sell our products at farmer's markets, terminal markets, restaurants, food service, chain stores, school cafeterias, and food banks. The world is our marketplace; our strawberries can be airfreighted to the other side of the world faster than we can get them to the state next door. We have learned to partner with other growers in other countries and teach them how to grow the products we want to sell year round. Not surprisingly, with time, the transfer of knowledge turns the table and we find out that our farm partners have learned to grow crops better than we do and we now learn from each other how to be better, safer, and more efficient. This leap-frogging of talent and technology is accelerating at unprecedented levels.

The enormous global disruption caused by the COVID-19 pandemic must be viewed from many angles. While it is clear that the impact across so many sectors of human activity was severe and unpredictable, it is also important to observe that many sectors responded with a never-before-seen competency and focus. The swift reaction of the food supply chain sectors was remarkable. Yes, weaknesses and vulnerabilities were exposed, and panic almost prevailed in some regions. We learned that essential services are defined in terms of critical infrastructure and that agriculture was among the most important core services to protect. The ability of the global agricultural food supply chain to turn and pivot and still deliver sustenance to a demanding public sector was admirable. For those who claim that the food system is broken, it may well be that the performance of our 21st-century agricultural system here in the US was more than resilient in the face of the food service shutdown—it was innovative and collaborative. One clear example of "pivot and turn" took place when the Navajo nation approached a desperate grower-shipper of fresh produce who had been disking down his fields of perishable lettuce and vegetables during the early days of the food service shutdown. Certain communities who live in so-called food deserts around the country found themselves with no backup food supply when their primary convenience or liquor store and restaurants shut down. The Navajo nation redirected their own revenue sources to work collaboratively with the farmer and in just days he was able to redirect his fresh produce to their own struggling communities. What happened next is a lesson in the unexpected consequences of innovative solutions. The families were given 30-pound boxes of farm-fresh produce delivered directly to their homes. These communities exist at the tail end of a food chain that delivers some of the oldest and worst-quality, end-of-life perishable products. The tears of joy from family members who had never seen or tasted such fresh produce exposed conditions that had become the norm. These communities suddenly became collaborative partners in a shift in priorities and resource alignment.

Disruption caused by the pandemic caused many producers to reassess their own farms and reimagine how to streamline their operations. Many are asking how they can become more productive members of their communities. We are in the process of significantly expanding our production of nutrient-dense foods for a direct link to regional food banks. For over 30 years we have been custom-growing food for our local food banks with small proof-of-concept community hunger projects of 2 to 8 acres annually. We asked ourselves, Why isn't it 20, 40, or 80 acres? Or 200, 400, to 800 acres? And suddenly we realized it was because our imagination had been stalled in single-minded thinking. Innovative collaboration has opened our eyes and minds to what's possible. We are focusing on being a "do tank" and no longer a "think tank" waiting for some perfect solution to leap forward. In an Agricultural Renaissance, the limitations we place on ourselves are ours to own.

As the agricultural sector plays an increasingly central role, perhaps this can be a time of dynamic transformation, even greater than in the past. We are currently watching a significant leap forward in artificial intelligence (AI), robotics, and data-driven decision making. Eye-opening systems and technologies are already being used: comprehensive farm monitoring and control systems that irrigate, chemigate, and feritgate autonomously; sound wave chamber pulverization of grains, volcanic rocks, waste by-products; mineral extraction from brackish water where commercial-grade potassium and phosphorous leave potable water as a by-product; atmospheric water extraction; temperature- and humidity-controlled clean rooms for nursery production that use 60 percent less energy; new plant breeding breakthroughs such as nitrogen-fixing grains, vitamin-fortified cultivars, plants that are tolerant of and resistant to drought, salinity, heat, and disease. We are witnessing the development and production of new and surprising foods, as well as their introduction to the consumer: novel protein products, seaweed, insects, earthworms, and grubs. How we eat, what we eat, and how we procure our daily bread continues to evolve. The capacity to feed a planet is improving at just the right moment.

The performance and future of agricultural supply chains has never been more exciting. These remarkable times are characterized by the unprecedented acceleration of invention, design, manufacturing, transport, and delivery. Humanity has moved to a new framework of whatever is possible is feasible and whatever is feasible is now achievable in record time. An Agricultural Renaissance thoughtfully guided and supported can deliver abundance and multiple benefits to society, the environment, and the economies of communities from rural towns to urban metropolises. Agriculture in all its different forms and sizes needs to be successful in order for the world to thrive. Anything less moves us toward a world of survival, not living.

7

Exploring Spatial Price Relationships
The Case of African Swine Fever in China

Michael Delgado, Meilin Ma, and H. Holly Wang

7.1 Introduction

As stated in Barrett and Li (2002), market integration is achieved when all arbitrage opportunities across markets are exhausted, which is often true in free market economies. Studies on market integration using time series data are abundant (Ravallion 1986; Goodwin and Schroeder 1991; Wang and Ke 2005; Shiue and Keller 2007; Negassa and Myers 2007; Ge, Wang, and Ahn 2010), though most have not carefully examined spatial relationships. Additionally, most existing studies on market integration focus on testing whether certain markets are integrated or not, and if not, few follow up with identifying the underlying driving forces. Other than consumer cultural preferences (Goyat 2011), which do not apply to generic commodities without place of origin information; political barriers (Fan 2002), which are mostly limited to the labor market; and processor market concentration (Goodwin and Schroeder 1991), risks due to animal epidemics may

Michael Delgado is a professor in the Department of Agricultural Economics at Purdue University.

Meilin Ma is an assistant professor in the Department of Agricultural Economics at Purdue University.

H. Holly Wang is a professor in the Department of Agricultural Economics at Purdue University.

The authors thank Fei Qin and Zhan Wang for excellent research assistance. We also thank the organizers and all participants of the 2021 NBER workshop, especially Barry Goodwin for insightful comments in the early version. All remaining errors are ours. For acknowledgments, sources of research support, and disclosure of the author's or authors' material financial relationships, if any, please see https://www.nber.org/books-and-chapters/risks-agricultural-supply-chains/exploring-spatial-price-relationships-case-african-swine-fever-china.

also prevent market integration. For example, the outbreak of BSE (bovine spongiform encephalopathy, or mad cow disease) disrupted the integration of US, Canadian, and Mexican beef markets (Sparling and Caswell 2006), and the most recent COVID-19 outbreak segmented vegetable markets in China (Ruan, Cai, and Jin 2021). These natural disasters bring tremendous market uncertainty, and producers and traders may decide to avert risks at the opportunity cost of reduced production (Sandmo 1971) and arbitrage, thus breaking the market integration.

The 2018 outbreak of African swine fever (ASF) in China provides a natural experiment for us to study market integration incorporating both spatial dimension and risks. Having the world's largest pork market, Chinese pork consumption is concentrated in large cities in coastal provinces while its production is in rural areas. Inter-province transportation of live hogs has been the major form of arbitrage to meet the pork demand with supply, resulting in a rather integrated domestic market. In response to the ASF outbreak, the central government immediately imposed an inter-province shipping ban for live hogs, which affected the spatial price relationships across provinces (Zhang et al. 2019). The shipping ban was later lifted for any province as it was officially cleared with ASF cases, but the provincial prices did not converge quickly.

In this study, we examine hog price responses to the ASF-induced supply shocks and the shipping ban over time and space and, particularly, the process for provincial hog markets to re-integrate after the ban was lifted. A recently developed spatial panel data model (de Paula, Rasul, and Souza 2018) is adopted to estimate the strength of price co-movement between each pair of provinces over time. It parameterizes the price links across provinces to facilitate estimation of those connections via generalized method of moments (GMM) for high-dimensional models—these estimates provide insight into which provincial hog markets are most closely linked in a given period, while controlling for province- and time-specific factors. We then use variables such as the geographic distance and the length of time period under ban for any pair of provinces to explain the slow market reintegration process measured by the price relationships estimated previously. We explain the slow reintegration by producers'/processors' reluctance to reassume the trading with distant partners compared with partners nearby, when the public information of ASF is incomplete.

Our study has important policy lessons, primarily related to the importance of information transparency about contagious animal diseases. A strong policy response may have dramatic economic effects, and the key to quick economic recovery is ensuring producers access to information needed to manage private risks in the recovery stage. The insights are of value to many countries that suffer or may suffer from animal epidemics and human pandemics.

7.2 Background

The Chinese hog market and the situation of ASF breakout in China from 2018 to 2019 are described in this section. Implementation of the inter-province shipping ban on live hogs is also summarized.

7.2.1 Chinese Pork Supply Chain

China is the world's largest producer and consumer of pork, with pork being the dominant meat in the Chinese diet. Every year, over 600 million hogs, or one-half of the world's total production, are produced and consumed in China. Per capita annual consumption of pork is around 40 kilograms from 2015 to 2018 (Ma et al. 2021) and accounts for 60 percent of Chinese consumers' total meat consumption (i.e., consumption of pork, poultry, beef, and mutton).

In normal times, or pre-ASF years, the stocks of hogs and sows are around 350 million and 35 million heads, respectively. Figure 7.1 depicts the monthly stocks from January 2016 to November 2020 and shows the sharp declines in hog and sow stocks caused by ASF. Within the first year of ASF, the stock of hogs decreased from 321 million to 191 million, a loss of 40.5 percent, while the stock of sows fell from 31 million to 19 million, or 39.3 percent. Since the last quarter of 2019, both stocks have been gradually built back. By November 2020, both reached 80 percent of their pre-ASF levels.

For decades, backyard farms had been predominant hog producers in China. In 2002, small farms with an annual output of fewer than 50 heads

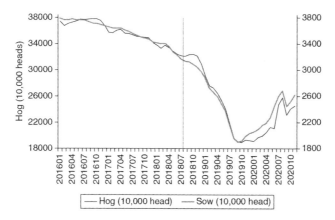

Figure 7.1   Hog and sow stock in China 2016–2020

Note: The figure covers January 2016 to November 2020. The horizontal axis indicates year and month. For example, 202011 refers to the 11th month of 2020, namely, November 2020. The dotted line indicates August 2018, when the ASF first broke out in China.

Source: Ministry of Agriculture and Rural Affairs of China.

accounted for 99 percent of all hog farms and contributed nearly 73 percent of the hogs slaughtered (Kuhn et al. 2020). In 2012, small farms still accounted for 95 percent of the farms but only contributed about 30 percent of the total output. Despite the significant structural transition in hog production from backyard toward industrialized, large-scale farms (Qiao et al. 2016), China's pork supply chain consists of a large number of producers and processors in all provinces (Zhang, Rao, and Wang 2019) and has much lower concentration ratios in production and processing compared with hog sectors in developed economies. For instance, the collective market share of the largest five slaughtering firms in China was merely 5 percent in 2018, which is in sharp contrast with the US, where the ratio is 74 percent (Wen and Liu 2019).

Pork is produced and consumed in every Chinese province. However, major pork-consuming provinces and major producing ones do not overlap. Major consuming provinces include Beijing, Guangdong, Shanghai, and Zhejiang, all of which are most economically advanced and populated in China, while major producing provinces include Henan, Hunan, Shangdong, and Sichuan, which are relatively less developed. Excess demand or excess supply at the province level, coupled with a strong preference for fresh, un-chilled pork (Wang et al. 2018) and underdeveloped cold chains, creates a need for inter-province shipments of live hogs. Large numbers of live hogs are transported by processors or logistics firms across provinces every day, mostly using open trailer trucks, and processed near the retail markets.

The inter-province shipping of live hogs in trailer trucks makes the spread of virus easy for two main reasons. One is that trucks from various locations meet at a slaughter plant and may spread the virus to each other if at least one of the trucks carries the virus. In particular, relatively large slaughtering plants often process hogs both from local farms and farms in other provinces. They own or hire trucks to ship in hogs from a number of hog farms. Trucks traveling within and across provinces meet at the slaughter plant frequently. Because trailers are not confined, the virus can easily move from one trailer to another. As trucks travel to load another batch of hogs from local or other provinces, they may spread the virus to those farms. The other way is via animal inspection stations set along inter-province highways. Trucks have to stop multiple times for inspection of various animal diseases at those stations when traveling from one province to another, and the virus may spread during an inspection.

7.2.2   ASF Outbreak in China and Policy Responses

ASF is a highly contagious disease among swine, wild or domestic, via the ASF virus. Once infected, the death rate is 100 percent. In addition to being passed among live hogs, the virus can also infect and be passed by leeches, birds, and mice, and can contaminate water and feed. The virus is able to survive in the air for days and remain active in blood, organs, and droppings of infected hogs for years, and it may spread through carcasses, pork cuts, and people who touch and carry the virus (Mason-D'Croz et al. 2020).

The first confirmed case of ASF was reported in a county located in Liaoning Province (Northeastern China) on August 3, 2018. To prevent ASF from spreading in the province and beyond, two actions were taken shortly after. First, all hogs on any *infected farm* and *farms within 3 kilometers* were culled, and the farms were thoroughly sanitized. Producers were compensated at 1,200 RMB per hog culled, which matched the materials cost of fed hogs. So far, nearly 1.2 million hogs were culled due to ASF.[1]

Second, live and slaughtered hogs in an *infected county* were not allowed to be shipped to other counties in the home province, and live hogs in an *infected province* were not allowed to be shipped to other provinces, starting August 31, 2018. Hereafter, we refer to the ban on inter-province shipments of live hogs as the *ban*. By September 10, six provinces were infected and put under the ban. Ten other provinces adjacent to these six were added to the list a day later. Despite these shipping restrictions, the virus kept spreading and the list kept growing. By the end of 2018, 95 ASF cases were officially reported in China (see table 7A.1), and all mainland provinces except for Hainan, the island province, were under the ban. However, if an infected county becomes clear of new cases for six weeks, it can be reopened after an inspection, and an infected province can be removed from the list if all of its counties are cleared. Thus, almost all provinces had their bans lifted by mid-March 2019, albeit the reported cases rose to 144 by the end of 2019.

Not surprisingly, the ban on inter-province shipment of live hogs greatly disrupted market integration, and substantial price divergence appeared across provinces. Specifically, net importing provinces, such as Beijing and Shanghai, experienced rapid and large price increases due to a sharp fall in the supply of live hogs. In contrast, net exporting provinces, such as Henan, Liaoning, and Inner Mongolia, saw large price decreases during the period due to a shift-in of hog demand. See figure 7.2, where the mean and ± two standard deviations of hog prices from the beginning of 2016 to late 2020 for 29 provincial level regions are shown. These, including all Chinese mainland provinces, municipalities, and minority autonomous regions with the exception of Tibet and Qinghai, are all referred to as *provinces* thereafter. Before the outbreak of ASF, the band around the national average price was narrow, indicating close co-movements of province-level prices. After the bans were lifted, prices began to converge, and markets began to reintegrate. It is clear, however, that this market reintegration is slow. As shown in figure 7.2, the weekly two-standard-deviation band of the national average hog price still did not narrow down to pre-ASF levels by November 2020.

---

1. The exact amount of compensation can be adjusted by provincial-level governments. The policy on culling hogs was revised in late February 2019, so that hogs on farms within 3 kilometers from the infected farm didn't need to be culled unless they tested positive.

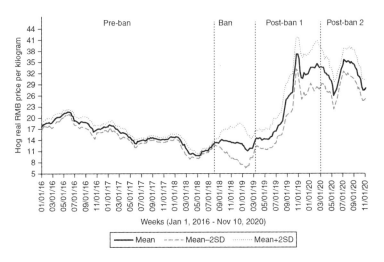

Figure 7.2   Weekly national average hog price

Note: The dotted curves represent the two-standard-deviation bands of the national average hog price (real RMB/kilogram). Each observation on the upper dotted curve represents the mean price plus two times the corresponding standard deviation, and each observation on the lower dotted curve represents the mean price minus two times the corresponding standard deviation. The horizontal axis represents all weeks from January 1, 2016 to November 10, 2020. From left to right, the three dotted vertical lines indicate the end of Period 1, the end of Period 2, and the end of Period 3, respectively.

Source: http://www.zhujiage.com.cn.

Throughout the article, we divide the data from January 1, 2016 to November 10, 2020 into four periods based on the outbreak of ASF and the implementation of the ban. Period 1 lasts from January 1, 2016 to August 5, 2018 and is the pre-ASF period. Period 2 covers the rest of 2018 through March 18, 2019 and is the ban period. We divide the post-ban period into two segments: the immediate post-ban but pre-COVID period (March 19, 2019 to February 29, 2020) and the post-COVID period. This division of the post-ban period into pre- and post-COVID allows us to isolate any potential confounding market effects of COVID-19. The three dotted vertical lines in figure 7.2 indicate the four periods.

Note that carcass shipments across provinces, which were allowed, did not help maintain integration of provincial hog markets for at least three reasons. First, the demand for frozen carcasses from other provinces is limited because of a strong consumer preference for un-chilled, fresh-cut pork (Wang et al. 2018; Mason-D'Croz et al. 2020). Second, because local slaughtering capacity was predetermined to meet the daily demand for fresh pork within a province, net exporting provinces would not be able to process the extra live hogs and produce more carcasses for net importing provinces. Third, there is insufficient cold chain capacity to ship more frozen or chilled carcasses over a long distance. Hence, even if additional hogs could be slaughtered in net exporting provinces, the carcasses would not be able to be shipped to net importing provinces in time.

7.3   Econometric Approaches

We construct two econometric models in this section. First, we will identify the spatial connectivity among provincial markets through their price relationships in each period. Second, we will identify factors affecting the spatial market relationships.

7.3.1   Spatial Model

To develop the spatial regression model, we define a standard panel-data spatial regression structure as:

$$(1) \qquad p_{it} - \bar{p}_t = \rho \sum_{j=1}^{n} w_{ij}(p_{jt} - \bar{p}_t) + v_i + \mu_t + \varepsilon_{it},$$

where the index, $i = 1, 2, \ldots, n$, references provinces, and $t = 1, 2, \ldots, T$ represents weeks. The variable $(p_{it} - \bar{p}_t)$ on the left-hand side of the equation denotes the price deviation in the hog price time series where p_{it} is the hog price for province i in week t, and $\bar{p}_t$ is the average price across all provinces in week t.[2] In the model, this price deviation is explained by the weighted average of all its spatial lags, $\sum_{j=1}^{n} w_{ij}(p_{jt} - \bar{p}_t)$, where $w_{ii} = 0$. The model is applied to each of the four periods defined in the second section, respectively.

Stationarity tests between the price series and price deviation series confirm appropriate use of the price deviation series in our regression models: the price series is not stationary, but the price deviation series is stationary. Variable v_i is a province-specific effect that may be unobserved (a province-level fixed effect), μ_t is a potentially unobservable month-specific seasonal effect (a month-level fixed effect), and ε_{it} is the regression error.

As is standard spatial regression formulation, w_{ij} are the elements of an $(n \times n)$ proximity matrix, W, whereby each element represents the pairwise spatial link among provinces i and j; the spatial links are constant over weeks within each period. The diagonal elements of W are constrained to be zero, so that each province's own price deviation is not used to explain itself on the right-hand side. Thus, for any province i, $\sum_{j=1}^{n} w_{ij}(p_{jt} - \bar{p}_t)$ captures the spatially weighted average of hog price deviations of all other provinces. Then the parameter ρ is the coefficient for the spatially weighted sum of hog price deviations of the province's trading partner provinces, and it captures the effect of the price deviations in other partner provinces on each province's price deviation series: the larger the value of ρ, the more closely related are the price deviation series across provinces.

In traditional spatial models, the elements of W are assumed to follow a

---

2. In the model, we use the price deviation instead of price level itself to stabilize the price time series, as co-movement in the untransformed price series renders estimation challenging.

prespecified spatial structure; for instance, proximate, contiguous neighbors (Florkowski and Sarmiento 2005; Tian, Wang, and Chen 2010; Wetzstein et al. 2021). Estimation then amounts to estimating while accounting for the fixed effects, and is typically done using maximum likelihood. Econometric consistency hinges, in particular, on accurate specification of the spatial structure. Indeed, in many empirical settings, the investigator likely does not know the exact spatial structure and merely imposes a particular structure based on geographic location. In our case of hog prices with a shipping ban, no prior knowledge about spatial relationships is available and, to make things more complex, the ban was imposed and then lifted.

In the newly developed de Paula, Rasul, and Souza (2018) model, the elements of W are treated as parameters to be estimated. The primary advantage of this generalized spatial modeling approach is that one needs not prespecify a fixed spatial structure, instead allowing for data-driven detection of spatial links (which may be constrained to be binary or allowed to be continuous, or ranging within 0 to 1 as in our study). Estimation of the spatial structure is a novel and robust way of determining the extent to which different hog prices are correlated across provinces.

It is worth pointing out that, distinct from traditional spatial econometric models, an alternative spatial-temporal approach would be a spatial transition model (see Fackler and Goodwin 2001 for a review of that literature), in which one would estimate a temporal transition probability or transition rate at which the province moves from one price regime to another. There is an important difference between our approach and this transition approach; that is, we are not required to specify price regimes as transition models do. The price connectivity among provinces is hence not constrained to fall between a small set of (specified) regimes. The data-driven approach allows for minimal structural assumptions on price connectivity, which ensures a more robust and likely more accurate estimation of spatial price relationships.

To this end, we recognize that in a complex trading environment, of which Chinese inter-province hog trading is a good example, it is unlikely that spatial price connectivity follows a straightforward geographic-oriented spatial structure or is confined to a known and small set of regimes. In the event that the drivers of spatial connectivity are multivariate, perhaps stemming from geographical proximity, road/rail accessibility, provincial or regional trade policies, and established supply chain infrastructure, a prespecified W or transition model that does not account for these factors or assign appropriate relative weights will be misspecified and leads to bias. Using the de Paula, Rasul, and Souza (2018) approach allows us to avoid this type of bias. Of course, the econometric consistency properties derived by de Paula, Rasul, and Souza (2018) ensure that this method is able to recover a variety of spatial patterns, whether simple or complex, and in light of evidence of a complex spatial connectivity structure, we can develop a deeper analysis of the estimated spatial links to better understand the nature of the price connectivity across Chinese provinces.

It is important to acknowledge that the parameterization of the spatial connectivity matrix leads to a large number of parameters to be estimated. After imposing the (necessary) diagonal constraint that each province is not able to directly influence itself, there remain $n(n-1)$ parameters to estimate. One might further choose to impose a symmetry constraint that the influence of province i on province j is equivalent to j's influence on i in order to reduce the number of remaining parameters to $n(n-1)/2$ parameters. Regardless, there are still a large number of parameters to estimate—large meaning greater than n. Fortunately, we follow de Paula, Rasul, and Souza (2018) and deploy recently developed GMM methods designed for estimating econometric models with a high-dimensioned parameter vector. The estimator is solved numerically, and so to ensure robustness of the numerical solution we follow a multiple starting value approach, initially setting the starting values of spatial connectivity to be in the set 0, 0.25, 0.5, 0.75, and 1. We then use an Akaike information criterion for each optimization set to determine the optimal solution.

7.3.2   Reduced form Econometric Model

We construct reduced form regressions to identify factors affecting the spatial relationships found from equation (1). We propose as the dependent variable the estimated inter-province price links, w_{ij}^m, which measures the degree to which province i's hog price follows the partner-province j's hog price. Superscript m is added to denote the weights for the mth period, $m = 1, \ldots, 4$ for the four periods defined in figure 7.2 with pre-ASF as period 1 and so on. The goal is to test if w_{ij}^m depends on the distance between provinces i and j and the number of weeks that the pair of provinces stayed under the ban, controlling for the average price of the partner province in the period (i.e., $\ln(\overline{p_{jm}})$).

The distance variable is denoted by D_{ij} and is constant over time. To estimate the impact of the shipping ban, we use variable Γ_{ij} to measure the total number of weeks that at least one of the provinces of the pair was under the ban. Additional exogenous variables are included in the regression. The provincial level hog output and province trading status pre-ASF are included in the baseline regression and denoted by vector Ω_j for province j. The period-specific specification is expressed as:

$$(2) \quad \ln(w_{ij}^m) = c^m + \alpha^m \ln(D_{ij}) + \beta^m \ln(\overline{p_{jm}}) + \varphi^m \Gamma_{ij} + \omega^m \Omega_j + F_i + e_{ij}^m,$$

$$m = 1, \ldots, 4,$$

where F_i is the fixed effect of the home province, and e_{ij}^m is the error term. The fixed effect captures any effect that is province-i-specific, including province i's average hog price in the period. Because the error term may be correlated among multiple observations related to the same home province, we cluster e_{ij}^m at the province level. When estimating the effect for the second to the fourth periods, we also add pre-ban estimated $\ln(w_{ij}^1)$ as a control variable to account for potential path dependence of the trading relationship. Taking logarithm on the weight, right-hand-side coefficients can be interpreted as percentage change in w brought by one unit change in corresponding variables.

7.4   Data

Data used in this study come from various sources and include hog prices and production, provincial-level trade status, geo-distances among provinces, and time and province of shipping bans. In this section, we explain how the data were collected and processed, and present key summary statistics.

Daily county-level hog price data are obtained from http://www.zhujiage .com.cn/, for the period between January 1, 2016 and November 10, 2020. They are then aggregated to the provincial level by a simple average, as the focus of our study is on inter-province trade and market integration. Before 2018, there are missing days in a fairly large number of weeks, and so we take the simple average of prices across all available days in each week to generate the weekly price.

The raw data set contains 31 provinces of China. Two provinces, Qinghai and Tibet, are excluded because their hog prices are not reported for 80 percent and 90 percent of the weeks, respectively. All other provinces are observed for at least 252 weeks, except for Ningxia (209 weeks), Shanghai (221 weeks), Hainan (230 weeks), and Guizhou (245 weeks). A linear interpolation is used to back out for the missing weeks of the 29 provinces.

Real prices measured as RMB per kilogram are obtained by deflating the nominal prices with the monthly Consumer Price Index (CPI) reported by the National Bureau of Statistics of China (http://www.stats.gov.cn). Setting January 2018 as the base month with a value of 100, the CPI series starts with a value of 96.2 in January 2016 and ends at 105.2 in November 2020. The finalized price data set is a panel of 29 provinces and 255 weeks. Summary statistics of the price data are displayed on the top four rows in table 7.1. Average prices in the post-ban periods are considerably higher compared with earlier periods due to the sharp reduction in hog supply caused by ASF.

The linear distance between the capital cities of any pair of provinces is collected from geodesic distance computed via the *Imap* package in R and measured in units of 1,000 kilometers. This distance is fixed, given that provincial boundaries do not change. The Ministry of Agriculture and Rural Affairs of China (http://www.moa.gov.cn/gk/yjgl_1/) has reported officially confirmed ASF cases since the outbreak. We collect information regarding ban imposition, cross-checked with news reports to pin down the starting

Table 7.1   **Summary statistics of additional variables**

Variables	Mean	SD	Min	Max	Unit
Province hog price in Period 1	15.81	0.34	15.11	16.69	RMB/kg
Province hog price in Period 2	13.05	1.56	10.45	16.71	RMB/kg
Province hog price in Period 3	24.56	1.53	20.98	27.04	RMB/kg
Province hog price in Period 4	31.71	1.59	28.79	35.73	RMB/kg
Distance D_{ij}	1.31	0.70	0.11	3.46	1000km
Province hog outputs	2.42	1.90	0.11	6.58	10 mil head
Province net importer (0,1 with 1=yes)	0.55	0.50	0.00	1.00	-
Number of weeks province under ban	25.16	4.64	12	34	Week

Note: The number of observations is 812. Statistics are weighted by observations.
Source: Authors' calculation.

week of the ban for each province. Yet, there is hardly any news on ban lifting time for each province. We define the ending week of a ban for a province as the week when the ban on the last reported case in the province was lifted, confirming each ending week with an official announcement claiming that almost all bans on inter-province hog shipment were lifted by April 2019. Except for Hainan, all mainland provinces were under the ban for some weeks during the ban period, with the number of ban weeks per province ranging from 12 to 34.

Provincial-level hog output is reported by the National Bureau of Statistics of China. We use hog output in 2017 as a control variable in the econometric models as a proxy for the regular production scale of the province. The production scale may affect trade relationships among provinces. Second, according to industry reports, some provinces are net importers and some are net exporters of pork in "normal times."[3] We add the provincial-level importer/exporter status in 2016 as another control variable to account for the impact of trade directions on trade relationships. Table 7.1 also presents the summary of statistics for these additional variables.

7.5   Empirical Results

Empirical results from the spatial model and the reduced form model are presented and discussed in this section.

7.5.1   Spatial Regression Outcomes

For each of the 29 provinces in our sample, there are 28 partner provinces, leaving us with $29 \times (29 - 1) = 812$ estimated w_{ij}, or $\widehat{w}_{ij}$, in each period. The summary of statistics of the estimated price links from the GMM model

---

3. Information in Chinese: http://pg.jrj.com.cn/acc/Res/CN_RES/INDUS/2018/11/19/0699 a384-c292-461e-aa98-74a0a019ec7d.pdf.

Table 7.2   **Summary statistics of estimated spatial matrices and distances**

Variables	Mean	SD	Min	Max
Estimated w_{ij} in Period 1, $\widehat{w_{ij}^1}$	0.16	0.14	0.00	0.98
Estimated w_{ij} in Period 2, $\widehat{w_{ij}^2}$	0.27	0.25	0.00	1.00
Estimated w_{ij} in Period 3, $\widehat{w_{ij}^3}$	0.51	0.31	0.00	1.00
Estimated w_{ij} in Period 4, $\widehat{w_{ij}^4}$	0.32	0.14	0.00	0.84

Note: The number of observations is 812. Statistics are weighted by observations.
Source: Authors' calculation.

are reported in table 7.2, instead of the $812 \times 4 = 3{,}248$ estimates. It is important to be clear that w_{ij} asures the relative strength of the connection between provinces i and j. For instance, one might interpret the strength of ties relative to the mean, median, or maximum strength, or, as in our case, seek to understand drivers of the strength of connection via reduced form regressions.

To gain preliminary insight, we can see, for instance, that the standard deviation of the links is lowest in Periods 1 and 4, indicating a greater degree of similarity in estimated spatial links in the pre-ASF and final post-ban periods. The higher standard deviations in Periods 2 and 3 indicate periods with more heterogeneity in links across provinces.

7.5.2   Reduced Form Regressions

Regression results of equation (2) are summarized in the left four columns of table 7.3. R-squared is fairly high across periods, suggesting the good fit of our model. A few patterns can be recognized. First, before ASF, the distance between two provinces does not have any significant impact on the co-movement of their prices. During the ban, the distance does not matter in a significant way either, as inter-province shipping was not allowed for any province near or far.

In the post-ban periods, provinces that were under the shipping ban for a relatively large number of weeks tended to have a significantly weaker price link in Period 3. If the two provinces were under the ban for one more week, the strength of their price link would fall by 2 percent. It is likely because the ban temporarily broke some of the original trading relationships across provinces. The longer two provinces stayed under the ban, the more likely that original trader partners had to build new trade relationships. Thus, the longer two provinces were under the ban, the more their trading relationships broke and the less their prices connected. In Period 4, the number of weeks under the ban no longer has any significant negative impact on the price link, suggesting some recovery of the original trading relationships.

More interestingly, the inter-province distance has a significant impact on the price link post the ban. Within the first 10 months after the ban was lifted (i.e., Period 3), inter-province distance has a significant and negative impact on the co-movement of prices in two provinces. When the distance increases by 10 percent, the strength of price connectivity drops by 1 percent. In Period 4, the negative effect of D_{ij} continues to be significant and enlarges to a 3 percent drop for each 10 percent increase in distance. It suggests that the newly formed trade relationships among nearby provinces in Period 3 were strengthened. There seems evidence of path-dependence in developing new trading relationships, after an integrated market fell segmented.

The negative effect of inter-province distance is likely to be driven by the lack of public information on ASF, after the ban was lifted. Recall that table 7A.1 suggests a considerably larger number of ASF cases than what was officially announced. A farm manager who decides whether to ship live hogs from the home province to another province has to weigh the potential gain from arbitrage and the potential loss due to catching ASF. The gain depends on the price spread between the two provinces, which the farm takes as given and known to all. The loss is determined by the risk of catching ASF. Without accurate public information, the farm manager has to rely on his/her own information sources to evaluate the risk.

The risk of catching ASF tends to increase in the distance of shipping for two major reasons. First, the more accurate the information, the lower the risk, because the farm can choose to trade with a safe processor located in the province, *with other conditions remaining the same.* Farmers obtain private information about ASF through personal networks. Because it tends to be more costly to collect information of slaughtering plants located farther away, the risk of catching ASF tends to be higher when trading with provinces farther away. Second, with the same amount and quality of information, the risk simply grows in the number of inspection stations that the truck has to go through to reach a slaughtering plant. As a result, inter-province arbitrage opportunities are less likely to be taken by farms and slaughtering plants located in relatively faraway provinces during the post-ban periods, leaving corresponding inter-province price links weaker.

Controlling for the fixed effect of province i, the average hog price of province j has a significant effect on the co-movement of prices both before and after the ASF shipping ban. In Period 1, a positive coefficient of the partner-province price suggests that inter-province trade is intensified if the hog price in the partner province increases. This can be rationalized by the arbitrage behavior of hog farms that export hogs. Similarly, a negative coefficient of the partner-province's price can be rationalized by the arbitrage behavior of hog importers or processing plants. In terms of the magnitude, effects of partner-province prices on w_{ij}^{m} are considerably lower in the post-ban periods compared with Period 1. This indicates that, prior to ASF, inter-province trade is more strongly motivated by arbitrage opportunities among provinces, while other incentives such as risks may have weakened the effect of price signals in leading inter-province trade of hogs in later periods.

One possible concern may be that the control variables defined for province j in the baseline regression may not have captured all the province-specific characteristics that affect the number of weeks that two provinces were under the ban and their price links. To address this possible concern, we add fixed effects for both provinces (F_i and F_j) as control variables via the alternative specification (2').

(2') $\ln(w_{ij}^m) = c^m + \alpha^m \ln(D_{ij}) + \varphi^m \Gamma_{ij} + \omega^m \Omega_j + F_i + F_j + e_{ij}^m, m = 1 \ldots 4$.

Estimates from this alternative specification are displayed in columns (5) to (8) in table 7.3. As expected, the R-squared increases relative to the previous model, suggesting that some unobservable factors of province j help explain the estimated inter-province price links. The coefficients of inter-province distance and the number of weeks under the ban stay robust in terms of both statistical significance and magnitude.

7.6   Concluding Remarks

The outbreak of ASF in China has caused a drastic shock to the hog market with a supply shortage reflected by considerable price jumps (Li and Chavas 2020; Ma et al. 2021). In addition to necessary culling of infected hogs, the inter-province shipping ban broke up the market integration and resulted in high prices in net consuming provinces and low prices in net producing provinces, a clear social welfare loss for the whole country.

We apply a novel method in studying spatial price transmission among trading partners by harnessing recently developed methods in spatial econometrics and network analysis that, itself, makes use of recent advances in GMM estimation. Our analysis demonstrates the empirical effects of this shipping ban on market integration, and the speed and manner at which markets reintegrate following a lifting of the ban, but in a setting in which uncertainty of information regarding the spread of the virus persists. We use the combination of the GMM spatial panel data model and reduced form regressions to analyze the spatial connectivity in live hog price series across provinces. These empirical models confirm the observations that the once highly integrated live hog markets across Chinese provinces quickly fractured under the ban, and were slow to recover after the ban was lifted.

One reason for this relatively slow recovery is a difference between public and private information about the spread of ASF, leading to uncertainty for producers and processors. The uncertainty in ASF information, absent the public mandate, leads to privately borne ASF risk for private operators. An immediate policy lesson from our analysis is that maintaining certainty

Table 7.3   Inter-province estimated price links and the determinants

	Without fixed effects for province j				With fixed effects for province j			
	Pre-ban (1)	Ban (2)	Post-ban 1 (3)	Post-ban 2 (4)	Pre-ban (5)	Ban (6)	Post-ban 1 (7)	Post-ban 2 (8)
Distance between provinces i and j	0.08 (0.10) [0.42]	0.07 (0.12) [0.56]	−0.12** (0.06) [0.05]	−0.26*** (0.08) [0.00]	0.09 (0.10) [0.39]	−0.12 (0.09) [0.22]	−0.21*** (0.07) [0.00]	−0.25*** (0.08) [0.00]
#weeks under the ban provinces i and j		−0.02* (0.01)	−0.02** (0.01)	−0.01 (0.01)		−0.03** (0.01)	−0.01*** (0.00)	−0.02 (0.01)
Province j average price in the period	6.29* (3.16)	−1.27*** (0.45)	−1.02** (0.39)	−1.04* (0.53)				
Pre-ban $\widehat{w_{ij}}$	NO	YES	YES	YES	NO	YES	YES	YES
Province i fixed effect	YES	YES	YES	YES	YES	YES	YES	YES
Province j controls	YES	YES	YES	YES	NO	NO	NO	NO
Province j fixed effect	NO	NO	NO	NO	YES	YES	YES	YES
R^2	0.57	0.48	0.63	0.38	0.59	0.60	0.66	0.42
# observations	812	812	812	812	812	812	812	812

Note: *** $p<0.01$, ** $p<0.05$, * $p<0.10$. Standard errors in parentheses and p-values in the square brackets. Standard errors are clustered at the province level. "Province j controls" include hog outputs in the partner province and an indicator whether the partner province is a net importer of pork.

and transparency in public information on an infectious animal disease promotes efficient trade among regional markets.

Another implication is that cold chain logistics may be an effective measurement to limit live hog shipping from production regions to consumer centers where the slaughtering plants are located. Many contagious animal diseases have happened in recent years, including the blue ear disease, swine flu, hoof-and-mouth disease, and now ASF in China. Although viruses can survive in carcasses, the survival period and rate are much shorter and lower than in live animals. With the fast development of the modern retail sector and home cold storage in emerging economies, cold chain logistics form the last link to close the meat distribution system. The existing slaughter facilities near consumer centers may be an obstacle to the cold chain development.

Given the slow recovery of market integration in the post-ban periods, it is likely that welfare losses were incurred; expanded use of cold chain logistics might be a way to minimize such losses in future disease-outbreak cases both within China and in other emerging economies beyond China. Besides, our methodological approach has application beyond the current Chinese hog market context for studying spatial price transmission.

Appendix
Officially Reported ASF Cases in China

Table 7A.1 summarizes the numbers of officially reported ASF cases in 2018 and 2019 by province in mainland China. The number of hogs affected is the reported number of hogs on all directly infected farms. Hogs raised on nearby farms may be culled as well.

Table 7A.1   Officially reported cases of African swine fever

Province	No. cases 2018	No. cases 2019	No. cases	No. hogs affected
Anhui	8	0	8	10,981
Beijing	3	0	3	14,050
Chongqing	2	1	3	423
Fujian	3	0	3	22,247
Gansu	0	3	3	586
Guangdong	3	0	3	6,167
Guangxi	0	5	5	27,619
Guizhou	4	4	8	1,666
Hainan	0	6	6	1,238
Hebei	0	1	1	5,600
Henan	3	0	3	260
Heilongjiang	5	1	6	74,649
Hubei	4	3	7	2,026
Hunan	7	1	8	13,443
Inner Mongolia	5	1	6	995
Jilin	4	0	4	1,458
Jiangsu	2	1	3	69,066
Jiangxi	3	0	3	463
Liaoning	16	0	16	35,342
Ningxia	0	4	4	465
Qinghai	1	1	2	101
Shandong	0	1	1	4,504
Shanxi	5	0	5	8,379
Shaanxi	3	2	5	11,857
Shanghai	1	0	1	314
Sichuan	5	3	8	1,608
Tianjin	2	0	2	1,000
Tibet	0	1	1	N/A
Xinjiang	0	3	3	1,124
Yunnan	4	7	11	1,919
Zhejiang	2	0	2	2,280
All	95	49	144	321,830

Note: "No. hogs affected" is the total number of hogs on the infected farms in the reported cases.

Source: Authors' summary from http://www.moa.gov.cn/gk/yjgl_1/yqfb/.

References

Barrett, Christopher B., and Jau Rong Li. 2002. "Distinguishing between Equilibrium and Integration in Spatial Price Analysis." *American Journal of Agricultural Economics* 84 (2): 292–307.

de Paula, Aureo, Imran Rasul, and Pedro Souza. 2018. "Recovering Social Networks from Panel Data: Identification, Simulations and an Application." Working paper. https://ssrn.com/abstract=3322049.

Fackler, Paul L., and Barry K. Goodwin. 2001. "Spatial Price Analysis." *Handbook of Agricultural Economics* 1: 971–1024.

Fan, C. Cindy. 2002. "The Elite, the Natives, and the Outsiders: Migration and Labor Market Segmentation in Urban China." *Annals of the Association of American Geographers* 92 (1): 103–24.

Florkowski, J. Wojciech, and Camilo Sarmiento. 2005. "The Examination of Pecan Price Differences Using Spatial Correlation Estimation." *Applied Economics* 37 (3): 271–78.

Ge, Yuanlong, H. Holly Wang, and Sung K. Ahn. 2010. "Cotton Market Integration and the Impact of China's New Exchange Rate Regime." *Agricultural Economics* 41 (5): 443–51.

Goodwin, Barry K., and Ted C. Schroeder. 1991. "Cointegration Tests and Spatial Price Linkages in Regional Cattle Markets." *American Journal of Agricultural Economics* 73 (2): 452–64.

Goyat, Sulekha. 2011. "The Basis of Market Segmentation: A Critical Review of Literature." *European Journal of Business and Management* 3 (9): 45–54.

Kuhn, Lena, Tomas Balezentis, Lingling Hou, and Dan Wang. 2020. "Technical and Environmental Efficiency of Livestock Farms in China: A Slacks-Based DEA Approach." *China Economic Review* 62: 101213.

Li, Jian, and Jean-Paul Chavas. 2020. "The Impacts of African Swine Fever on Vertical and Spatial Hog Pricing and Market Integration in China." Selected Paper, AAEA Annual Meetings, Kansas City, MO, July 2020. https://ageconsearch.umn .edu/record/304516/files/18994.pdf.

Ma, Meilin, H. Holly Wang, Yizhou Hua, Fei Qin, and Jing Yang. 2021. "African Swine Fever in China: Impacts, Responses, and Policy Implications." *Food Policy* 102065. doi:10.1016/j.foodpol.2021.102065.

Mason-D'Croz, Daniel, Jessica R. Bogard, Mario Herrero, Sherman Robinson, Timothy B. Sulser, Keith Wiebe, Dirk Willenbockel, and H. Charles J. Godfray. 2020. "Modelling the Global Economic Consequences of a Major African Swine Fever Outbreak in China." *Nature Food* 1 (4): 221–28.

Negassa, Asfaw, and Robert J. Myers. 2007. "Estimating Policy Effects on Spatial Market Efficiency: An Extension to the Parity Bounds Model." *American Journal of Agricultural Economics* 89 (2): 338–52.

Qiao, Fangbin, Jikun Huang, Dan Wang, Huaiju Liu, and Bryan Lohmar. 2016. "China's Hog Production: From Backyard to Large-Scale." *China Economic Review* 38: 199–208.

Ravallion, Martin. 1986. "Testing Market Integration." *American Journal of Agricultural Economics* 68 (1): 102–9.

Ruan, Jianqing, Qingwen Cai, and Songqing Jin. 2021. "Impact of COVID-19 and Nationwide Lockdowns on Vegetable Prices: Evidence from Wholesale Markets in China." *American Journal of Agricultural Economics* https://doi.org/10.1111/ajae .12211.

Sandmo, Agnar. 1971. "On the Theory of the Competitive Firm under Price Uncertainty." *American Economic Review* 61 (1): 65–73.

Shiue, Carol H., and Wolfgang Keller. 2007. "Markets in China and Europe on the Eve of the Industrial Revolution." *American Economic Review* 97 (4): 1189–216.

Sparling, David H., and Julie A. Caswell. 2006. "Risking Market Integration without Regulatory Integration: The Case of NAFTA and BSE." *Review of Agricultural Economics* 28 (2): 212–28.

Tian, Lei, H. Holly Wang, and Yongjun Chen. 2010. "Spatial Externalities in China Regional Economic Growth." *China Economic Review* 21 (S1): S20–S31.

Wang, H. Holly, and Bingfan Ke. 2005. "Efficiency Tests of Agricultural Commodity Futures Markets in China." *Australian Journal of Agricultural and Resource Economics* 49 (2): 125–41.

Wang, H. Holly, Junhong Chen, Junfei Bai, and John Lai. 2018. "Meat Packaging, Preservation, and Marketing Implications: Consumer Preferences in an Emerging Economy." *Meat Science* 145: 300–307.

Wen, Xian, and Biao Liu. 2019. "Overview of Hog Slaughtering Industry." In Chinese. http://pdf.dfcfw.com/pdf/H3_AP201909161360005225_1.pdf.

Wetzstein, Brian, Raymond Florax, Kenneth Foster, and James Binkley. 2021. "Transportation Costs: Mississippi River Barge Rates." *Journal of Commodity Markets* 21: 100123.

Zhang, Wendong, Dermot J. Hayes, Yongjie Ji, Minghao Li, and Tao Xiong. 2019. "African Swine Fever in China: An Update." *Agricultural Policy Review* 2019 (1): 2.

Zhang, Yuehua, Xudong Rao, and H. Holly Wang. 2019. "Organization, Technology and Management Innovations through Acquisition in China's Pork Value Chains: The Case of the Smithfield Acquisition by Shuanghui." *Food Policy* 83: 337–45.

Concentration and Resilience in the US Meat Supply Chains

Meilin Ma and Jayson L. Lusk

8.1 Introduction

Concentration in the US meat packing sector has increased markedly from the 1960s to the 1990s (MacDonald et al. 1999). In 2019, the 22 largest beef packing plants, representing just 3.3 percent of all plants, were responsible for 71.7 percent of federal inspected cattle processing in the US (National Agricultural Statistics Service or NASS 2020). Pork packing is similarly concentrated with the largest 15 plants, representing only 2.5 percent of all plants, responsible for 61.9 percent of all federally inspected hogs slaughtered (see appendix A). The high level of horizontal concentration can be explained, at least in part, by the economies of scale in meat packing (Koontz and Lawrence 2010; MacDonald 2003; MacDonald and Ollinger 2005; Morrison Paul 2001), implying that, in normal times, large and cost-efficient packing plants result in more affordable meat for consumers and higher livestock demand than would be the case with a more diffuse and higher-cost packing system.

However, times are not always normal, and unexpected events can lead to plant shutdowns. For example, in August 2019, a fire at a beef packing plant in Kansas, responsible for about 5 percent of the total US processing capacity, caused a spike in the farm-to-retail price spread and led to law-

Meilin Ma is an assistant professor in the Department of Agricultural Economics at Purdue University.

Jayson L. Lusk is Distinguished Professor and Head of the Department of Agricultural Economics at Purdue University.

For acknowledgments, sources of research support, and disclosure of the authors' material financial relationships, if any, please see https://www.nber.org/books-and-chapters/risks -agricultural-supply-chains/concentration-and-resiliency-us-meat-supply-chains.

suits and a federal investigation (USDA 2020). Then, in April and May 2020, worker illnesses from COVID-19 led to the shutdown of a number of large beef and pork packing plants, as roughly 40 percent of processing capacity was brought offline, leading to an unprecedented increase in the farm-to-wholesale price spread and serious concerns over food security and meat supply (Lusk, Tonsor, and Schulz 2021). These recent events have raised questions about the resilience of the beef and pork supply chains, and policy makers have sought ways to encourage the entry of more small- and medium-sized processors, hoping to enhance the resilience (Bustillo 2020; Nickelsburg 2020; Pitt 2021). Despite these efforts, at present, it remains unclear whether and to what extent a less concentrated meat packing sector would have performed better during the pandemic, a knowledge gap this paper aims to rectify.

Resilience is a widely discussed topic across disciplines, like ecology, sociology, and management, and the definition of resilience is disciplinary specific (Bhamra, Dani, and Burnard 2011). Regarding the resilience of the supply chain, researchers mainly study the short-run as well as long-run adaptive capability of a supply chain to respond to disruptions and maintain operations at the desired level (Ponomarov and Holcomb 2009). In our context, we evaluate resilience of the US meat supply chain based on *the short-run performance of different horizontal structures in achieving target output and producer/consumer welfare, in response to an exogenous chance of shutdown faced by packing plants.*

Our model of the US meat supply chain captures key features of the meat packing sector, including its concentrated nature and economies of scale. The concentrated nature of meat packing has been the subject of much attention, and numerous studies have attempted to estimate and determine the presence or extent of imperfect competition in the sector, finding mixed evidence (e.g., see Wohlgenant 2013 for one review). Our model allows heterogeneous packers to exercise market power under Cournot competition, though packers may not exercise much seller or buyer power under a particular horizontal structure.

Legal complaints and livestock producer concerns have focused on the farm-to-wholesale or farm-to-retail price spreads as evidence of market power, and concerns about widening price spreads, have been reignited by price dynamics following recent plant shutdowns. Our model and findings reinforce Brester, Marsh, and Atwood's (2009) results that price spreads, in isolation, are uninformative as they relate to market power. A few recent papers have explored the market impacts that occur when a firm decides to close one of its packing plants (e.g., McKendree, Saitone, and Schaefer 2021; Raper, Cheney, and Punjabi 2006). Our paper goes beyond this prior work by introducing a broader framework that allows us to explore outcomes resulting from differing horizontal structures, and when plants in the industry face an exogenous risk of shutdown rather than the endogenous choice to reduce capacity.

This paper is organized as follows. In section 8.2, we set up a three-stage theoretical model to characterize the interactions among livestock farmers, meat packing plants, and retailers. Because entering the meat packing sector requires considerable fixed investment in constructing the plant (i.e., sunk costs), the processing capacity of each plant is assumed to be fixed in our short-run context. We allow the plants to Cournot-compete by choosing the optimal production scale in the scenario with no exogenous risk of shutdown, given size-specific heterogeneous processing cost functions. Under Cournot competition, the degree of seller and buyer power exercised by a packing plant is determined by its volume share in the sector.

To calibrate the model, we impose linear functions to beef demand and cattle supply to obtain analytical solutions for equilibrium prices, quantities, and welfare measurements in section 8.3. The demand elasticity, supply elasticity, and marginal costs of retailing are collected from recent empirical studies and government statistics. Given these parameters, marginal costs of processing are specified to ensure that the equilibrium size distribution of plants in the risk-free scenario matches the actual horizontal structure of US beef packing in 2019.

In section 8.4, we conduct simulations to study counter-factual equilibria in the beef industry under various risk levels and different horizontal structures. For each simulation, a particular level of risk is randomly imposed on all packing plants, causing some plants to shut down. In addition to the actual structure of the beef-packing sector, we consider two alternative structures: a market with small-sized plants only (i.e., the diffuse structure) and a market with large-sized plants only (i.e., the concentrated structure). The actual structure lies in between the two extreme structures.

Simulation outcomes reveal the complexity in the relative resilience across horizontal structures of meat packing. When each plant in the industry faces chance of shutdown equal to 10–30 percent, for example, simulation results show that a more concentrated packing sector performs better in ensuring a relatively high level of output (e.g., less than 20 percent output reductions), and thus food security, than a diffuse packing sector, while the reverse is true if the goal is to ensure that output does not fall below a minimal threshold (e.g., more than 40 percent output reductions). On average, though, differences across horizontal structures are typically not of large economic magnitudes. What distinguishes the three structures is the variation in the prices and quantities across simulations. A more diffuse packing sector has lower variability in output and consumer and producer welfare for any given shutdown risk than a more concentrated packing sector. While lower variability might be interpreted as a benefit of a diffuse packing sector, it need not be the case as it might imply certainty of a poor outcome. Sensitivity analysis suggests that these patterns are robust to alternative values of key parameters, including supply elasticity, and alternative structures and assumptions on the plant-level output. Similar conclusions apply to the pork supply chain, which has similar structural features as the beef supply chain.

As discussed in section 8.5, these results help illustrate the consequences of policies and industry efforts aimed at increasing the resilience of the food supply chain. Policy proposals, academic writings, and popular discussions have tended to focus on lessening the degree of concentration as key to improving resilience (e.g., Hendrickson 2015; Pitt 2021; Rotz and Fraser 2015). Using the beef supply chain as an example, our research shows that the relationship between concentration and resilience is complex. Odds of output, or producer or consumer surplus, falling below a given level is sometimes lower and sometimes higher when the packing sector is less concentrated; however, it is generally the case that a more diffuse packing sector has slightly lower odds of witnessing the worst possible outcomes. However, total expected welfare is typically lower under a more diffuse packing sector because of the lost economies of scale, a result related to findings such as that by Azzam and Schroeter Jr. (1995), who show welfare losses from market power are more than offset by improved cost efficiencies. However, if the social planner is risk averse, especially loss averse, a more diffuse structure may be preferred (see section 8.4.3).

Despite the sizable literature on concentration and market power in meat packing, our study is among the first to relate these issues to the short-run resilience to exogenous (or "disaster") shutdown risks on packing plants. Given the severe adverse impacts of COVID-19 on livestock and meat packing sectors, and impending policy changes and legal challenges to the present system, it is of high importance to understand how short-run resilience may be impacted by degree of concentration.

8.2   Conceptual Model

Given heterogeneity in size of processors in the US meat packing industry, we employ a Cournot competition model to characterize plant interactions. The Cournot model offers an appropriate framework for our context because a meat processor is committed to producing at a particular scale upon building its plant.[1] Once the plant is built, the processor tries to, and often does, produce near full capacity where costs are minimized (Koontz and Lawrence 2010; Bina et al. 2021). It is hence reasonable to model plants competing in quantity, which implies rising marginal costs of processing at

1. This model does not account for spatial factors related to plant location. In reality, all the largest beef packing plants are located in a tight geographic region around the Texas panhandle, Western Kanas, and Nebraska, suggesting that distance is unlikely to be a predominant factor affecting competition.

the full capacity or increasing shadow value of relaxing the capacity constraint of a given plant. The model also allows for imperfect competition in the cattle as well as beef retail markets, and can consider various counterfactual structures of the meat packing sector.

Let there be n processing plants of different sizes. The plants are denoted by $i \in \{1, 2, 3, \ldots n\}$. Relatively large processors enjoy economies of scale and have relatively low marginal costs of processing than smaller processors (Koontz and Lawrence 2010; MacDonald 2003; MacDonald and Ollinger 2005). Under Cournot competition, a processor with lower marginal costs always produces at a larger scale in equilibrium.

Prior studies find that meat processors exercise buyer power against livestock producers and may also exercise seller power against retailers (Wohlgenant 2013). We hence specify an upward sloping supply function and a downward sloping inverse demand function faced by the processors. The inverse demand function that processors face is derived from the inverse demand function for beef less a constant retailing marginal cost (c^r):

(1a) $$P^r = D(Q^r | X),$$

(1b) $$P^w = P^r - c^r = D(Q^r | X) - c^r,$$

where P^r is the retail price, P^w the wholesale price, and X demand shifters. The inverse farm supply of cattle is expressed as:

(1c) $$P^f = S(Q^f | Y),$$

where P^f is the farm-gate price and Y supply shifters.

Assume for convenience that the processing technology satisfies quasi-fixed proportions, so that no substitution is permitted between cattle and other processing inputs like labor and energy in producing beef products. Without loss of generality, we can hence measure total quantities at farm, processor, and retail stages in the supply chain as $Q^r = Q^w = Q^f = Q = \sum_n q_i$ where q_i denotes the output of a packing plant.

Assuming a constant marginal cost of processing for each packing plant, we express the total cost of plant i as:

(2) $$C_i^w = c_i^w q_i + P^f(Q)q_i,$$

where c_i^w is a constant marginal cost of processing and decreases in the size of the plant. We then write a profit-maximizing processor's objective function as:

(3) $$\pi_i^w = (D(Q | X) - c^r)q_i - [c_i^w + P^f(Q | Y)]q_i.$$

Taking the derivative with respect to q_i gives the first order condition:

(4) $$P^r\left(1 - \frac{\xi_i^w}{\eta^w}\right) - c^r = P^f\left(1 + \frac{\theta_i^f}{\varepsilon^f}\right) + c_i^w,$$

where $\xi_i^w = (\partial Q / \partial q_i)(q_i / Q) \in [0,1]$ is the market power parameter of a particular processor against retailers and indicates processor's seller power (Perloff, Karp, and Golan 2007), η^w is the absolute value of demand elasticity for the meat, θ_i^f is the market power parameter of a particular processor against farmers and measures processor's buyer power, and ε^f is the elasticity of farm supply. When the market power parameter equals zero, there is perfect competition in the corresponding market. The closer the market power parameter is to 1.0, the more market power exercised by the processing plant.

Under Cournot competition, $\xi_i^w = (\partial Q / \partial q_i)(q_i / Q) = [(\partial Q / Q) / (\partial q_i / Q_i)]$ $= s_i = \theta_i^f$, meaning that the market power parameter of a processor equals its output share in the market.[2] As illustrated in section 8.3, we calibrate output shares of plants based on the actual distribution of plant sizes. Taking the actual horizontal structure of beef packing in 2019 as an example, the market shares of largest plants are merely 3–5 percent, implying limited exercise of market power in the processing sector.

8.3   Parameterization

To apply this framework to the US livestock industry, we need to obtain analytical solutions from the general model by assigning functional forms, choosing plant sizes to be considered, and obtaining values of parameters. Referring to NASS (2020), we take the most recent, pre-COVID size distribution of beef packers in the US as the benchmark to characterize the risk-free horizontal structure. The pork packing sector has a similar structure.

As detailed in appendix A, the nine size groups reported by NASS are consolidated into three groups. Plants with yearly output of 1–49,999 head account for 91.8 percent of all plants but contribute only 3.1 percent of the industry output. Their average annual output is 1.7 thousand head per plant. Plants with yearly output of 50,000–499,999 head account for 4.9 percent of all plants and contribute 25.2 percent of the total output. On average, their annual output is 252.3 thousand head per plant. Finally, 3.3 percent of the plants slaughter over half million head per year and contribute 71.7 percent of industry output. Their average annual output per plant is as large as 1.1 million head. Throughout the rest of this article, we rely on the three output groups referred to as the small-sized, medium-sized, and large-sized beef packers, respectively.

---

2. One might be concerned about the common ownership across packing plants in the meat industry. For instance, the largest four meat packing companies own most of the large-sized plants. Our model is readily able to incorporate common ownership by letting $\partial Q / \partial q_i$ be larger than 1. That is, when a plant changes its output levels, other plants belonging to the same company would do the same. Doing so results in a smaller Q^* and gives large-sized plants more market power, but would not change our central insights in the distribution of simulated outcomes across structures. Moreover, our main focus is on risks of shutdown, which occur at the plant, not ownership level.

8.3.1   Analytical Solutions

We utilize linear inverse demand and supply functions faced by meat packers, respectively:

$$(5a) \qquad P^r = a - \alpha Q,$$

$$(5b) \qquad P^f = b + \beta Q.$$

Assume that perfect competition is achieved with a large number of small-sized processors in the industry. Normalizing the equilibrium retail price and quantity under perfect competition to 1, we can express the competitive wholesale price as $1 - c^r$ and the competitive farm price as $f = 1 - c^r - c_S^w$, where the S subscript indicates small-sized plants. It follows that $\alpha = 1/\eta^r$, $\beta = f/\varepsilon^f$, $a = 1 + 1/\eta^r$, and $b = f - \beta$.

Rewriting the first order condition of a processing plant i as:

$$(6) \qquad P^r - c^r - P^f - c_i^w = -q_i \left(\frac{\partial P^r}{\partial q_i} - \frac{\partial P^f}{\partial q_i} \right),$$

we obtain:

$$(7a) \qquad (a - \alpha Q) - (b + \beta Q) - c^r - c_i^w = (\alpha + \beta) Q \frac{\partial Q}{\partial q_i} \frac{q_i}{Q}.$$

Because $(\partial Q / \partial q_i)(q_i / Q)$ equals the production share of plant i, adding up over the n plants yields:

$$(7b) \qquad n(a - b) - n(\alpha + \beta)Q - nc^r - \sum_i^n c_i^w = (\alpha + \beta)Q.$$

Equation (7b) implies the equilibrium industry output is:

$$(8a) \qquad Q^* = \frac{n}{n + 1} \frac{(a - b) - c^r - \overline{c^w}}{\alpha + \beta},$$

where $\overline{c^w} = \sum_i^n c_i^w / n$ is the industry-level average processing marginal cost.

With Q^*, it is easy to compute the equilibrium prices P^{r*} and P^{f*}. Because we assume linear functional forms for demand and supply, we compute consumer surplus (CS), producer surplus (PS), and processor profits (Π) as:

$$(8b) \qquad CS = \frac{(a - P^{r*})Q^*}{2},$$

$$(8c) \qquad PS = \frac{(P^{f*} - b)Q^*}{2}, \text{ and}$$

$$(8d) \qquad \Pi = (P^{r*} - c^r - P^{f*})Q^* - \sum_i^n c_i^w q_i^*.$$

The equilibrium production of plant i is solved by plugging Q^* into equation (7a). Rearranging the equation, we see that plant i's output is given by:

(8e)
$$q_i^* = \frac{(a-b) - c^r - c_i^w}{\alpha + \beta} - Q^*.$$

Given a shutdown shock imposed on each plant, some plants stop operation, leaving n' active plants in the sector. In the short run, the remaining n' plants are unable to produce more than the initial equilibrium output, q_i^*, because of the fixed production capacity. Thus, the new total quantity processed is:

(9a)
$$Q' = \sum_{n'} q_i^* < Q^*.$$

Correspondingly, the new market equilibrium retail price and farm price can be found based on the demand and supply functions that are unchanged under the shock on processing plants. In the new equilibrium, we consider an *implied* c_i^w that makes the initial outputs equilibrium outputs with n' active plants. The implied processing marginal cost reflects additional costs with producing just beyond the capacity and additional costs in a risky environment (e.g., sanitation and social distancing). It is higher than the initial c_i^w and equals:

(9b)
$$c_i^{w\prime} = (a-b) - c^r - (\alpha + \beta)(q_i^* + Q').$$

In sensitivity analysis, we relax the assumption of fixed q_i^* and show that main conclusions remain unchanged.

8.3.2   Parameter Values

The key parameters in our simulation model are the own-price demand elasticity for beef (η^r), the short-run supply elasticity of cattle (ε^f), the retail marginal costs (c^r), marginal costs of processing for different sizes of slaughter plants (c_i^w), and the competitive farm share of retail beef value (f). We survey the literature and public statistics to assign appropriate values to the parameters in our baseline simulation model.

To find the plausible value for η^r, we surveyed recent US-focused empirical studies on beef demand. These studies use a variety of data sources at different frequencies ranging from individual-consumer survey data, to weekly retail scanner data, to quarterly or annual, aggregate nationwide data. We summarize seven recent studies providing 31 point estimates of demand elasticity in table 8B.1. The estimates range widely and roughly fall in two domains: a low domain from -0.5 to -1, suggesting inelastic demand, and a high domain from -1.7 to -2.3, implying elastic demand. The relatively elastic magnitudes are generally from studies using high-frequency data. We take the mean value of the high domain as the baseline value of η^r because our study focuses on short-run changes in the market equilibrium.

Estimating supply responses for products with biological cycles has long been a challenge (Aadland and Bailey 2001). There are relatively few recent studies providing estimates of cattle supply elasticities in the US (see table 8B.2 for a few estimated values). The values are quite consistent, suggesting inelastic cattle supply in the short run, with ε^f equal to about 0.2. With respect to our simulation model, however, letting ε^f be smaller than 1.0 might lead to cases where the equilibrium farm price is negative. Such cases happen when a sufficiently large number of plants shut down, and imply that farmers need to pay plants to get their animals slaughtered to make room for new feeder animals. While these outcomes would be highly unusual, the market might approximate the outcome, as in the case of COVID-19, when hog producers resorted to euthanizing hogs (e.g., Dipietre and Mulberry 2021). For the purpose of simulations, we restrict P^f to be non-negative by setting the supply elasticity to 1.0, assuming that farmers may enjoy some flexibility in holding the stock for a few days to a couple of weeks if the farm price falls too low. Less elastic supply is considered in section 8.4.2, where we conduct sensitivity analysis.

The retail marginal cost parameter is approximated by price spreads reported by USDA, Economic Research Service (2021). We assume that a common c^r applies to all sizes of slaughter plants and c^r is independent from shutdown risks. USDA monthly beef price spread data are measured in retail-weight equivalent units based on fixed conversion rates from cattle to processed beef and from processed beef to retail beef (Hahn 2004). The average monthly wholesale-to-retail price spread margin in 2019 accounts for 41–43 percent of the retail beef value. In the base simulation, we hence set c^r at the mean value or 0.42 given the competitive retail price is normalized to 1.

To replicate the actual distribution of plant sizes grouped into three levels, we set processing marginal costs for the three sizes of plants such that their risk-free, relative output sizes under Cournot competition match with the actual statistics reported by USDA (see table 8A.1). Normalizing the risk-free output of small-sized plants to 1, the scale of medium-sized plants is 154, and the scale of large-sized plants is 660. Once the marginal costs of processing for the small-sized plants are determined, the farm share under perfect competition is found by $f = 1 - c^r - c_S^w$. The value of f also matches with the farmer share of beef reported by USDA (2021). Baseline parameter values are summarized in table 8.1.

8.4   Simulation Results

The calibrated model is flexible in considering various horizontal structures of the US beef packing sector. We consider various risk levels and present baseline simulation outcomes for three horizontal structures of interest. Sensitivity analysis suggests that the baseline outcomes are robust to alternative parameter values and assumptions.

Table 8.1   Parameter values in the base simulation

Parameter	Definition	Value
η^r	Magnitude of demand elasticity for beef	1.94
ε^f	Supply elasticity of cattle	1.00
c^r	Retail marginal costs	0.42
f	Farm share of the retail value under no risk	0.43
c_S^w	Processing marginal costs, small-sized under no risk	0.16
c_M^w	Processing marginal costs, medium-sized under no risk	0.15
c_L^w	Processing marginal costs, large-sized under no risk	0.12

Table 8.2   Plant size distributions under different structures

Scenario	No. small plants	No. medium plants	No. large plants	No. plants
Current	615	33	22	670
All small	22,000	0	0	22,000
All large	0	0	30	30

8.4.1   Baseline Outcomes

In addition to the actual structure, we are interested in two counter-factual horizontal structures of the beef packing sector: small-sized-only and large-sized-only. In the rest of this article, we refer to the actual structure as the "current scenario" where the size distribution of packing plants matches exactly the actual distribution in 2019, when collapsed to three size groups. The small-sized-only is referred to as the "all-small scenario" and characterizes a diffuse structure which is completely occupied by small-sized plants. The third structure is called the "all-large scenario" and characterizes an oligopoly-oligopsony market which is occupied by a few large-scale plants.

For easier comparison across different horizontal structures, we let all the scenarios reach the same equilibrium industry output under no risk.[3] The number of different sized plants are adjusted accordingly. The distribution of plant sizes in each scenario is displayed in table 8.2. Because the output scale of a small-sized plant is only 1/660th of a large-sized plant, it is no surprise the see many more small-sized plants in the all-small scenario and only a few large-sized plants in the all-large scenario.

We consider various shutdown risks, including 5 percent, 10 percent, 20 percent, 30 percent, 40 percent, and 50 percent. The risk is common to all plants in a scenario and is independently and randomly realized. The risk is not set as a function of the plant size, because there is no evidence

3. Strictly speaking, the total output by 30 large plants is slightly lower under no risk compared with the current and all-small scenarios. Because the number of plants has to be an integer, 30 plants already give us an output level closest to the other two scenarios.

against this setup. For example, capacity reductions in beef slaughter plants during COVID-19 did not depend on plant sizes (Bina et al. 2021). Other supply-side risks such as fire outbreak and machinery breakdown could be higher for smaller plants due to their use of older buildings/facilities (Williams 2018) or lower because of more careful supervision in daily operation. By imposing a common risk to all plants, we are able to isolate the effect of changing the structure on industry outputs and prices under a particular risk.

Given a scenario and a risk level, 1,000 simulations are conducted to generate equilibrium prices and outputs. At each iteration, a [0, 1] uniform random draw is taken for each plant. If the draw exceeds the assigned shutdown risk level (e.g., 0.3), the plant stays open, otherwise the plant closes and produces zero output. Once the risk is realized for each plant, industry output and prices and welfare measurements are recomputed for packing plants that remain open.

To judge the fitness of the model, we begin by comparing simulation outcomes from the current scenario to actual price and output changes witnessed during COVID-19, confirming that this scenario indeed captures key features of the US beef industry. In April and May 2020, the US beef packing sector experienced substantial supply-side disruptions due to slowdown and shutdown of packing plants. Daily number of federally inspected cattle processed fell 20–40 percent year-over-year for eight weeks (Lusk, Tonsor, and Schulz 2021). From February to mid-May, the farm-to-wholesale price spread increased by over 250 percent. Our simulation outcomes depict a similar picture. When the risk of shutdown is 30 percent, the farm-to-wholesale price spread rises from 0.16 to 0.44, an increase of 179 percent. With a 40 percent risk, the increase becomes 241 percent. The large increases in the price spread, however, do not mean an increase in packer profits because the price spread increases as much in a competitive-market setup as under imperfect competition.

We proceed to compare the current horizontal structure to the two counter-factual structures. One general insight is that the new equilibrium prices and outputs after plant shutdowns have almost identical mean values, regardless of the structure. The structure matters only when we consider the variation in new equilibrium prices and outputs across the 1,000 iterations: there is much less variation in a diffuse sector than in more concentrated ones.

The intuition is straightforward and captured by panel (a) of figure 8.1. With a large number of small plants, outcomes from imposing random shocks always converge to the expected level. For example, if each plant faces a 30 percent chance of shutdown in the all-small scenario, approximately 30 percent of plants will close and, because all plants are the same small size, output will fall approximately 30 percent in every iteration. Therefore, its distribution of simulated outputs is highly concentrated around the mean of

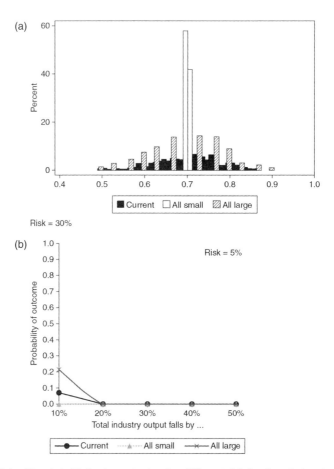

Figure 8.1   Simulated industry output under different risk levels and structures

Note: In panel (a), the horizontal axis is the normalized simulated total output ranging from 0.4 to 1. The vertical axis is the percentage of 1,000 simulated cases that produce the corresponding output under a particular structure. In panels (b) (c) (d), the horizontal axis indicates the reduction in total industry output with "X%" meaning that "total output falls by more than X% compared with the risk-free output." The vertical axis measures the corresponding probability of experiencing a reduction in total output larger than X%. Plant outputs under risks are fixed at the risk-free levels.

Source: Author's simulation outcomes.

0.70 (i.e., the green bars in the figure). With a small number of plants, however, a simulation outcome of imposing random shocks could vary widely around the expected level, particularly if a large plant happens to receive a "good" or "bad" draw in an iteration. The distribution of simulated outputs under the all-large scenario has wide tails or high variance (i.e., the blue bars in the figure). The current scenario generates outcomes that lie in between the two extreme structures.

Panel (b) of figure 8.1 shows the probability of avoiding different reductions (i.e., target levels of operation) in the sector's total output given a

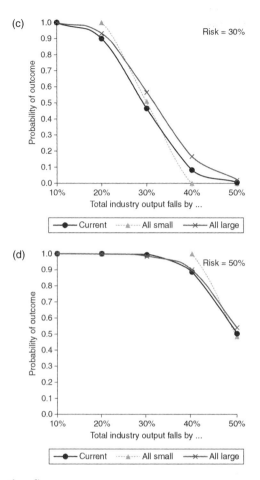

Figure 8.1   (continued)

shutdown risk and a horizontal structure. When the risk is small (e.g., 5 percent), the all-small scenario always outperforms the other two scenarios in achieving the lowest probability of experiencing any output reduction, and the all-large scenario is always the worst. When the risk level is medium (e.g., 30 percent), the all-small scenario outperforms only in achieving the lowest probability of experiencing large output reductions such as 40 percent+ (i.e., more than 40 percent) and 50 percent+. The current scenario performs the best regarding relatively small output reductions. When the risk level is high (e.g., 50 percent), the three scenarios perform equally in experiencing 10 percent+ and 20 percent+ reductions. The all-large scenario performs slightly better in avoiding 30 percent+ reductions. The current scenario outperforms regarding 40 percent+ reductions, while the all-small scenario remains the best in avoiding 50 percent+ reductions.

Given the patterns, we argue that the short-run resilience of a horizontal

Table 8.3   Simulated mean values under different structures

Scenario	Risk = 5%	Risk = 10%	Risk = 20%	Risk = 30%	Risk = 40%	Risk = 50%
Price spread						
Current	0.622	0.671	0.762	0.856	0.951	1.045
All small	0.623	0.670	0.764	0.858	0.952	1.046
All large	0.624	0.671	0.765	0.859	0.950	1.042
Packer profits						
Current	0.023	0.021	0.019	0.017	0.014	0.012
All small	0.000	0.000	0.000	0.000	0.000	0.000
All large	0.030	0.028	0.025	0.022	0.019	0.016
CS						
Current	0.233	0.208	0.167	0.128	0.095	0.066
All small	0.232	0.209	0.165	0.126	0.093	0.064
All large	0.232	0.209	0.166	0.128	0.095	0.067
PS						
Current	0.192	0.172	0.137	0.106	0.078	0.054
All small	0.191	0.172	0.136	0.104	0.076	0.053
All large	0.191	0.172	0.136	0.105	0.078	0.056
Total welfare						
Current	0.448	0.402	0.323	0.251	0.187	0.133
All small	0.424	0.381	0.301	0.230	0.169	0.118
All large	0.453	0.409	0.327	0.255	0.192	0.139

Note: "Price spread" refers to the farm-to-retail price spread. "CS" means consumer surplus and "PS" means producer surplus. "Total welfare" equals the summation of consumer surplus, producer surplus, and packer profits.
Source: Authors' simulation outcomes.

structure depends on the goal of a policy as well as the risk of shutdown. If the goal is to ensure a level of output close to the "normal" level (and thus food security), a relatively concentrated processing sector performs better than a more diffuse packing sector for a medium or large risk of plant shutdown, while a diffuse sector outperforms under a small risk. If the policy aims to ensure output does not fall below a minimal threshold, then the diffuse structure tends to outperform under all risk levels considered.

Table 8.3 summarizes the mean farm-to-retail price spread under different horizontal structures and risk levels. The mean values under the three structures are almost the same and all increase with shutdown risk, but there is considerably more variation in the price spread across simulations in a less concentrated market. The price spread widens as shutdown risk increases, intuitively, because the retail price increases as the quantity of processed beef decreases and the farm price falls. Even in a perfectly competitive market (i.e., the all-small scenario), the price spread widens at the same rate as the other scenarios with an increasing shutdown risk.[4]

4. By construction of our model, the farm-to-wholesale price spread increases by the same increments as the farm-to-retail price spread because the marginal costs of retailing are fixed at $c^r = 0.42$.

In the meantime, the profits made by packing plants drop given the implied marginal costs. In the perfectly competitive scenario, of course, the packers never make profits by construction, and the packer profits remain at zero regardless of the risk. In the two other scenarios, the packing plants exercise some buyer and seller power. Their profits do not increase with the widening price spread because the increase in the spread is not due to packers' markups over retailers or markdowns over farmers. Instead, the increasing spread is driven by the loss of processing capacity of shutdown plants. Implied marginal costs of processing increase considerably as the industry's total capacity falls, more than canceling out any potential profits to packers from reducing industry-level outputs. If the actual marginal costs do not increase as much, of course, processor profits could increase after shutdowns, but still less than what the increased price spread would suggest.

Worth noticing from table 8.3, consumer and producer (farmer) surpluses fall with an increasing shutdown risk. In expectation, the three scenarios lead to the same consumer and producer surpluses under a given risk. Total social welfare, which is the summation of consumer and farmer surpluses and packer profits, is the largest in the all-large scenario, thanks to the high cost efficiency of large-sized processing plants. The finding echoes prior studies such as Azzam and Schroeter Jr. (1995), who find that welfare losses from market power are more than offset by higher cost efficiencies of large-sized packing plants. We revisit the evaluation of social welfare in section 8.4.3.

Figure 8.2 summarizes changes in the marginal processing costs of small-sized, medium-sized, and large-sized plants in the current scenario. The mean increases are similar in the other two scenarios. Changes in the implied marginal processing costs for three size groups follow similar trends as the shutdown risk increases. Because the processing capacity of each plant is fixed in the short run, the implied marginal costs increase with the decreasing total outputs as indicated by equation (9b). For example, when the average reduction in total outputs is 30 percdent, the implied marginal costs of small, medium, and large plants increase by 180 percent, 189 percent, and 224 percent, respectively, relative to the risk-free level. The substantial cost increases imply a tight bottleneck in processing at the (near) full capacity and some increased operational costs in a risky environment like COVID-19 (e.g., Lusk, Tonsor, and Schulz 2021).[5]

8.4.2   Sensitivity Analysis

We test the robustness of baseline simulation outcomes by considering alternative parameter values and assumptions. First, we relax the assumption

---

5. Marginal costs of manufacturing rise substantially at a binding capacity constraint regardless of the commodity. See a recent example from the electricity industry in Texas. https://www.usnews.com/news/us/articles/2021-02-18/texas-power-consumers-to-pay-the-price-of-winter-storm.

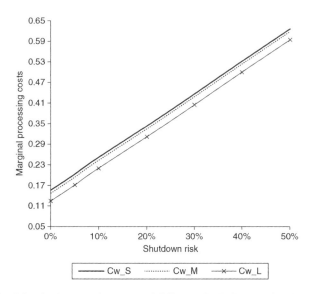

Figure 8.2   Marginal processing costs of different sized plants under risks

Note: The small-, medium-, and large-sized plants are defined in the modeling section under the current structure. See table 1 for plant sizes. "Cw_S" refers to the marginal costs of processing for small-sized plants, "Cw_M" for medium-sized plants, and "Cw_L" for large-sized plants.

Source: Authors' simulation outcomes.

of unit supply elasticity. According to the literature, the short-run supply of beef is likely to be quite low (see table 8B.2). Letting ε^f be 0.8, 0.6, and 0.4, respectively, we rerun the simulations. The general patterns observed in the baseline stay unchanged. Using smaller demand elasticity values makes no significant changes in simulation outcomes, either.

Taking the cases where the shutdown risk is 30 percent as an example, figure 8.3 shows output reductions under less elastic supply. Again, the relative resilience of a horizontal structure depends on the goal of a policy. If the goal is to ensure a high level of output, a concentrated processing sector performs better than a more diffuse packing sector. If the goal is to ensure output does not fall below a minimal threshold, then the diffuse structure tends to outperform.

Worth noticing, with less elastic supply of cattle, the farm-gate price may fall negative if the shutdown risk is large. For instance, when $\varepsilon^f = 0.4$ and the risk is 30 percent, P^f falls to –0.03 if the industry-level output drops by 43.2 percent from the risk-free level. A negative P^f implies that the farmers must pay the processing plants for slaughtering their animals, when the processing capacity is very low. Consequently, the farm-to-retail price spread tends to be larger the more inelastic the cattle supply.

Second, we consider simultaneous negative shocks on the demand and

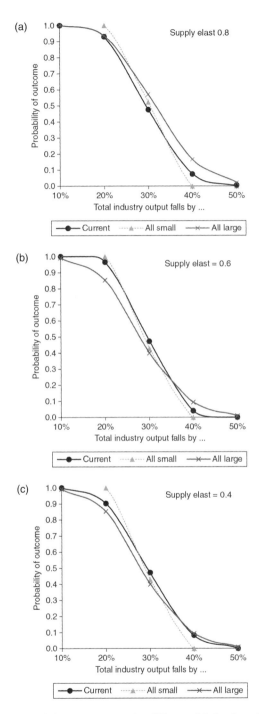

Figure 8.3   Simulated industry output under different risk levels and inelastic cattle supply

Note: same as figure 8.1.

Source: Author's simulation outcomes.

Table 8.4   Mean price spreads under different demand shocks

	Risk = 30%			
Scenario	$a' = a$	$a' = 0.95a$	$a' = 0.9a$	$a' = 0.85a$
Price spread				
Current	0.856	0.780	0.636	0.442
All-small	0.858	0.780	0.638	0.444
All-large	0.859	0.783	0.639	0.445

Note: "Price spread" refers to the farm-to-retail price spread.
Source: Authors' simulation outcomes.

supply. For example, consumer demand may fall in a pandemic due to decreased visits to restaurants and reduced visits to grocery markets (Chetty et al. 2020), reductions in income, or the concern about getting the virus from consuming potentially contaminated products (McFadden et al. 2021). If the demand curve shifts inwards, we need to update the demand function as:

(10) $P^r = a' - \alpha Q,$

where a'. All other calculation steps remain the same.

Following this approach, we rerun the simulations by setting $a' = 0.95a$, $0.9a$, and $0.85a$, respectively. By construction, changes in the industry output follow the same patterns as shown in figure 8.1, because the supply would not be affected by a parallel shift in the demand curve. Only equilibrium prices at the farm gate and retail would be different. Specifically, the increase in P^r would be smaller if both demand and supply curves shift in. The change in P^f is not affected by a', leaving the price spread smaller with smaller a', with other conditions remaining the same (see table 8.4).

Thirdly, we assume that demand remains unchanged, but allow operating plants to increase their outputs under supply-side shocks. Amid COVID-19 disruptions, for example, some packing plants made changes to fabrication and produced more whole cuts instead of small cuts or ran extra shifts on weekends in order to increase the total output with the same facilities and rising operational costs (Lusk, Tonsor, and Schulz 2021). Being able to increase outputs beyond the full capacity is expected to add resilience in the supply chain.

In this simulation, we let plants that do not shut down find new equilibrium outputs given higher marginal processing costs. With a shutdown risk of 30 percent, for example, we bring up the marginal costs of small-sized, medium-sized, and large-sized plants by 100 percent, 104.5 percent, and 120 percent, respectively. These cost increases are chosen to ensure that all plants achieve higher outputs, after some plants shut down, and that their output increases are not too large to be realistic or so large that their size rankings change.

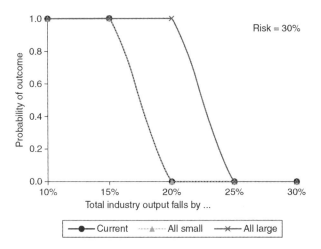

Figure 8.4   Simulated industry output with adjustable plant outputs
Note: same as figure 8.1. Plant equilibrium outputs increased after the supply shocks.
Source: Author's simulation outcomes.

Given the cost increases listed here, the new equilibrium outputs of small-sized, medium-sized, and large-sized plants on average become 2.27, 1.07, and 1.19 times as large as their outputs under no risk, respectively. The average reduction in industry output is only 16.6 percent instead of 29.8 percent in the baseline, showing considerably more resilience in the beef supply chain. Besides, the probability of industry output falling by more than 20 percent drops to zero. Across all three scenarios, figure 8.4 shows that the decreases in industry outputs become smaller if we allow plants to increase outputs under supply shocks. The current and all-small structures result in almost identical outcomes, and both outperform the all-large structure.

Lastly, we consider an alternative structure that is less extreme than all-large and all-small—some large-sized plants are replaced by small-sized plants, and the number of medium-sized plants remain unchanged. Specifically, we let there be 12 large-sized plants, 33 medium-sized plants, and 7,215 small-sized plants, which is a structure lying in between the current and all-small structures. Figure 8.5 is directly comparable with panel (b) of figure 8.1. As expected, the simulation outcomes under this "in-between" structure are in-between outcomes from the current and all-small structures. Baseline insights remain unchanged.[6]

6. We also change the way of imposing risks. Instead of assuming that we know the level of risk, we can draw the level of risk from a normal distribution. Then we generate multiple rounds of outcomes under an unknown risk. Again, the core insight that more concentrated structure leads to more variance in outcomes and similar mean stays robust.

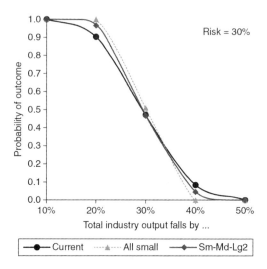

Figure 8.5   Simulated industry output under the fourth structure
Note: same as figure 8.1. "Sm-Md_Lg2" refers to the structure with 12 large-sized plants, 33 medium-sized plants, and 7,215 small-sized plants.
Source: Author's simulation outcomes.

8.4.3   Welfare Implications

Regarding social welfare, the criterion of welfare affects the ranking of alternative horizontal structures of meat packing. Table 8.3 indicates that if a social planner only cares about the expected total welfare, the concentrated structure is preferred thanks to the economies of scale and lower marginal costs in processing. However, a social planner may care more than the mean welfare. In particular, the planner may want to avoid extreme losses in CS and PS. For instance, the planner may maximize a utility function that imposes a penalty if CS or PS falls below a lower bar (Holthausen 1981).

To see how the alternative welfare criterion changes the ranking of various structures, we consider a linear loss avoidance utility function:

$$(11) \qquad \begin{cases} U(x) = x, \ \forall x > \underline{x} \\ U(x) = x - \kappa(\underline{x} - x), \ \forall x \le \underline{x}, \end{cases}$$

where $x \in \{CS, PS\}$, $\underline{x}$ is the bar triggering penalty, and κ is the loss avoidance parameter. The larger is κ, the more loss averse is the planner. The total social welfare is the summation of $U = U(CS) + U(PS) + \Pi$ with Π being the collective profits of packers.

We consider a common risk of 30 percent as an example. Let the planner set $\underline{x}$ at 49 percent of the CS (PS) value without risk and maximizes the expected U. We find that the ranking of the three alternative structures varies

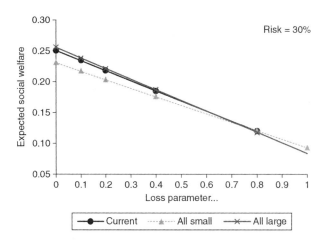

Figure 8.6   Simulated social welfare under different loss avoidance parameters

Note: The vertical axis measures the expected social welfare. The horizontal axis measures the loss avoidance parameter, κ, in equation (11).

Source: Author's simulation outcomes.

with the magnitude of κ. Figure 8.6 indicates that, when the planner is not loss averse or κ is small, the all-large scenario outperforms due to efficiency gains discussed earlier. As the planner becomes sufficiently loss averse, the diffuse scenario starts to be preferred by being better at avoiding severe CS (PS) losses. Similarly, if the planner is risk averse and treats variance in the total welfare as disutility, the all-large scenario would tend to be less preferred than the other two structures.

8.5   Policy Discussions

Several states have recently considered or adopted legislation to subsidize the introduction of small- or medium-sized meat packers. At the federal level, bills have been proposed to encourage more capital investments and allow small processors to access larger markets (e.g., Feedstuffs 2020; Hagstrom 2020). The implicit assumption behind such policy proposals is that they would result in more short-run resilience in the packing system faced with shocks like COVID-19. As the foregoing simulations suggest, however, a less concentrated packing system on average would not necessarily have produced outcomes much different than what was observed during April and May 2020, when cattle and hog slaughter dropped by almost 40 percent. One, perhaps counterintuitive, simulation result is that total welfare is typically lower under a more diffuse packing sector because of the lost economies of scale.

In addition to policies aimed at promoting more small- and medium-sized packers, a number of lawsuits have been levied at large meat packers, and a Justice Department investigation has been launched, following the packing plant shutdowns (e.g., Bunge and Kendall 2020). Complaints tend to focus on the dramatic increase in the farm-to-wholesale price spread that occurred as a result of the plant shutdowns (Lusk, Tonsor, and Schulz 2021). Our simulation provides insight into this phenomenon and the controversy surrounding it. In particular, regardless of the degree of concentration, the price spread rises when the industry is faced with an exogenous risk of shutdown. This finding is entirely consistent with the theory of marketing margins (Wohlgenant 2001), and we show that widening price spreads result from disruptions to processing even if all packers are small-sized and there is no market power.

These simulation outcomes reveal complex consequences of government and industry efforts aimed at increasing the resilience of the food supply chain through changing the horizontal structure. The consequences depend critically on the exogenous risk as well as the target level of industry output. Neither a diffuse nor a concentrated horizontal structure dominates. More comprehensive policy designs may be needed to add short-run resilience in the supply chain under supply-side disruptions. Though long-run resilience is not discussed in this article, biological cycles of livestock production, fixed investments, and other factors are likely to make the role of horizontal structure even more complex and imply even more difficulty in policy design. We leave the long-run resilience in US meat supply chains for future research.

Appendix A

Size Distribution of Processing Plants in the US

Table 8A.1 summarizes the distribution of plant sizes in the beef and pork processing sectors, respectively. Their horizontal structures are similar.

Table 8A.1   Size distributions of US meat packing plants

Size group	# plants	% plants	Head/ year	Head/ plant/year	% total output
Beef					
1–999	480	71.6%	163.2	340.0	0.5%
1,000–9,999	107	16.0%	261.5	2,443.9	0.8%
10,000–49,999	28	4.2%	604.9	21,603.6	1.8%
50,000–99,999	6	0.9%	483.0	80,500.0	1.5%
100,000–199,999	9	1.3%	1,270.7	141,188.9	3.8%
200,000–299,999	4	0.6%	1,018.8	254,700.0	3.1%
300,000–499,999	14	2.1%	5,554.3	396,735.7	16.8%
500,000–999,999	10	1.5%	6,394.2	639,420.0	19.3%
1,000,000+	12	1.8%	17,318.8	1,443,233.3	52.4%
All	670	100%	33069.4		100%
Pork					
1–999	396	64.0%	125.4	316.7	0.1%
1,000–9,999	123	19.9%	337.9	2,747.2	0.3%
10,000–99,999	39	6.3%	1,529.4	39,215.4	1.2%
100,000–249,999	18	2.9%	2,967.6	164,866.7	2.3%
250,000–499,999	7	1.1%	2,501.0	357,285.7	1.9%
500,000–999,999	3	0.5%	2,074.1	691,366.7	1.6%
1,000,000–1,999,999	6	1.0%	7,849.1	1,308,183.3	6.1%
2,000,000–2,999,999	12	1.9%	31,794.8	2,649,566.7	24.6%
3,000,000+	15	2.5%	80,031.5	5,335,433.3	61.9%
All	619	100%	129210.8		100%

Note: The column of "head/year" shows the number of animals slaughtered by plants in the size group in a year and uses the unit of 1,000 head.
Source: National Agricultural Statistics Service (2020).

Appendix B

Elasticities of US Beef Demand and Cattle Supply

The two tables below summarize estimates of beef demand and cattle supply in the United States from recent empirical studies.

Table 8B.1   **Demand elasticities of US beef in recent studies**

Source	Data period	Data frequency/type	Demand elasticities	Notes
Lusk and Tonsor (2016)	2013–14	Monthly, Choice experiment	−1.959	Low income, Ground beef, Price increase
			−1.834	Middle income, Ground beef, Price increase
			−1.703	High income, Ground beef, Price increase
			−2.511	Low income, Ground beef, Price decrease
			−2.377	Middle income, Ground beef, Price decrease
			−2.075	High income, Ground beef, Price decrease
			−1.738	Low income, Steak, Price increase
			−1.836	Middle income, Steak, Price increase
			−1.674	High income, Steak, Price increase
			−2.625	Low income, Steak, Price decrease
			−2.606	Middle income, Steak, Price decrease
			−2.061	High income, Steak, Price decrease
Mutondo and Henneberry (2007)	1995–2005	Quarterly, USDA/ERS, USDA/FAS	−0.712	U.S. grain-fed beef, Uncompensated
			−0.507	U.S. grass-fed beef, Uncompensated
Shang and Tonsor (2017)	2009–14	Monthly, Scanner Data from IRI FreshLook Perishable Service	−0.998	Beef, Total US
			−0.830	Ground beef, Total US
			−0.700	Other beef, Total US
Taylor and Tonsor (2013)	2007–11	Monthly, Scanner Data collected by Fresh Look Marketing Group	−1.274	Beef, Uncompensated, Meat separable
			−0.944	Beef, Uncompensated, Food separable
			−2.011	Beef loin, Uncompensated, Meat separable
			−1.242	Ground beef, Uncompensated, Meat separable
			−1.254	Other beef, Uncompensated, Meat separable
Tonsor et al. (2018)	1970–2017	Quarterly, USDA/ERS	−0.479	Beef, All-Fresh, 1988–2017
			−0.645	Beef, All-Fresh, 1988–2007
			−0.450	Beef, All-Fresh, 2008–2017
			−0.593	Beef, Choice, 1970–2017
			−0.490	Beef, Choice, 1988–2017
			−0.594	Beef, Choice, 1970–1994
			−0.468	Beef, Choice, 1995–2017
Tonsor et al. (2010)	1982–2007	Quarterly, USDA/ERS	−0.420	Beef, Compensated
Tonsor and Olynk (2011)	1982–2008	Quarterly, USDA/ERS	−0.493	Beef, Compensated

Table 8B.2   **Supply elasticities of US cattle in recent studies**

Source	Data period	Data frequency/type	Supply elasticities	Note for demand elasticities
Marsh (2003)	1970–99	Annual, USDA's red meats yearbook	0.26	Short-run elasticity of slaughter supply
			0.59	Long-run elasticity of slaughter supply
			0.22	Short-run price elasticity of feeder supply
			2.82	Long-run price elasticity of feeder supply
McKendree (2020)	1996–2016	Quarterly, Livestock marketing information center (LMIC)	0.10	Short-run fed cattle supply elasticity
			0.24	Long-run fed cattle supply elasticity
			0.17	Short-run feeder cattle supply elasticity
			0.24	Long-run feeder cattle supply elasticity
Suh and Moss (2017)	1981–2011	Annual, FAOSTAT, USDA/ERS	0.12	Supply elasticity of cattle

References

Aadland, David, and DeeVon Bailey. 2001. "Short-Run Supply Responses in the U.S. Beef-Cattle Industry." *American Journal of Agricultural Economics* 83 (4): 826–39.

Azzam, Azzeddine M., and John R. Schroeter Jr. 1995. "The Tradeoff between Oligopsony Power and Cost Efficiency in Horizontal Consolidation: An Example from Beef Packing." *American Journal of Agricultural Economics* 77 (4): 825–36.

Bina, Justin D., Glynn T. Tonsor, Lee L. Schulz, and William F. Hahn. 2021. "Balancing Beef Processing Efficiency and Resiliency Post-COVID-19." Working Paper.

Bhamra, Ran, Samir Dani, and Kevin Burnard. 2011. "Resilience: The Concept, A Literature Review and Future Directions." *International Journal of Production Research* 49 (18): 5375–93.

Brester, Gary W., John M. Marsh, and Joseph A. Atwood. 2009. "Evaluating the Farmer's-Share-of-the-Retail-Dollar Statistic." *Journal of Agricultural and Resource Economics* 34 (2): 213–36.

Bunge, Jacob, and Brent Kendall. 2020. "Justice Department Issues Subpoenas to Beef-Processing Giants." *Wall Street Journal, June 5.* https://www.wsj.com/articles/justice-department-issues-subpoenas-to-beef-processing-giants-11591371745.

Bustillo, Ximena. 2020. "Small Meat Processors Get Little Aid as Demand Grows." *Politico, June 15.* https://www.politico.com/news/2020/06/15/small-meat-processors-financial-aid-319822.

Chetty, Raj, John N. Friedman, Nathaniel Hendren, and Michael Stepner. 2020. "The Economic Impacts of COVID-19: Evidence from A New Public Database Built Using Private Sector Data." National Bureau of Economic Research, No. w27431.

Dipietre, Dennis, and Lance Mulberry. 2021. "How Do the Profitability Puzzle Pieces Align for 2021?" *Pork Business* https://www.porkbusiness.com/news/hog-production/how-do-profitability-puzzle-pieces-align-2021.

Feedstuffs. 2020. "RAMP-UP Act Helps Meat Processors Upgrade Plants." https://www.feedstuffs.com/news/ramp-act-helps-meat-processors-upgrade-plants.

Hagstrom, Jerry. 2020. "Small Packer Processing Bill Introduced in House." *Ag Policy Blog. DTN.* https://www.dtnpf.com/agriculture/web/ag/blogs/ag-policy-blog/blog-post/2020/09/30/small-packer-processing-bill-house.

Hahn, William. 2004. *Beef and Pork Values and Price Spreads Explained.* Livestock, Dairy, and Poultry Outlook No. (LDPM-11801) 30. Washington D.C.: US Department of Agriculture, Economic Research Service.

Hendrickson, Mary K. 2015. "Resilience in a Concentrated and Consolidated Food System." *Journal of Environmental Studies and Sciences* 5 (3): 418–31.

Holthausen, Duncan M. 1981. "A Risk-Return Model with Risk and Return Measured as Deviations from A Target Return." *American Economic Review* 71 (1): 182–8.

Koontz, Stephen R., and John D. Lawrence. 2010. "Impacts of Alternative Marketing Agreement Cattle Procurement on Packer Costs, Gross Margins, and Profits: Evidence from Plant-Level Profit and Loss Data." *Agribusiness* 26 (1): 1–24.

Lusk, Jayson L., and Glynn T. Tonsor. 2016. "How Meat Demand Elasticities Vary with Price, Income, and Product Category." *Applied Economic Perspectives and Policy* 38 (4): 673–711.

Lusk, Jayson L., Glynn T. Tonsor, and Lee L. Schulz. 2021. "Beef and Pork Marketing Margins and Price Spreads during COVID-19." *Applied Economic Perspectives and Policy* 43 (1): 4–23.

MacDonald, James M., Michael E. Ollinger, Kenneth E. Nelson, and Charles R. Handy. 1999. *Consolidation in U.S. Meatpacking*. Washington, DC: U.S. Department of Agriculture, Economic Research. Agricultural Economics Report no. AER-785, March.

MacDonald, James M. 2003. "Beef and Pork Packing Industries." *The Veterinary Clinics of North America. Food Animal Practice* 19 (2): 419–43.

MacDonald, James M., and Michael E. Ollinger. 2005. "Technology, Labor Wars, and Producer Dynamics: Explaining Consolidation in Beefpacking." *American Journal of Agricultural Economics* 87 (4): 1020–33.

Marsh, John M. 2003. "Impacts of Declining U.S. Retail Beef Demand on Farm-Level Beef Prices and Production." *American Journal of Agricultural Economics* 85 (4): 902–13.

McFadden, Brandon R., Trey Malone, Maik Kecinski, and Kent D. Messer. 2021. "COVID-19 Induced Stigma in US Consumers: Evidence and Implications." American Journal of Agricultural Economics 103 (2): 486-497.

McKendree, Melissa G. S., Tina L. Saitone, and K. Aleks Schaefer. 2021. "Oligopsonistic Input Substitution in a Thin Market." American Journal of Agricultural Economics 103 (4): 1414-32.

McKendree, Melissa G. S., Glynn T. Tonsor, Ted C. Schroeder, and Nathan P. Hendricks. 2020. "Impacts of Retail and Export Demand on United States Cattle Producers." *American Journal of Agricultural Economics* 102 (3): 866–83.

Morrison Paul, Catherine J. 2001. "Market and Cost Structure in the U.S. Beef Packing Industry: A Plant-Level Analysis." *American Journal of Agricultural Economics* 83 (1): 64–76.

National Agricultural Statistics Service (NASS). 2020. *Livestock Slaughter 2019 Summary*. U.S. Department of Agriculture, April.

Mutondo, Joao E., and Shida Rastegari Henneberry. 2007. "A Source-Differentiated Analysis of 9U.S. Meat Demand." *Journal of Agricultural and Resource Economics* 32 (3): 515–33.

Nickelsburg, Monica. 2020. "The Pandemic Has the Potential to Finally Transform Meat Processing in the U.S." *Civil Eats, October 19*. https://civileats.com/2020/10/19/the-pandemic-has-the-potential-to-finally-transform-meat-processing-in-the-u-s/.

Perloff, Jeffrey M., Larry S. Karp, and Amos Golan. 2007. *Estimating Market Power and Strategies*. Cambridge University Press.

Pitt, David. 2021. "USDA Unveils $500 Million Plan to Help Build More, Smaller

Meat Processing Plants." *PBS*, July 9. https://www.pbs.org/newshour/economy/usda-unveils-500-million-plan-to-help-build-more-smaller-meat-processing-plants.

Ponomarov, Serhiy Y., and Mary C. Holcomb. 2009. "Understanding the Concept of Supply Chain Resilience." *International Journal of Logistics Management* 20 (1): 124–43.

Raper, Kellie Curry, Laura M. Cheney, and Meeta Punjabi. 2006. "Regional Impacts of a U.S. Hog Slaughter Plant Closing: The Thorn Apple Valley Case." *Review of Agricultural Economics* 28 (4): 531–42.

Rotz, Sarah, and Evan D. G. Fraser. 2015. "Resilience and the Industrial Food System: Analyzing the Impacts of Agricultural Industrialization on Food System Vulnerability." *Journal of Environmental Studies and Sciences* 5 (3): 459–73.

Shang, Xia, and Glynn T. Tonsor. 2017. "Food Safety Recall Effects across Meat Products and Regions." *Food Policy* 69: 145–53.

Suh, Dong Hee, and Charles B. Moss. 2017. "Decompositions of Corn Price Effects: Implications for Feed Grain Demand and Livestock Supply." *Agricultural Economics* 48 (4): 491–500.

Taylor, Mykel R., and Glynn T. Tonsor. 2013. "Revealed Demand for Country-of-Origin Labeling of Meat in the United States." *Journal of Agricultural and Resource Economics* 38 (2): 235–47.

Tonsor, Glynn T., Jayson L. Lusk, and Ted C. Schroeder. 2018. "Assessing Beef Demand Determinants." Report for Cattlemen's Beef Board.

Tonsor, Glynn T., James R. Mintert, and Ted C. Schroeder. 2010. "U.S. Meat Demand: Household Dynamics and Media Information Impacts." *Journal of Agricultural and Resource Economics* 35 (1): 1–17.

Tonsor, Glynn T., and Nicole J. Olynk. 2011. "Impacts of Animal Well-Being and Welfare Media on Meat Demand." *Journal of Agricultural Economics* 62 (1): 59–72.

U.S. Department of Agriculture. 2020. *Boxed Beef & Fed Cattle Price Spread Investigation Report*. Agricultural Marketing Service (AMS). July.

U.S. Department of Agriculture. 2021. *Meat Price Spreads*. https://www.ers.usda.gov/data-products/meat-price-spreads/.

Williams, Cole. 2018. "The Basics of Fire Insurance for Small Meat Plants." *The National Provisioner*, June 12. https://www.provisioneronline.com/articles/106353-the-basics-of-fire-insurance-for-small-meat-plants.

Wohlgenant, Michael K. 2001. "Marketing Margins: Empirical Analysis." *Handbook of Agricultural Economics* 1: 933–70.

———. 2013. "Competition in the U.S. Meatpacking Industry." *Annual Review of Resource Economics* 5 (1): 1–12.

9

Labor Dynamics and Supply Chain Disruption in Food Manufacturing

A. Ford Ramsey, Barry K. Goodwin,
and Mildred M. Haley

9.1 Introduction

Agricultural supply chains link agricultural producers to consumers and end users. The nature and organization of the agricultural supply chain has changed drastically over time with increased vertical integration, increased prevalence of contract farming, and specialization in different supply activities (Adjemian et al. 2016; Boehlje 1999). Firms strategically design supply chains in response to new innovations and technologies (Zilberman, Lu, and Reardon 2019). In designing and adopting different organizational structures or technologies, firm owners and managers in the supply chain act in entrepeneurial capacities by reacting to disequilibria in their environment (Schultz 1975). Disequilibria are uncertain in both frequency and magnitude, resulting in a variety of risks for supply chain participants.

Just as supply chains have changed over time, supply chain risk has also evolved. Many organizational structures and technologies introduced into

A. Ford Ramsey is an assistant professor in the Department of Agricultural and Applied Economics at Virginia Tech.

Barry K. Goodwin is the William Neal Reynolds Distinguished Professor and Graduate Alumni Distinguished Professor in the Departments of Economics and Agricultural and Resource Economics at North Carolina State University.

Mildred M. Haley is an agricultural economist with the Economic Research Service of the US Department of Agriculture.

The findings and conclusions in this paper are those of the authors and should not be construed to represent any official USDA or US Government determination or policy. This research was supported in part by the US Department of Agriculture, Economic Research Service and NIFA-AFRI Grant Number 2020–67023–32760: "COVID-19 Rapid Response: Coronavirus Disease 2019, Price Transmission, and the Farm-Retail Price Spread in U.S. Livestock." For acknowledgments, sources of research support, and disclosure of the authors' material financial relationships, if any, please see https://www.nber.org/books-and-chapters/risks-agricultural-supply-chains/labor-dynamics-and-supply-chain-disruption-food-manufacturing.

food supply chains have been aimed at reducing risks faced by participants (Antle 1996; Knoeber and Thurman 1995; McCluskey and O'Rourke 2000). Supply chain risks can be broadly characterized as either operational risks or disruption risks. Tang (2006) defines operational risk as risks that are inherent to the business, such as uncertain market conditions. In contrast, disruption risks arise from natural disasters or other extreme events. Operational and disruption risks can be closely linked as the same elements of the supply chain that are subject to inherent uncertainty—consumer demand, for example—can serve as transmission mechanisms for disruptive events.

A major risk in agricultural supply chains arises from the diverse skills required of workers in the agriculture and food industry labor forces. These risks are compounded by consolidation and increased concentration in food manufacturing and processing, including meatpacking, which has resulted in increased plant size (MacDonald 2014; MacDonald et al. 2000; Wohlgenant 2013). Although varying in significance by industry within the food manufacturing sector, labor is a critical input to most manufacturing operations. Huang (2003) shows that changes in labor inputs to food manufacturing are heterogeneous across industries; meat products and miscellaneous foods saw increased employment between 1975 and 1997, while other food industries saw decreased employment of production workers. The meatpacking industry employs the most production workers of all food manufacturing industries. Given heterogeneity in the types and uses of labor in food manufacturing, firms face an array of operational and disruption risks related to their labor inputs.

Operational risks can be characterized by empirically modeling industry operation and assessing the flexibility of supply chain participants in responding to changes in the operating environment. For instance, if meatpacking labor is more specialized and harder to acquire than labor in other areas of food manufacturing, we might expect employment in the meatpacking sector to respond more slowly to changes in demand or other factors. There may be significant temporal relationships that affect the ability of firms to adjust to changing market conditions. Accurate assessment of labor and wage flexibility is necessary for characterizing labor-related operational risks faced by firms.

In contrast to operational risks, disruption risk arises from events that may entail a sudden and complete break in the supply chain or firm operations. Probabilities of loss and magnitudes of loss are difficult to assess for disruption risk as disruptive incidents usually occur with low probability and potentially large losses. These characteristics of disruption risk make it difficult for firms to perform cost-benefit analyses or other studies for risk management as the results of such studies can be highly dependent on a small number of disruptive events (Tang 2006). Firm management may view the probability of such events to be so low that they are not worthy of incorporation in risk management strategies (Kunreuther and Useem 2018).

Despite difficulties in modeling disruptive events, such events often lead to calls for public policy actions to improve resilience of a system.

The COVID-19 pandemic illustrates the impact of a major disruption in the food manufacturing sector. Impacts occurred at all stages of the supply chain with effects across both demand and supply sides of markets. In particular, labor inputs to food manufacturing were disrupted due to the nature of work in manufacturing facilities. Work routines in food manufacturing plants make workers particularly susceptible to infection by respiratory viruses such as SARS-CoV-2. Disruption was most evident in the animal slaughtering and processing sector. On April 12, 2020 Smithfield Foods announced that it would temporarily suspend operations at a plant in Sioux Falls, Idaho, in response to a surge in the number of infected workers. At the time, the plant was one of the largest sources of COVID-19 infection in the US (Bunge 2020a, 2020b). Many other plants experienced similar local outbreaks of COVID-19 resulting in temporary closures. Plants that remained open and operated at increased speed were associated with higher rates of infection in the counties in which they were located (Taylor, Boulos, and Almond 2020).

The supply chain implications of COVID-19 in agriculture have received significant attention. Hobbs (2020) discussed the potential for supply-side disruption due to labor shortages in downstream food processing and transportation. She notes that the nature of the COVID-19 pandemic afforded manufacturing facilities a period of time to make adjustments to manufacturing processes and working environments. Labor issues up and down the supply chain are discussed in Larue (2020). Within food manufacturing, he notes that firms have the ability to reallocate capacity and an industry-wide shutdown would be the most difficult to manage. However, complete shutdowns are extreme measures—likely to be only temporary—and he suggests the sector will switch to operation below capacity to implement mitigation measures.

Temporary plant closures and changes in capacity utilization have the potential to result in stockouts and shortages of food at retail. Stockouts were observed in retail establishments for specific products as consumers stockpiled in the early days of the pandemic. However, widespread shortages of food, whether meat, vegetables, processed items, or other items, did not occur (Hobbs 2021). Many manufacturing plants were operating near capacity by the middle of 2020. While COVID-19 did create a major and unprecedented disruption for food manufacturers and meat processors, rapid response on the part of market participants indicates a degree of resilience.

Using the COVID-19 pandemic as an example of a major disruptive event related to manufacturing labor (and other market conditions), we investigate labor dynamics in food manufacturing and animal processing and slaughtering using county-level data from the Current Employment Survey compiled by the Bureau of Labor Statistics. We model employment and wage dynamics using dynamic panel models estimated using generalized method of moments (GMM). We then compare employment and wages under the estimated dynamic models with employment and wages during the onset of the COVID-19 pandemic in early 2020.

The dynamic labor demand and wage models allow for interdependencies across space and time to be taken into account when evaluating the impacts of economic shocks. The response of market participants to changes in wages and other relevant economic variables can be assessed. Dynamics in the estimated models are useful in evaluating operational risk; they highlight factors resulting in employment and wage changes, and capture the speed of adjustment to changes in these factors. Therefore, the combination of the dynamic models with a COVID-19 event study provides assessment of both operational and disruption risks in food manufacturing and the agricultural supply chain.

9.2   Labor and the Food Manufacturing Link in Agricultural Supply Chains

In spite of increased mechanization in manufacturing, labor remains a major input for food manufacturers and animal processors. The food manufacturing sector defined by the North American Industry Classification System (NAICS) consists of nine constituent industries of which animal slaughtering and processing is one. While farm labor has received extensive treatment in the literature, labor in food manufacturing has garnered less attention (Hertz and Zahniser 2013; Richards 2018). However, labor disruption as a result of the COVID-19 pandemic has brought new focus to employment in food manufacturing.

Among several studies investigating historical changes in the structure of food manufacturing, Goodwin and Brester (1995) showed that demand elasticities for labor decreased and that the degree of substitutability between inputs increased over much of the second half of the 21st century. Their findings with respect to labor were in line with an earlier study of factor demand in food manufacturing conducted by Huang (1991). Contemporary statistics compiled by the Bureau of Labor Statistics show that both total output and employment in food manufacturing have increased over the past thirty years as shown in figure 9.1. While employment in food manufacturing fell in the early 2000s, a sharp increase in employment occurred from 2010. Also shown in figure 9.1, sector labor productivity grew until 2005, but has since experienced a modest decline.

Labor is the largest component of the marketing bill for food products. The marketing bill is the difference between the farm value of food and what consumers actually pay for food. In a review of food costs between 1950 and 1997, Elitzak (1999) found labor costs contributed to 55 percent

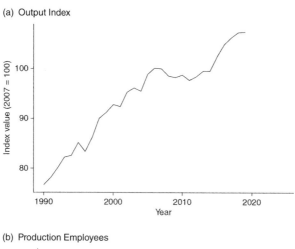

(a) Output Index

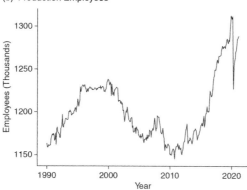

(b) Production Employees

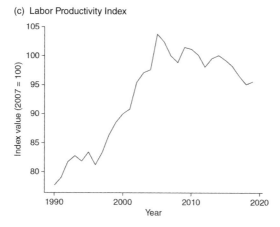

(c) Labor Productivity Index

Figure 9.1   Food manufacturing sector output, employment, and labor productivity
Source: All data from Bureau of Labor Statistics.

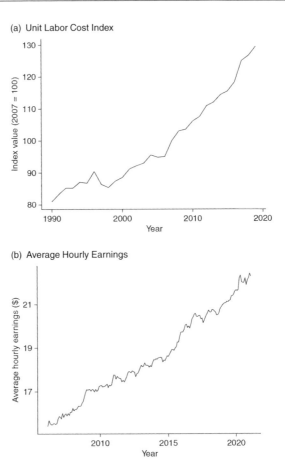

Figure 9.2   Food manufacturing sector unit labor cost and hourly wages
Source: All data from Bureau of Labor Statistics.

of rising marketing bills and that 38.5 cents of every food dollar in 1997 was spent on labor associated with the food industry. Larger price spreads—between farm and retail levels—are typically observed for highly processed foods. Figure 9.2 shows unit labor costs and average hourly earnings in food manufacturing. Both average hourly earnings and unit labor costs have risen over the past two decades. Unit labor costs increased by nearly 70 percent between 1990 and 2020. Trends of increasing employment and labor costs suggest that labor is an important input to food manufacturing and a potential source of supply chain risk.

Figures 9.3 and 9.4 show the distribution of employment and weekly wages in food manufacturing as a whole, and meat processing specifically,

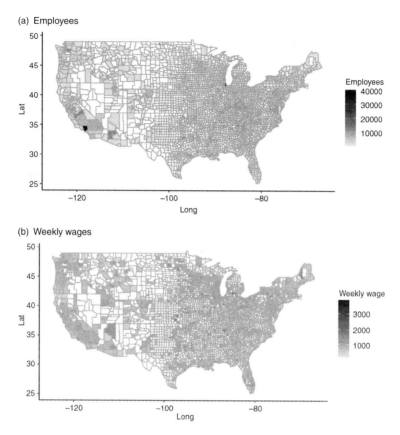

Figure 9.3   Food manufacturing sector employees and weekly wage by county, 2019
Source: All data from Bureau of Labor Statistics.

across the US. The meat processing sector is significantly more concentrated compared to food manufacturing. In contrast to the early 20th century, when meat processing was largely conducted in urban areas, processing facilities are mostly in rural counties with close proximity to livestock inputs. Rural labor pools may be relatively shallow, resulting in increased frictions in the adjustment of employees and wages.

Figure 9.5 shows kernel density estimates of the 2019 wage and employment distributions by county for both food manufacturing and animal slaughtering and processing. The average weekly wage in food manufacturing was approximately $802 with standard deviation of $292. In animal slaughtering and processing the average weekly wage was $779 with standard deviation of $272. The mean number of employees per establishment was 52 in food manufacturing versus 92 in animal slaughtering and processing. All

(a) Employees

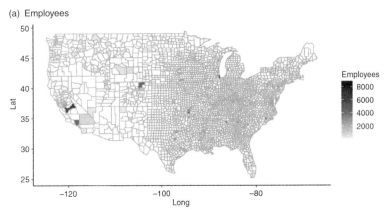

(b) Weekly wages

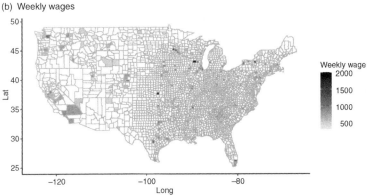

Figure 9.4   Animal processing sector employees and weekly wage by county, 2019
Source: All data from Bureau of Labor Statistics.

of the distributions are strongly right skewed. In general, animal slaughtering and processing facilities were larger and employed more workers compared to the average food manufacturing operation in 2019.

Much of the risks associated with labor in food manufacturing are likely to be heterogeneous across firms within an industry. McGuckin, Nguyen, and Reznek (1998) note significant impacts of plant ownership changes in food manufacturing on increased productivity and employment. More generally, variation in wages and frequency of job changes have been shown to be greater within industries compared to across industries (Davis and Haltiwanger 1992). Wage and employment dynamics are expected to differ between industries in food manufacturing. For instance, animal processing has tended to make higher use of immigrant and undocumented labor, which could result in supply chain risk related to immigration policy.

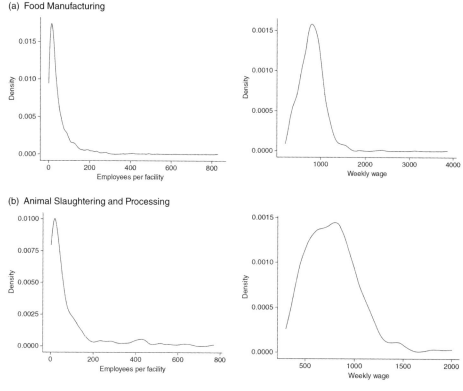

Figure 9.5   Wage and employment distributions for food manufacturing sector and animal processing sector, 2019

Source: All data from Bureau of Labor Statistics.

Other industries make less use of this type of labor and are insulated from unanticipated policy changes.

The labor demand created by food manufacturing plants can have large impacts on local economic outcomes, especially when food manufacturing operations are located in rural or otherwise sparsely populated counties. The meatpacking industry is a major source of jobs for low-income and immigrant workers. Artz, Jackson, and Orazem (2010) find that meatpacking plants alter the demographics of communities in which they are located, being associated with immigrant populations, as well as populations with limited English-speaking ability. These changing demographics are reflected in local school systems and poverty rates. However, they found little evidence of per capita increases in government spending as a result of this demographic change. Their conclusive findings are similar to those of Artz, Orazem, and Otto (2007).

Plant siting decisions and food manufacturing growth are also related to local labor market conditions. Goetz (1997) shows that establishment growth is associated with lower labor costs, higher educational attainment, higher unemployment rates, and a larger population. Similarly, among other factors, Henderson and McNamara (2000) found that food manufacturing facilities were more likely to locate in counties with lower average wages. Lambert and McNamara (2009) indicate that both labor availability and the skill level of labor are important for attracting manufacturers. They argue that deeper and more diversified labor pools increase the likelihood of being able to hire workers for all positions. Labor heterogeneity is one of the most important factors attracting food manufacturing operations (Davis and Schluter 2005).

There are relatively few comprehensive studies of labor disruption in food manufacturing, which may reflect the low probability of widespread disruptive events. However, case studies of labor disruption in specific firms have been mentioned in the literature. Artz, Jackson, and Orazem (2010) described a 2008 Immigration and Customs Enforcement raid on an Iowa meatpacking facility in which one-third of all employees were arrested. The operating firm subsequently filed for bankruptcy and closed the plant down. Other notable food manufacturing supply chain disruptions have occurred, but did not arise through labor disruption: for instance, the Tyson meatpacking fire of 2019.

The COVID-19 pandemic caused widespread disruption in food manufacturing with news reports concentrating on the meatpacking sector. These disruptions were the result of working conditions that put workers at high risk of contracting COVID-19. However, Asher, Deb, and Gangaram (2021) found COVID-19 cases and deaths to be heterogenously associated with industries in food manufacturing. Meatpacking plants were associated with higher cases and deaths, but so were seafood processing facilities and bakeries. In contrast, dairy manufacturing facilities were associated with less cases. Asher, Deb, and Gangaram (2021) suggest that this disparity is related to capital-labor ratios, which are low in meat processing and baking, and much higher in dairy manufacturing.

Cho, Lee, and Winters (2020) report findings on the impacts of COVID-19 on the employment status of food sector workers—including manufacturing workers—up through April 2020. COVID-19 infection rates locally were found to be associated with a decreased likelihood of continuing to work in the same food industry and increased temporary absence for food manufacturing workers. The percentage of previously employed food and beverage workers who were unemployed increased from March 2020 to April 2020. Their findings imply that the impact of COVID-19 on labor in food manufacturing arose not only through plant shutdowns but also through the individual actions of workers to protect themselves from possible exposure.

The COVID-19 pandemic has prompted calls for increased regulation of meatpacking facilities, and potentially other food manufacturers, due to plant shutdowns. Increasing price spreads between farm and retail levels were observed at the start of the pandemic. However, increased marketing margins can result from a competitive market environment (Lusk, Tonsor, and Schulz 2021). Any potential policy actions will need to consider issues of operational and disruption risks in food manufacturing and resilience to shocks. The question is, how flexible are firms during normal operation in terms of adjusting employment, wages, and output, and was their adjustment to the pandemic faster or slower? Both of these elements of labor risk in food manufacturing are addressed in the empirical analysis that follows.

9.3   Methodology

We estimate a panel dynamic model of the framework of Holtz-Eakin, Newey, and Rosen (1988), Arellano and Bond (1991), and Blundell and Bond (1998). The general formulation is given by

$$(1) \qquad y_{it} = \sum_{j=1}^{L} \phi_j \, y_{i,t-j} + \sum_{k=1}^{K} x_{itk} \beta_k + \mu_i + \varepsilon_{it},$$

where y_{it} is an $m \times 1$ vector of endogenous variables for the ith unit of observation in time t. Then $y_{i,t-j}$ are lagged endogenous variables and x_{itk} is a matrix of exogenous variables. The errors ε_{it} are assumed to be independent from x_{it}. The fixed effect μ_i is correlated with lagged values of y which induces endogeneity in the lagged values.

As noted above, the data in this case are large in cross section but the time dimension is relatively small. Estimating a dynamic panel model via ordinary least squares would result in biased estimators as noted in Nickell (1981). If one differences equation (1), then the differenced endogenous variable is correlated with the differenced error term. However, several authors have addressed estimation problems in dynamic panel settings with generalized method of moments (GMM) estimators. These include Holtz-Eakin, Newey, and Rosen (1988), Arellano and Bond (1991), Blundell and Bond (1998), and Binder, Hsiao, and Pesaran (2005).

Consider the case of equation (1) where both L and K are equal to one. The basic problem is that the moment condition,

$$(2) \qquad E[\Delta y_{it-1} \nu_{it}] = 0,$$

where ν_{it} is the differenced error term, is violated. Instruments that are relevant for $\Delta y_{i,t-1}$ and satisfy the moment condition can be used to correct for endogeneity bias. As shown in Arellano and Bond (1991), an intuitive set of instruments is given by all other previous realizations of y_i. The lagged endogenous variables will not be correlated with the contemporaneous error term and are relevant for the contemporaneous value of the dependent variable because the model is autoregressive.

The differenced model for individual i is given by

$$(3) \qquad\qquad y_i^d = X_i^d \gamma + v_i^d,$$

where

$$
y_i^d = \begin{pmatrix} \Delta y_{i3} \\ \Delta y_{i4} \\ \vdots \\ \Delta y_{iT} \end{pmatrix}
\quad
X_i^d = \begin{pmatrix} \Delta y_{i2} & \Delta x_{i3} \\ \Delta y_{i3} & \Delta x_{i4} \\ \vdots & \vdots \\ \Delta y_{i,T-1} & \Delta x_{iT} \end{pmatrix}
\quad
\gamma = \begin{pmatrix} \phi \\ \beta \end{pmatrix}
\quad
v_i^d = \begin{pmatrix} v_{i3} \\ v_{i4} \\ \vdots \\ v_{iT} \end{pmatrix},
$$

with the matrix of instruments given by

$$
Z_i^d = \begin{pmatrix}
y_{i1} & 0 & 0 & 0 & 0 & 0 & \cdots & 0 & 0 & 0 \\
0 & y_{i1} & y_{i2} & 0 & 0 & 0 & \cdots & 0 & 0 & 0 \\
0 & 0 & 0 & y_{i1} & y_{i2} & y_{i3} & 0 & \cdots & 0 & 0 \\
\vdots & \vdots & \vdots & \vdots & \vdots & \vdots & \ddots & \vdots & \vdots & \vdots \\
0 & 0 & 0 & 0 & 0 & 0 & 0 & y_{i1} & \cdots & y_{i,T-2}
\end{pmatrix}.
$$

Blundell and Bond (1998) implement a system GMM estimator that makes use of additional moment conditions. The gains from the additional moment conditions are typically larger when there is a high degree of autocorrelation in the dependent variable (ϕ is large). The set of equations in equation (3) are augmented by level equations where

$$y_i^\ell = X_i^\ell + \varepsilon_i^\ell$$

and

$$
y_i^\ell = \begin{pmatrix} y_{i2} \\ y_{i3} \\ \vdots \\ y_{iT} \end{pmatrix}
\quad
X_i^\ell = \begin{pmatrix} y_{i1} & x_{i2} \\ y_{i2} & x_{i3} \\ \vdots & \vdots \\ y_{i,T-1} & x_{iT} \end{pmatrix}
\quad
\varepsilon_i^\ell = \begin{pmatrix} v_i + \varepsilon_{i2} \\ v_i + \varepsilon_{i3} \\ \vdots \\ v_i + \varepsilon_{iT} \end{pmatrix}.
$$

The instrument matrix for the full system is given by

$$
Z_i = \begin{pmatrix} Z_i^d & 0 & D_i \\ 0 & Z_i^\ell & 0 \end{pmatrix}.
$$

The general formulation is easily extended to settings where both L and K are greater than 1.

Robust two-step estimators of the finite sample variance in this setting are biased. Windmeijer (2005) notes the potential for severe downward bias in small samples and proposes a corrected estimator. The proposed corrected estimator is found to perform well in approximating the finite sample variance in simulation, thus resulting in more accurate inference. The Windmeijer (2005) correction essentially involves the use of an additional correction term in estimation of the variance with the correction term disappearing as the sample size grows larger. Although the sample size in the following empirical analysis is relatively large, we utilize the bias-corrected estimator of the variance in estimating the employment and wage equations (as well as a single-equation dynamic model of industry output).

Using dynamic employment and wage models estimated via GMM, we then project employment and wages in each county through 2020 and compare the projections to actual employment and wages in an event study framework (Campbell, Lo, and MacKinlay 2012; Kothari and Warner 2007). It is important to note that this approach does not constitute a natural experiment because we do not observe a counterfactual. Any results only describe changes in employment and wages under COVID-19 and any other conditions prevailing in the market in 2020.

In spite of our inability to isolate labor effects of the COVID-19 pandemic, the event study provides potentially useful evidence about food manufacturing and animal processing resilience in the face of a disruptive event. Firms take equilibrating actions given constraints in the face of disruption. If these actions return employment and wage levels to those implied by the model, and do so quickly, then the food manufacturing and animal processing sectors are by definition resilient. By using county-level data, the event study also permits us to examine if the initial impacts of COVID-19 and the degree of resilience is heterogeneous across counties, which we might expect by virtue of different rates of infection and industry structures.

9.4   Empirical Results

Our empirical application utilizes data collected from the US Bureau of Labor Statistics (BLS) and the US Bureau of Economic Analysis (BEA). A county-level consumer price index (CPI) deflator was constructed using the metropolitan statistical area (MSA) implicit price deflators. MSA and regional data were translated to the county level using the National Bureau of Economic Research (NBER) MSA to County crosswalk data tool. For those counties that were not covered by a BLS-defined MSA or regional area, the state-level non-urban household CPI was used. Price data are taken from the BLS CPI database. We consider four classes of commodities—food, pork, poultry, and beef. All price, income, and wage data were deflated using the county-specific CPI.

County-level wages and employment were taken from the BLS Quarterly Census of Employment and Wages. These data include annual and monthly employment statistics for 3- and 4-digit NAICS industry classifications. Two specific industries are of interest in this analysis—food manufacturing and processing (NAICS 311) and animal slaughter and processing (NAICS 3116). As noted previously, the data for food manufacturing and processing include animal slaughter and processing as a constituent industry. The data provide a rich assessment of employment and wage patterns at the county level. However, the data do suffer from one shortcoming—wage and employment data are not reported when such reporting would disclose proprietary details of individual firms.

We only consider the subset of counties for which wages and employment are reported.[1] This likely omits those counties with a small number of workers or employees in the relevant sectors. We also consider county-level data taken from the BEA's Regional Economic Information System (REIS). This data source reports county-level income, population, and a range of potentially relevant economic variables. Our data are observed annually at the county level. However, the BLS reported wages for the first three quarters of 2020. Monthly employment was also available for the associated nine months of 2020. These data allow an evaluation of COVID-19 pandemic effects on wages and employment levels in these two specific industries in 2020.

The goal of our empirical analysis is to evaluate the factors associated with the level of wages and numbers of employees in the food manufacturing sector and animal slaughter and processing industry. These sectors were impacted significantly by the COVID-19 pandemic suffering widespread disruptions. The drop in capital utilization and industry output was especially acute in these two sectors. This is demonstrated in figure 9.6, where a significant decline in output and plant capacity utilization is apparent in 2020. However, capacity utilization and output recovered within the first three quarters of 2020 and exceeded levels observed at the end of 2019 by the end of the year.

We jointly estimated wage and employment equations using the dynamic panel estimation procedures described above for all food manufacturing and for animal slaughter and processing. Summary statistics for the variables used to explain wage and employment levels are presented in table 9.1. Food manufacturing as a whole tends to have higher wages and levels of employment over the entirety of the sample. Wages and employment also tend to be less historically variable in food manufacturing as shown by the historical coefficient of variation (CV) for wages and employees in the two industries. Per capita wage income is slightly higher in the counties with meat processing facilities.

We assume that employment and wages are jointly endogenous and are

---

1. The number of establishments is reported for all counties in the US. A valuable future research direction would address possible specification biases that may result from nondisclosure data reporting considerations.

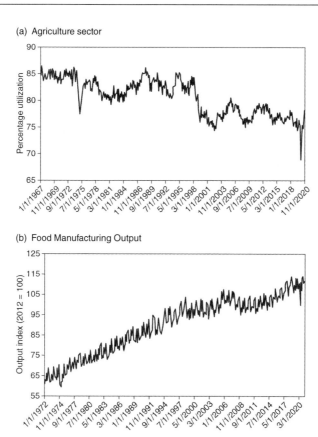

(a) Agriculture sector

(b) Food Manufacturing Output

Figure 9.6   Food manufacturing sector capacity utilization and output

influenced by adjustment lags, which are represented using lagged employment and wages. These adjustment lags may represent labor and wage contracts and agreements or other factors causing frictions in the adjustment process. Preliminary results indicated a faster adjustment for wages, where only a single lagged value was significant. Employment is slower to adjust and required two lags.

We estimated the following specifications for the employment and wage equations. In the food manufacturing sector, the employment equation is given by

$$(4) \quad employees_{it} = \mu_i + employees_{it-1} + employees_{it-2} + establishments_{it}$$
$$+ foodcpi_{it} + wage_{it} + wagecv_{it} + employeescv_{it}$$
$$+ pcwageincome_{it} + \varepsilon_{it} .$$

Table 9.1   **Variable definitions and summary statistics**

Variable	Definition	Food Manufacturing		Animal Processing	
		Mean	Standard Deviation	Mean	Standard Deviation
Per-Capita Income	Log of Real Per-Capita Income	3.7763	0.2259		
No. Establishments	Number of Industry Establishments	2.3630	0.9452	1.7272	0.6298
CV of Wages	CV of Real Wage Rate (previous 8 quarters)	17.1946	30.7891	25.2171	41.9651
CV of Employment	CV of Employment (previous 12 months)	15.7715	31.2680	22.6170	42.7803
Per-Capita Wage Income	Log of Real Per-Capita Wage Income	2.8543	0.3931	3.0378	0.4032
No. Employees	Number of Industry Employees	5.6864	1.6492	5.2038	1.8154
Average Weekly Wage	Log of Real Average Weekly Wage	6.5454	0.3918	6.4935	0.3548
Food Total Output	Real Income in Food Processing Industry	0.0759	0.1865		
Food CPI	Log of Regional Food CPI	5.5401	0.0242		
Pork CPI	Log of Regional Pork CPI			5.3979	0.0424
Poultry CPI	Log of Regional Poultry CPI			5.4774	0.0333
Beef CPI	Log of Regional Beef CPI			5.6728	0.0935

Note: Numbers of observations are 14,187 for the food processing sector employment and wages, 13,726 for food processing industry output, and 2,300 for the meat processing sector.

while the wage equation is given by

$$(5) \quad wage_{it} = \mu_i + wage_{it-1} + establishments_{it} + foodcpi_{it} + employees_{it}$$
$$+ wagecv_{it} + employeescv_{it} + pcwageincome_{it} + \varepsilon_{it} .$$

For the animal slaughter and processing industry, the employment equation is given by

$$(6) \quad employees_{it} = \mu_i + employees_{it-1} + employees_{it-2} + establishments_{it}$$
$$+ porkcpi_{it} + poultrycpi_{it} + beefcpi_{it} + wage_{it}$$
$$+ wagecv_{it} + employeescv_{it} + pcwageincome_{it} + \varepsilon_{it} .$$

and the wage equation is given by

$$(7) \quad wage_{it} = \mu_i + wage_{it-1} + establishments_{it} + porkcpi_{it} + poultrycpi_{it}$$
$$+ beefcpi_{it} + employees_{it} + wagecv_{it} + employeescv_{it}$$
$$+ pcwageincome_{it} + \varepsilon_{it} ,$$

Table 9.2   **Dynamic panel model of food manufacturing sector weekly wages and employment**

Variable	Average Weekly Wages			No. Employees		
	Parameter Estimate	Standard Error	t Ratio	Parameter Estimate	Standard Error	t Ratio
Intercept	−2.1271	0.5975	−3.56	1.2128	0.9462	1.28
Weekly Wage$_{t-1}$	0.7347	0.0418	17.58			
No. Employees$_{t-1}$				0.9009	0.0431	20.92
No. Employees$_{t-2}$				−0.0495	0.0180	−2.75
No. Establishments	0.0048	0.0129	0.37	0.3890	0.0281	13.84
Food CPI	0.6334	0.1081	5.86	−0.3186	0.1807	−1.76
Weekly Wage				0.0797	0.0533	1.50
No. Employees	0.0288	0.0086	3.37			
CV of Wages	0.0044	0.0005	8.90	−0.0013	0.0005	−2.62
CV of Employment	−0.0041	0.0005	−8.27	0.0006	0.0005	1.17
Per-Capita Wage Income	0.0625	0.0288	2.17	−0.0133	0.0456	−0.29
R^2		0.90			0.97	
Number of Cross Sections		1378			1378	
Time Series Length		12			12	
Number of Instruments		92			71	

where counties are indexed by i and time is indexed by t. Employment and wages are affected by lagged values, contemporary values of employment and wages, the number of establishments in a county, prices of food and/or meat, historical variation in employment and wages, and per capita wage income in a county.

Parameter estimates and related statistics for the dynamic models for food manufacturing are presented in table 9.2. The results indicate that average weekly wages in the food processing sector are positively associated with the price of output, as represented by the food CPI. Historical volatility in wages, which is represented using the wage CV, tends to increase real wages. This likely represents a risk premium to workers in counties and years that had volatile wages. In contrast, greater volatility in the number of employees tends to be associated with lower wages. Greater volatility in the availability of labor would be expected to result in lower real wages. Finally, counties and years that realized a higher average wage per person also tended to have higher wages in the food manufacturing sector.

Strong lagged effects are apparent for the number of employees in the food manufacturing sector. The first-order autoregressive coefficient is 0.90, which represents a very slow adjustment over time. This is consistent with expectations that although wages may be more easily adjusted in response to economic conditions, the actual number of employees is much slower to adjust. This requires hiring and firing of workers and therefore is more likely

Table 9.3   Dynamic panel model of food manufacturing sector output

Variable	Parameter Estimate	Standard Error	t Ratio
Intercept	−0.5225	0.1321	−3.96
Food Total Output$_{t-1}$	0.9961	0.0410	24.30
Food Total Output$_{t-2}$	−0.0408	0.0473	−0.86
No. Establishments	−0.0032	0.0019	−1.68
Food CPI	0.1040	0.0265	3.92
No. Employees	0.0107	0.0056	1.92
Weekly Wage	−0.0164	0.0078	−2.11
CV of Wages	0.0001	0.0000	2.21
CV of Employment	−0.0001	0.0000	−1.83
Per-Capita Wage Income	0.0016	0.0066	0.24
R^2		0.98	
Number of Cross Sections		1324	
Time Series Length		12	
Number of Instruments		91	

to involve significant frictions that impair adjustment. Long-term employment agreements are one factor that is likely to slow adjustments in the number of workers.

A scale effect on the number of workers is reflected in the number of establishments. More manufacturing plants would be expected to require a greater number of workers. The real price of food tends to lower the number of workers employed in the food manufacturing sector. This is counter to expectations but may reflect the cost of other unobservable inputs. The endogenous weekly wage does not have a significant effect on the number of workers. A higher historical volatility of wages tends to lower employment. A greater degree of wage volatility may suggest a higher level of risk to both workers and plant managers, thereby leading to a lower level of employment.

We also considered a single-equation dynamic panel model of the value of total output from the food industry. This was represented using the industry-specific total personal income for food, beverage, and tobacco manufacturing. A strong lagged effect with a near unitary autoregressive parameter was found for total output. The number of plants in a county and year is associated with lower total output. However, a higher value for the output, as represented by the food CPI, was associated with greater output. The number of employees was associated with greater output. Higher average wages for workers lower the value of output. Greater volatility of average wages is associated with higher output. However, volatility in the number of workers tends to lower the value of output. This suggests that volatility in the availability of workers tends to have a negative effect on the supply chain and reduces the value of output.

The wage and employment analysis was repeated for a much more finely defined industry—animal slaughter and processing. COVID-19 had signifi-

Table 9.4   **Dynamic panel model of animal processing industry weekly wages and employment**

	Average Weekly Wages			No. Employees		
Variable	Parameter Estimate	Standard Error	t Ratio	Parameter Estimate	Standard Error	t Ratio
Intercept	1.9945	0.7800	2.56	−1.3635	1.7477	−0.78
Weekly Wage$_{t-1}$	0.8000	0.0549	14.57			
No. Employees$_{t-1}$				0.9584	0.0827	11.58
No. Employees$_{t-2}$				−0.1577	0.0421	−3.75
No. Establishments	−0.0221	0.0356	−0.62	0.2642	0.0727	3.63
Pork CPI	−0.3586	0.0962	−3.73	−0.0041	0.1734	−0.02
Poultry CPI	0.1080	0.1416	0.76	0.1182	0.2772	0.43
Beef CPI	0.0596	0.0593	1.00	0.0066	0.1615	0.04
Weekly Wage				0.1299	0.1163	1.12
No. Employees	0.0300	0.0120	2.51			
CV of Wages	0.0017	0.0007	2.27	−0.0005	0.0009	−0.51
CV of Employment	−0.0014	0.0007	−1.84	−0.0005	0.0009	−0.60
Per-Capita Wage Income	0.0622	0.0538	1.16	0.1582	0.2176	0.73
R^2	0.90			0.98		
Number of Cross Sections	266			266		
Time Series Length	12			12		
Number of Instruments	94			73		

cant impacts on workers in the meat processing sector, although as noted, there is emerging evidence of similar but apparently less newsworthy effects in other areas of food manufacturing (Asher, Deb, and Gangaram 2021). Employees working on the animal slaughter and meat processing lines spent hours in close proximity to one another and the spread of the virus among plant workers was felt across the beef, pork, and poultry industries. Significant lags in adjustment are apparent for both wages and the number of workers in the industry. A greater number of processing plants increased the number of employees but had no statistically significant impact on wages. Wages were negatively related to pork prices but beef and poultry prices had no impact on wages or employment. A higher number of workers is associated with higher wages. Wages are increased as the volatility of wages rises but are decreased as the volatility of the number of workers increases.

A central objective of our analysis is to assess the impacts of COVID-19 on wages and employment in the food and animal processing sectors as a study of disruption risk in the sector. To this end, we utilized BLS wage data for the first three quarters of 2020 and monthly employment through September 2020. We predicted wages and the number of workers holding all other factors at their 2019 levels. Figure 9.7 illustrates the implied impact on average wages in the food manufacturing sector across the first three quarters of 2020. The predicted and realized values of wages are plotted alongside

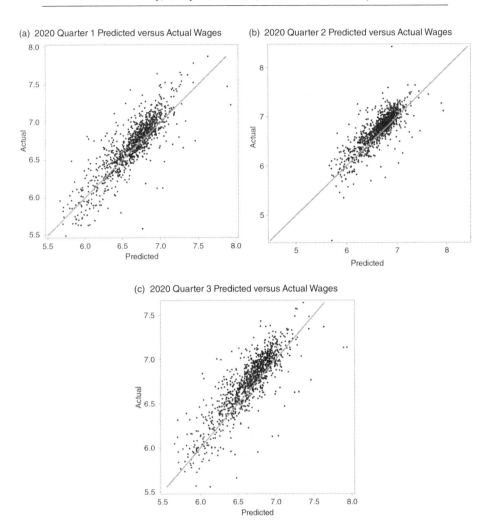

Figure 9.7   COVID-19 related changes in average weekly wages in the food manu-facturing sector

a 45° line. Observations above the line indicate wages that are higher than expected while the converse is true for observations below the line.

In general, wages appear to have been slightly higher than one might have expected, conditional on other economic factors being held constant. The cross-sectional volatility of wages appears to have fallen in the second quarter of 2020. Panel (b) of figure 9.7 shows a much lower level of dispersion of wages. Higher wages may have been necessary to induce employment in the plants during COVID-19. The lower cross-sectional volatility of wages in the second quarter of 2020 may have been associated with a general slowdown in the entire economy.

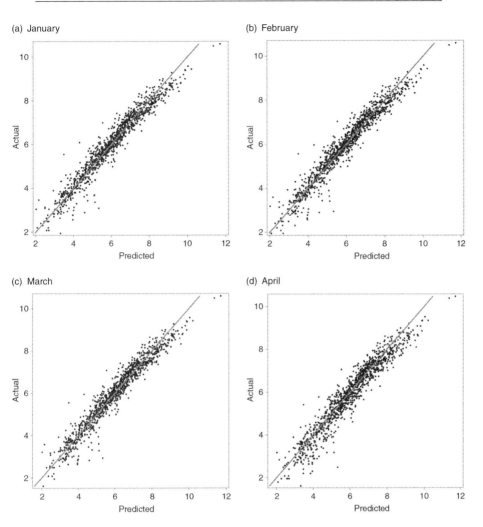

Figure 9.8   2020 monthly differences in predicted and actual employment in the food manufacturing sector

Employment over the first nine months of 2020 is illustrated in figure 9.8. Again, observations below the 45° line represent a case where the number of workers is lower than the model predicts. A subtle pattern of declining employment in April and May is visible. Figure 9.9 illustrates the proportion of counties that had higher than predicted employment in the food manufacturing sector across the first nine months of 2020. A fall in employment relative to what would have been expected is apparent from March through June. This period was characterized by worsening conditions due to the pandemic.

Predictions of wages and employment in the livestock slaughter and processing sector are presented in figures 9.10 and 9.11. Again, wages appear

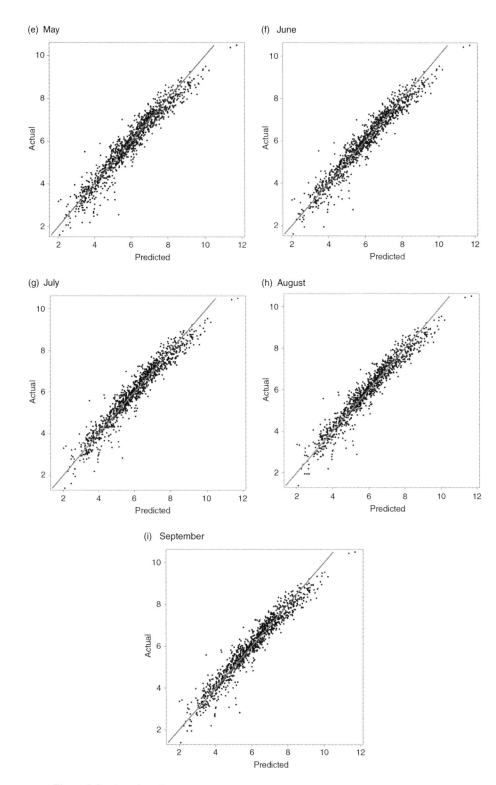

Figure 9.8 (continued)

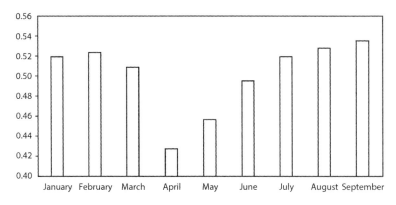

Figure 9.9   Unanticipated decreases in 2020 food manufacturing employment

to have been higher during the first three quarters of 2020 than the model predicted. A lower degree of cross-sectional volatility of wages is again notable for the second quarter. Figure 9.11 again suggests subtle decreases in employment relative to what was expected. Figure 9.12 repeats the analysis of the proportion of counties that realized lower and higher levels of employment than were expected. Again, a substantial drop in employment from March through May is apparent.

From the point of view of labor-related risks in food manufacturing, several conclusions are apparent from this analysis. First, in terms of operational risks, there are complicated dynamics at play for wages and employment in these industries. While wages are relatively quick to adjust, employment is slower. This lag suggests that labor inflexibilities in food manufacturing and animal processing may be a significant source of risk with implications throughout the supply chain. Second, historical variation in wages and employment have impacts on current wages and employment, possibly reflecting risk premia. In terms of disruption risk, there are noticeable impacts of the COVID-19 pandemic on employment and wages, particularly in March, April, and May 2020. Employment is lower than predicted and wages are higher for most (but not all) counties in the sample. These dynamics are indicative of equilibrating actions on the part of firms and market forces at work.

9.5   Conclusion

We model employment and wages in the food manufacturing sector and animal slaughter and processing industries using dynamic panel models and data at the county level. The estimated models allow us to characterize labor dynamics in these industries and provide insight into the operational risks faced by firms in this environment. We then compare estimated employ-

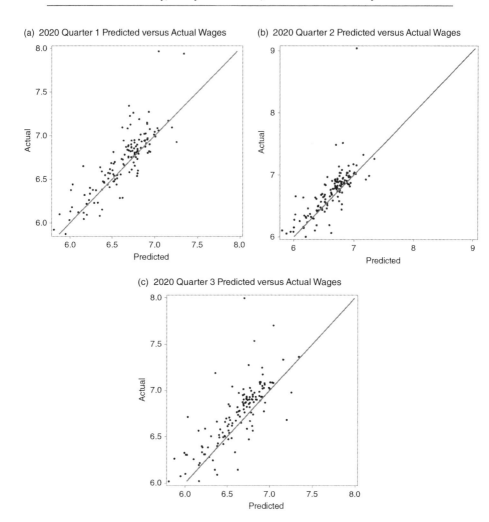

Figure 9.10   COVID-19 related changes in average weekly wages in the animal processing sector

ment and wages with these labor outcomes during a disruptive event. The COVID-19 pandemic had large impacts on employment and wages in early 2020. However, the food manufacturing industry recovered quickly returning to pre-pandemic levels. Taken together, these assessments of operational and disruption risk in food manufacturing suggest that labor risk is an important source of risk in the agricultural supply chain. However, the food manufacturing sector as currently organized is relatively resilient, at least to the types of labor shocks resulting from the pandemic.

This analysis of labor dynamics and disruption in food manufacturing points to several lines of research where the literature on agricultural supply

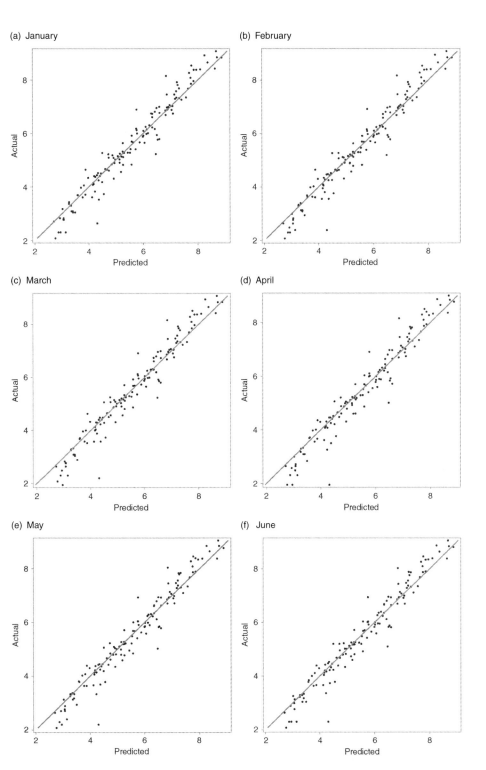

Figure 9.11   2020 monthly differences in predicted and actual employment in the animal processing sector

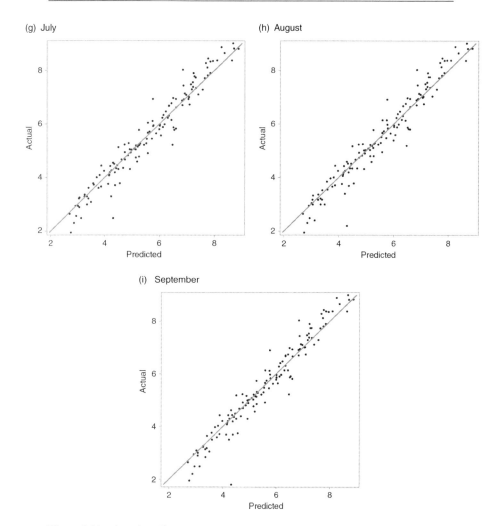

Figure 9.11   (continued)

chains might be advanced. First, there are a number of interesting outstanding questions related to food manufacturing and animal processing operations. While this analysis focuses on county-level employment, and makes no distinction between regular and production employees, later work could focus on plant-level analysis. By distinguishing between different types of employees, it would be possible to better understand intra-firm changes in the distribution of workers. Presumably any risks associated with labor could also differ across worker types.

Second, richer data sets will enable the use of increasingly sophisticated methodologies for the measurement and analysis of agricultural supply

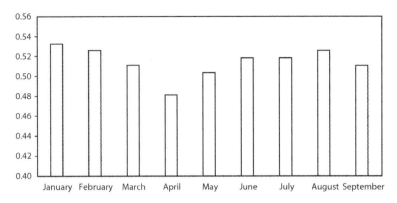

Figure 9.12   Unanticipated decreases in 2020 animal processing employment

chains. Difficulties in empirically modeling supply chains arise from the oftentimes limited availability of current data and the spatially and temporally dynamic nature of supply chains. On one hand, deterministic models of supply chains can be parameterized and used to examine counterfactual supply chain makeup. On the other, purely empirical models can be developed. In either case, computational and econometric methods will need to be increasingly flexible to account for the complexities of global value chains. Such advances are already being incorporated in supply chain research (Chor 2019; Yu and Nagurney 2013).

Lastly, the expanding literature on supply chain innovation and its relationship to supply chain risk could be expanded to manufacturing labor and labor flexibility. Among the growing literature in this area, Lu, Reardon, and Zilberman (2016) focus on machinery rental at the farm level. Du et al. (2016) consider a portfolio selection approach to supply chain design using the example of a firm that requires feedstock processing. The focus is on purchase of feedstock or production in-house. Few studies have explicitly considered labor issues in food manufacturing and animal processing although unique labor markets (such as heavy use of immigrant labor) characterize these sectors.

The COVID-19 pandemic presents an opportunity to understand how supply chains respond to major—and potentially prolonged—disruption. At the current time, any measured responses can only be considered short term. Important questions about firms' long run response to the pandemic, especially in the food sector, remain. Has disruption spurred food manufacturers to make permanent adjustments to supply chains and manufacturing operations? Anecdotal evidence suggests that animal processors have made increased use of robotization in processing facilities. If widespread, increased mechanization could lower the the number of production workers required in processing with concomitant changes in supply chain risk.

References

Adjemian, Michael, B. Wade Brorsen, William Hahn, Tina L. Saitone, and Richard J. Sexton. 2016. "Thinning Markets in U.S. Agriculture." Economic Information Bulletin 148. Economic Research Service.

Antle, John M. 1996. "Efficient Food Safety Regulation in the Food Manufacturing Sector." *American Journal of Agricultural Economics* 78 (5): 1242–1247.

Arellano, Manuel, and Stephen Bond. 1991. "Some Tests of Specification for Panel Data: Monte Carlo Evidence and an Application to Employment Equations." *Review of Economic Studies* 58 (2): 277–97.

Artz, Georgeanne, Rebecca Jackson, and Peter Orazem. 2010. "Is It a Jungle Out There? Meat Packing, Immigrants, and Rural Communities." *Journal of Agricultural and Resource Economics* 35 (2): 299–315.

Artz, Georgeanne, Peter Orazem, and Daniel Otto. 2007. "Measuring the Impact of Meat Packing and Processing Facilities in Nonmetropolitan Counties: A Difference-in-Differences Approach." *American Journal of Agricultural Economics* 89 (3): 557–70.

Asher, Twisha, Partha Deb, and Anjelica Gangaram. 2021. "Nursing Facilities, Food Manufacturing Plants and COVID-19 Cases and Deaths." *Economics Letters* 201, 109800.

Binder, Michael, Cheng Hsiao, and M. Hashem Pesaran. 2005. "Estimation and Inference in Short Panel Vector Autoregressions with Unit Roots and Cointegration." *Econometric Theory* 21: 795–837.

Blundell Richard, and Stephen Bond. 1998. "Initial Conditions and Moment Restrictions in Dynamic Panel Data Models." *Journal of Econometrics* 87 (1): 115–43.

Boehlje, Michael. 1999. "Structural Changes in the Agricultural Industries: How Do We Measure, Analyze and Understand Them?" *American Journal of Agricultural Economics* 81 (5): 1028–1041.

Bunge, Jacob. 2020a. "Smithfield CEO Warns of Risks to Pork Supply." *Wall Street Journal,* April 12.

Bunge, Jacob. 2020b. "Smithfield To Close More Pork Plants over Coronavirus Pandemic." *Wall Street Journal,* April 15.

Campbell, John Y., Andrew W. Lo, and A. Craig MacKinlay. 2012. "Event-Study Analysis." In *The Econometrics of Financial Markets*, John Y. Campbell, Andrew W. Lo, and A. Craig MacKinlay. Princeton University Press.

Cho, Seung Jin, Jun Yeong Lee, and John V. Winters. 2020. "COVID-19 Employment Status Impacts on Food Sector Workers." IZA Discussion Paper. Institute of Labor Economics.

Chor, Davin. 2019. "Modeling Global Value Chains: Approaches and Insights from Economics." In *Handbook on Global Value Chains*, edited by Stefano Ponte, Gary Gereffi, and Gale Raj-Reichert. Cheltenham, UK: Edward Elgar Publishing.

Davis, David E., and Gerald E. Schluter. 2005. "Labor-Force Heterogeneity as a Source of Agglomeration Economies in an Empirical Analysis of County-Level Determinants of Food Plant Entry." *Journal of Agricultural and Resource Economics* 30 (3): 480–501.

Davis, Steven, and John Haltiwanger. 1992. "Gross Job Creation, Gross Job Destruction, and Employment Reallocation." *Quarterly Journal of Economics* 107 (3): 819–63.

Du, Xiaoxue, Liang Lu, Thomas Reardon, and David Zilberman. 2016. "Economics of Agricultural Supply Chain Design: A Portfolio Selection Approach." *American Journal of Agricultural Economics* 98 (5): 1377–1388.

Elitzak, Howard. 1999. "Food Cost Review, 1950–97." Agricultural Economic Report 780. Economic Research Service.

Goetz, Stephan J. 1997. "State- and County-Level Determinants of Food Manufacturing Establishment Growth: 1987–93." *American Journal of Agricultural Economics* 79 (3): 838–50.

Goodwin, Barry K., and Gary W Brester. 1995. "Structural Change in Factor Demand Relationships in the US Food and Kindred Products Industry." *American Journal of Agricultural Economics* 77 (1): 69–79.

Henderson, Jason R., and Kevin T. McNamara. 2000. "The Location of Food Manufacturing Plant Investments in Corn Belt Counties." *Journal of Agricultural and Resource Economics* 25 (2): 680–97.

Hertz, Tom, and Steven Zahniser. 2013. "Is There a Farm Labor Shortage?" *American Journal of Agricultural Economics* 95 (2): 476–81.

Hobbs, Jill E., 2020. "Food Supply Chains during the COVID-19 Pandemic." *Canadian Journal of Agricultural Economics/Revue canadienne d'agroeconomie* 68 (2): 171–76.

Hobbs, Jill E. 2021. "The COVID-19 Pandemic and Meat Supply Chains." *Meat Science* 81, 108459.

Holtz-Eakin, Douglas, Whitney Newey, and Harvey S. Rosen. 1988. "Estimating Vector Autoregressions with Panel Data." *Econometrica* 56 (6): 1371–1395.

Huang, Kuo S. 1991. "Factor Demands in the US Food-Manufacturing Industry." *American Journal of Agricultural Economics* 73 (3): 615–20.

Huang, Kuo S. 2003. "Food Manufacturing Productivity and Its Economic Implications." Technical Bulletin 1905. Economic Research Service.

Knoeber, Charles R., and Walter N. Thurman. 1995. "Don't Count Your Chickens . . . : Risk and Risk Shifting in the Broiler Industry." *American Journal of Agricultural Economics* 77 (3): 486–96.

Kothari, Sagar P., and Jerold B. Warner. 2007. "Econometrics of Event Studies." In *Handbook of Empirical Corporate Finance*, edited by B. Espen Eckbo. Amsterdam: Elsevier.

Kunreuther, Howard, and Michael Useem. 2018. *Mastering Catastrophic Risk: How Companies Are Coping with Disruption*. Oxford University Press.

Lambert, Dayton M., and Kevin T. McNamara. 2009. "Location Determinants of Food Manufacturers in the United States, 2000–2004: Are Nonmetropolitan Counties Competitive?" *Agricultural Economics* 40 (6): 617–30.

Larue, Bruno. 2020. "Labor Issues and COVID-19." *Canadian Journal of Agricultural Economics/Revue canadienne d'agroeconomie* 68 (2): 231–37.

Lu, Liang, Thomas Reardon, and David Zilberman. 2016. "Supply Chain Design and Adoption of Indivisible Technology." *American Journal of Agricultural Economics* 98 (5): 1419–1431.

Lusk, Jayson L., Glynn T. Tonsor, and Lee L. Schulz. 2021. "Beef and Pork Marketing Margins and Price Spreads during COVID-19." *Applied Economic Perspectives and Policy* 43 (1): 4–23.

MacDonald, James M. 2014. "Technology, Organization, and Financial Performance in US Broiler Production." Economic Information Bulletin 126. Economic Research Service.

MacDonald, James M., Michael Ollinger, Kenneth E. Nelson, and Charles R. Handy. 2000. "Consolidation in US Meatpacking." Agricultural Economic Report 785. Economic Research Service.

McCluskey, Jill J., and A. Desmond O'Rourke. 2000. "Relationships between Produce Supply Firms and Retailers in the New Food Supply Chain." *Journal of Food Distribution Research* 31: 11–20.

McGuckin, Robert H., Sang V. Nguyen, and Arnold P. Reznek. 1998. "On Measuring the Impact of Ownership Change on Labor: Evidence from US Food-Manufacturing Plant-Level Data." In *Labor Statistics Measurement Issues*, Studies in Income and Wealth, volume 60, edited by John Haltiwanger, Marilyn E. Manser, and Robert Topel, 207–46. Chicago, IL: University of Chicago Press.

Nickell, Stephen. 1981. "Biases in Dynamic Models with Fixed Effects." *Econometrica* 49 (6): 1417–1426.

Richards, Timothy J. 2018. "Immigration Reform and Farm Labor Markets." *American Journal of Agricultural Economics* 100 (4): 1050–1071.

Schultz, Theodore W. 1975. "The Value of the Ability to Deal with Disequilibria." *Journal of Economic Literature* 13 (3): 827–46.

Tang, Christopher S. 2006. "Perspectives in Supply Chain Risk Management." *International Journal of Production Economics* 103 (2): 451–88.

Taylor, Charles A., Christopher Boulos, and Douglas Almond. 2020. "Livestock Plants and COVID-19 Transmission." *Proceedings of the National Academy of Sciences* 117 (50): 31706–31715.

Windmeijer, Frank. 2005. "A Finite Sample Correction for the Variance of Linear Efficient Two-Step GMM Estimators." *Journal of Econometrics* 126 (1): 25–51.

Wohlgenant, Michael K. 2013. "Competition in the US Meatpacking Industry." *Annual Review of Resource Economics* 5 (1): 1–12.

Yu, Min, and Anna Nagurney. 2013. "Competitive Food Supply Chain Networks with Application to Fresh Produce." *European Journal of Operational Research* 224 (2): 273–82.

Zilberman, David, Liang Lu, and Thomas Reardon. 2019. "Innovation-Induced Food Supply Chain Design." *Food Policy* 83: 289–97.

Has Global Agricultural Trade Been Resilient under COVID-19? Findings from an Econometric Assessment of 2020

Shawn Arita, Jason Grant, Sharon Sydow, and Jayson Beckman

10.1 Introduction

In 2020, the world economy suffered an immediate and significant global recession brought on by the coronavirus (COVID-19) pandemic. Global gross domestic product (GDP) shrank 3.2 percent (International Monetary Fund [IMF] 2021). In response to disease outbreaks, many national and sub-national governments imposed lockdowns, stay-at-home orders, and the promotion of remote business and education activities to thwart the spread of the virus. These actions contributed to significant disruptions of

Shawn Arita is a Senior Economist in the Office of the Chief Economist of the US Department of Agriculture.

Jason Grant is the W. G. Wysor Professor of Agriculture and Director of the Center for Agricultural Trade at Virginia Tech.

Sharon Sydow is a Senior Economist in the Office of the Chief Economist of the US Department of Agriculture.

Jayson Beckman is an Economist with the Economic Research Service of the US Department of Agriculture.

Versions of this paper were invited for presentation at the 2020 International Agricultural Trade Research Consortium (IATRC) Annual Meeting and the NBER Spring 2021 Conference on Risks in Agricultural Supply Chains, hosted by NBER and the Economic Research Service of the US Department of Agriculture. The authors are grateful for the discussion and helpful comments from Pol Antràs, David Zilberman, Wyatt Thompson, Thomas Hertel, Ian Sheldon, Kari Heerman, Titus Awokuse, Joseph Cooper, Callie McAdams, Mirvat Sewadeh, Patricia Deal, and participants at the IATRC and NBER conferences. All remaining errors are our own. The views expressed here are those of the authors and do not reflect the views of the Office of the Chief Economist, the Economic Research Service, or US Department of Agriculture. For acknowledgments, sources of research support, and disclosure of the authors' material financial relationships, if any, please see https://www.nber.org/books-and-chapters/risks-agricultural-supply-chains/has-global-agricultural-trade-been-resilient-under-covid-19-findings-econometric-assessment-2020.

non-essential businesses including restaurants, bars, shopping centers, and attractions.[1] Service and tourism industries have been particularly hard hit. For example, the year over year percentage change in weekly airline traffic plunged well over 50 percent for most industrialized nations in 2020 compared to 2019.[2] However, as countries have learned to manage the crisis, GDP forecasts for global economic growth in 2021 and 2022 have become more optimistic with forecasts of 6 and 4.9 percent growth, respectively (IMF 2021).[3]

In the early phases of the pandemic, initial 2020 forecasts for world trade were bleak. In April 2020, the World Trade Organization (WTO) forecasted declines in the value of real exports of −8.1 percent, −16.5 percent, and −20.4 percent under a V- (optimistic), U- (less optimistic), and L-shaped (pessimistic) set of economic recovery scenarios, relative to a baseline without pandemic (WTO 2020a).[4] However, even the most optimistic scenario turned out to overstate the actual decline in total trade in 2020, which, according to the WTO, was −5.3 percent (WTO 2021).[5] The WTO identified several reasons for the better-than-expected trade performance in 2020, including strong monetary and fiscal policies in many governments, business, and household innovation and adaptation that helped stabilize economic activity, and trade policy restraint (WTO 2021). While some trade restrictive measures were initially introduced when the pandemic began, including export restrictions for cereals, most of these measures were rescinded and new restrictions were not imposed. Countries also introduced trade facilitating measures in response to the pandemic, such as lowering import tariffs or taxes (Evenett et al. 2021).

Global trade in food and agricultural products also outperformed the WTO's initial projections, growing 3.5 percent in 2020. The smaller impact of the pandemic on global agricultural trade is likely related to several factors including a low-income elasticity of food demand, shipping channels that do not require substantial human interaction (i.e., bulk commodities), and the essential nature of the industry that many governments declared. Indeed, the WTO (2020b) describes agricultural trade during the COVID-19 pandemic as a "story of resilience" and one of the few "bright spots" in the

1. Experience with similar diseases (i.e., SARS, MERS, H1N1) reveals that while the human costs can be significant, the economic toll is due to the preventive behavior of individuals and the transmission control policies of governments (Brahmbhatt and Dutta 2008).
2. Flight data provided by Statista: https://www.statista.com/statistics/1104036/novel-coronavirus-weekly-flights-change-airlines-region/.
3. It should be noted that prior outlooks forecasted a larger contraction in GDP. In June 2020, the World Bank forecasted a 5.2 percent decline in global GDP growth; the International Monetary Fund (IMF 2020) projected a 4.2 percent decline. The World Bank forecasts growth of 5.6 percent in 2021 and 4.3 percent in 2022.
4. For agricultural exports, the projected decline was −6.5 percent, −11.2 percent, and −12.7 percent, respectively.
5. According to its latest projections, the WTO forecasts a growth in trade of 8.0 percent in 2021 and 4.0 percent in 2022.

global economy. Nevertheless, global food insecurity rose during the pandemic, with FAO estimating that 768 million people were facing hunger in 2020, 118 million more people than in 2019 (FAO et al. 2021).

While descriptive analyses may shed some light on the trade flow impacts of the pandemic, simple year over year changes are clouded by other confounding factors including ongoing animal disease challenges related to African swine fever (ASF) in pork and swine production, burgeoning feed demand by China related to a faster than expected recovery of its hog herd, policy changes such as the US-China Phase One trade agreement, and other factors. While global agricultural trade registered an overall increase in 2020, it is unclear to what extent COVID-19 affected trade flows conditional on other confounding factors. Identifying the pandemic effect from other factors is the key empirical objective of this paper.

A few studies have investigated the impacts of COVID-19 on international trade. Mallory (2020) analyzed early 2020 monthly data and found that beef and pork markets were temporarily impacted by lower exports during the initial onset of COVID-19, whereas grains and oilseeds markets were not affected. Friedt and Zhang (2020) estimate that the pandemic reduced Chinese exports by 40–45 percent during the initial wave. The authors estimate that China's domestic supply shocks contributed about 10–15 percent of the total reduction in Chinese exports, while international import demand shocks reduced the propensity of countries' purchases of Chinese exports by only 5–10 percent. Kejzar and Velic (2020) characterize the impacts of COVID-19 on supply chains in terms of the relative upstream or downstream position of an industry. Recently, Beckman and Countryman (2021) found that agricultural trade increased by 2.3 percent in 2020; but the information they present is at a highly aggregated level—and only accounts for total 2020 trade, without providing the decomposition done here. Arita, Grant, and Sydow (2021) provided a preliminary "early look" assessment of the impacts on agricultural trade using quarterly country-level data on imports of agricultural and non-agricultural commodities in a non-directional framework using data through August 2020. This paper builds off this analysis by using a more rigorous bilateral estimation framework across disaggregated agricultural commodities and market regions, adds non-agricultural and manufacturing trade to the analysis, and includes a longer time period (complete 2020 calendar year).

This article provides a comprehensive retrospective quantitative assessment of the impacts of COVID-19 on food and agricultural trade. Specifically, we develop a monthly reduced form, gravity-based model of bilateral agricultural and non-agricultural trade and econometrically assess different dimensions of the global pandemic effect. We examine the extent to which COVID-19 affected bilateral trade in 2020 relative to the pre-pandemic era, using high-frequency monthly data and detailed agricultural product sectors to account for the heterogeneous impact of the pandemic on economic outcomes and differences in underlying requirements of product distribution. As the governmental response to the pandemic was diverse and many countries experienced several surges of COVID-19 infections, we leverage variation in country-specific mobility restrictions and national lockdown stringency to identify trade impacts. To the best of our knowledge, this study is the first to systematically quantify the differential impacts of the pandemic on agricultural versus non-agricultural trade using a full calendar year of monthly data.

Our analysis aims to unpack various components of the COVID-19 pandemic effect on trade and is organized as follows. First, we examine the impacts of the overall agricultural sector and compare them to quantified impacts on the non-agricultural sector. Our estimated pandemic effect is decomposed between COVID-19 incidence rates, policy restrictions, *de facto* reduction in human mobility/lockdown effects and further between import demand and export supply disruptions. Second, we disaggregate impacts across product types and stratify which products were most affected by the pandemic compared to product sectors that were unaffected or even benefited from its indirect effects. Third, we illustrate the differential impact of the pandemic across countries with differing development levels and income classification, highlighting in particular the more severe impacts on low-income countries. Fourth, our analysis examines how the pandemic impacts on trade may have shifted throughout the year as industries learned to operate within the health and safety guidelines necessitated by the pandemic. Finally, we examine the pandemic's impact on the extensive margin of trade using monthly US port level shipments.

Potential impacts of trade restricting and trade facilitating policy responses to the pandemic were not incorporated into this analysis, although we believe that any positive or negative effects these measures had on agricultural trade during the period were likely minimal. First, these measures covered a relatively small share of total agricultural and food trade. Evenett et. al. (2021) estimate that export restraints applied to agriculture and food trade during January–October 2020 covered $39.4 billion (3 percent) of total 2019 trade, while import reforms covered $42.2 billion (4 percent). Second, Evenett et. al. (2021) found that trade policy intervention in food trade was not as geographically widespread and more likely to be temporary relative to medical products and personal protective equipment (PPE), which accounted for almost all of the COVID-19-related trade policy responses. Third, relatively stable food supplies and prices prior to the pandemic likely reduced the broad, open-ended use of export controls as observed in earlier periods (e.g., 2007/08 and 2010/11) when grain stocks were low, and prices spiked. Heterogeneous trade policy responses, both in terms of duration and type of measure, as well as some countries' concurrent use of both trade restricting and trade facilitating measures, adds a great deal of complexity to such an analysis.[6] While not the focus of this article, we view this topic as a fruitful area for further exploration, particularly looking at differential commodity effects.

10.2   COVID-19, Agricultural Markets, and Global Trade Trends

In this section, we provide an overview of the implications of COVID-19 on agriculture markets and trade. Specifically, we summarize the latest trade data and document the main stylized facts and trends before and during the global pandemic. Food and agricultural production and trade are generally considered an essential industry in most countries, which meant many agricultural workers, producers, wholesalers, retailers, and distributors were able to continue moving agricultural product through the supply chain (Chenarides, Manfredo, and Richards 2020). However, as Yaffe-Bellany and Corkery (2020) and Lusk, Tonsor, and Schulz (2021) found, the shuttering of restaurants, hotels, bars, entertainment attractions, and schools due to lockdown policies resulted in supply chain disruptions for certain agricultural products, leaving some producers with very few buyers. The COVID-19 pandemic is a complicated event because it affects both aggregate demand and supply and is dependent on the nature of the industry, the exposure of workers to illness (Luckstead, Nayga Jr., and Snell 2021), and the ability of supply chains to adapt to sharp changes in the way final products are consumed (i.e., food at home).

10.2.1   COVID-19 Trade Disruption Not Historically Large

Disruptions to food and agricultural trade resulting from economic, natural, or trade policy induced shocks are not new. Figure 10.1 plots the quarterly percent change of global agricultural and non-agricultural trade from 2005Q1 through 2020Q4. Figure 10.2 presents monthly values of global agricultural and non-agricultural trade during the 2018–2020 period. Several sharp declines in trade stand out. First, the Great Recession of 2007–2009 marked the most significant collapse in trade. Global manufacturing trade fell by 30 percent. Global agricultural trade fell by 20 percent (figure 10.1). However, the economic expansion period that followed was one of the longest on record. From 2009Q3 through 2014Q4, global agricultural and non-agricultural trade growth remained positive (the exception of 2012Q3 for non-agricultural trade). Second, beginning in 2015, world trade experienced a significant slowdown; commodity prices fell from their recent highs,

---

6. In a separate study, Ahn and Steinbach (2021) examined the determinants and factors that prompted countries to implement NTMs during the pandemic. Their study found that for the agricultural and food sector, the effects of COVID-19 cases were more correlated with facilitating trade than restricting it. Notably, they found a lower likelihood of trade-facilitating actions with domestic COVID-19 cases whereas they found a positive association for worldwide cases.

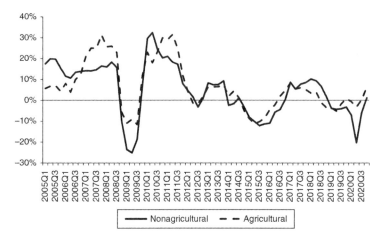

**Figure 10.1   Changes in the growth of the value of global trade in 2020 not histori-
cally large**

Note: Agricultural trade includes all HS codes defined under USDA's BICO definition of
Agricultural and Agricultural-related goods. Non-agricultural trade includes all other HS
codes.

Source: Author calculations using data from Trade Data Monitor, growth is in real terms.

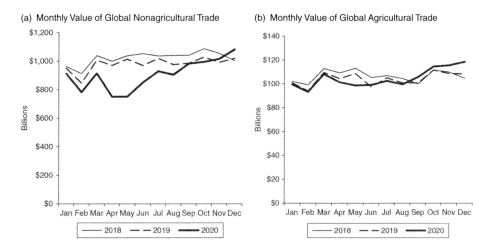

**Figure 10.2   Non-agricultural trade plunged in 2020; agricultural trade relatively
stable**

Note: Agricultural trade includes all HS codes defined under USDA's BICO definition of
Agricultural and Agricultural-related goods. Non-agricultural trade includes all other HS
codes (not including trade in services). Trade values in real terms.

Source: Author calculations using data from Trade Data Monitor.

the US dollar appreciated, and the IMF lowered its forecast for global economic growth (see also UNCTAD 2016). These global macro factors led to a slowdown in global trade, with US and global agricultural exports falling more than 10 percent, a steeper contraction than currently observed under COVID-19 (figure 10.1). Third, in 2018, a trade dispute between the US and China and several other trading partners led to a significant escalation in applied tariffs and a resulting decline in US-China agricultural and merchandise trade (Crowley 2019; Bown 2018; Bown 2019; Amiti, Redding, and Weinstein 2019; Grant et al. 2021); nevertheless, global quarterly trade growth fell only slightly below zero.

10.2.2   Agricultural Trade Relatively Stable under COVID-19

Agricultural trade under COVID-19 has been relatively stable. Global agricultural trade fell 2 percent in 2020Q2 during the initial wave of COVID-19 infections and lockdowns; however, food and agricultural trade rebounded significantly during 2020Q3 and 2020Q4 and ended the year up. On the other hand, non-agricultural trade under the COVID-19 pandemic in 2020Q2 experienced the second largest contraction in global trade since 2005. Non-agricultural trade subsequently experienced a strong recovery in Q3 and Q4, but still remained down by the end of 2020.[7] The smaller impact on agricultural trade may reflect the relatively lower income elasticity of food demand, particularly for staple food items, and the structure of the agricultural global value chains which is less fragmented than manufacturing and other merchandise trade. Additionally, agricultural trade, which occurs more substantially through bulk marine shipments, is likely to be less susceptible to disruption to transport restrictions in other sectors that require more human interaction (WTO, 2020b). Interestingly, compared to the Great Recession of 2007–2009, when agricultural trade fell by large amounts, trade under the pandemic has remained stable, even though in both instances global GDP fell (and the decline in GDP was larger for COVID-19).

10.2.3   Uneven Changes in Agricultural Trade

While overall aggregate changes in agricultural trade have been generally stable, there are differences at the product and country level. Figure 10.3 presents the percentage change in 2020 trade flows (in value and volume) relative to 2019 across product sector categories and trading countries. Products used to make higher-end goods such as hides and skins, cotton, rubber, and nursery are among the sectors that saw the largest contraction in trade during the COVID-19 pandemic. These sectors are more likely to have a higher income elasticity of demand and thus are relatively more sus-

---

7. Non-agriculture does not include trade in services. In 2020, global trade in services fell over 20 percent, reflecting a much more significant effect from the pandemic than merchandise trade.

Figure 10.3   Uneven changes in the value and volume of global agricultural trade

Source: Author calculations using data from Trade Data Monitor. Trade values in real terms.

ceptible to aggregate demand shocks and lockdowns. Retail sales of clothing and textiles plummeted as clothing and apparel stores closed, weaker demand for retail purchases due to stay at home orders, and lower incomes as unemployment increased or workers became furloughed. Secondly, there is a clear dichotomy between food products more likely to be consumed at home versus those being consumed away from home. For example, trade in sectors characterized by high restaurant or food away from home consumption, such as seafood, poultry, and beef products (Binkley and Liu 2019), have declined globally. In comparison, trade in staple products such as cereal grains and protein crops, which are more likely to be consumed at home or serve as intermediate inputs for processing, has increased. Finally, the role of workers falling ill at meat packaging plants and plant closures in the US, Brazil, and other major meat exporting countries was also expected to weigh on exports due to temporary supply disruptions (Lusk, Tonsor and Schulz 2021). However, on an annual basis, figure 10.3 illustrates that beef, poultry, and especially pork increased significantly compared to 2019 trade values.

10.2.4   Other Agricultural Trade Shocks Occurring in 2020:
          Record China Import Demand, African Swine Fever (ASF),
          and Policy Changes

When examining year over year changes in trade, it is important to recognize that there are additional trade shocks that have occurred outside COVID-19. Simple year over year changes indicate that pork and oilseeds have experienced among the highest growth in 2020, an increase driven by ASF that has ravaged herd populations in China, Asia, and other parts of the world. China— which prior to ASF consumed almost half the world's pork supply—has faced severe supply shortfalls (down more than 20 percent since 2018), and has imported record amounts of pork, raising global prices.

As China's pig herd recovered and was further consolidated into more grain-fed operations, China's import demand for grains and oilseeds grew substantially with soybean imports expanding by an additional $4 billion in 2020. Corn and coarse grain imports also surged on China's restocking efforts, increased demand from the larger and more grain intensive pig herd; wheat imports also increased as China has shifted some of the wheat grains to feed. The US-China Phase One agreement may also have supported further imports with selective waivers on retaliatory tariffs and liberalization of non-tariff measures on many key import sectors.

China, in fact, drives much of the overall observed global growth in 2020. Figure 10.4 shows that of the $20 billion increase in global agricultural trade in 2020, China accounted for over 95 percent of that growth and fueled higher global commodity prices. Excluding increased China demand, the world would have experienced virtually zero agricultural trade growth in 2020. East-Asia (excluding China) and North America (excluding US) stand out in particular in terms of weak import growth.

10.3   Econometric Approach and Data

10.3.1   Econometric Model

Descriptive analysis suggests that agricultural trade has been generally stable under COVID-19. However, most of this assessment has relied on

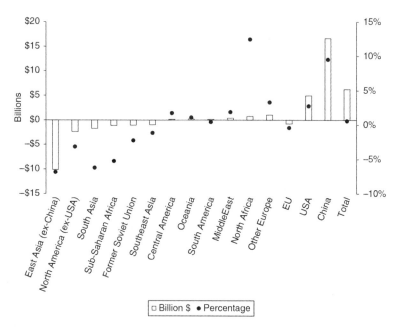

Figure 10.4   Agricultural trade growth in 2020 dominated by strong import demand in China. Figure shows change in value of agricultural imports year over year (2020 versus 2019).

Source: Author calculations using data from Trade Data Monitor, deflated into real dollars.

simple year over year changes that ignores confounding natural (i.e., ASF) and policy-induced (i.e., US-China Phase One) factors. To isolate the effect of COVID-19, we employ a rigorous monthly panel data econometric model of disaggregated product-line bilateral trade relationships. This approach exploits variation in country-and-month-specific indicators to estimate the (partial) direct trade effects of the pandemic-induced shock using a theoretically consistent model of bilateral trade flows at the product level as presented by Yotov et al. (2016), Peterson et al. (2013), Baldwin and Taglioni (2006), and Head and Mayer (2014). Following Grant et al. (2021), this approach is further extended by the use of a monthly dimension which provides a further source of within-year variation specific to many agricultural commodity exports. This framework has also been employed by Fajgelbaum et al. (2020) and Carter and Steinbach (2020), who investigated the impacts of the 2018–2019 trade war on manufacturing and agricultural product-line trade controlling for pre-trends and seasonality.

The gravity model used here is not fully structural as in Anderson and Yotov (2016) in conditional or full endowment general equilibrium (GE). By design, the GE gravity setup requires intra-national trade flows (i.e., trade with self) which is nearly impossible to obtain across months within years.

Thus, our results are consistent with best practices to estimate partial direct effects also advocated by Yotov et al. (2016) and Grant et al. (2021).

Denote exporting (importing) countries as i (j) and products, months, and years as k, m, and t, respectively. Using monthly panel data from January 2016 through December 2020 of bilateral-product-month relationships ($ijkm$), our baseline estimating equation to quantify the trade effect of COVID-19 on agricultural and non-agricultural exports is:

$$(1) \quad X_{ijkmt} = \exp\{\mu_{ijkm} + \pi_{it} + \varphi_{jt} + \kappa_{kt} + \xi_{mt} + \gamma_1 \text{Cov19}_{imt} + \gamma_2 \text{Cov19}_{jmt}\} + \varepsilon_{ijkmt},$$

where exp denotes the exponential function, X_{ijkmt} is the value of bilateral trade between exporting country i, importing country j, product group k, month m ($m = 1, 2, \ldots 12$), and year t ($t = 2016, 2017, \ldots 2019, 2020$). Equation (1) contains a comprehensive set of exporter-importer-product-month specific fixed effects,[8] μ_{ijkm}, designed to absorb all time-invariant product-and-month specific bilateral trade cost or natural trading partner effects.[9] Such trade cost factors include existing non-tariff measures (see Grant and Arita 2017; Ning and Grant 2019), transportation costs (i.e., distance), existing free trade agreements (i.e., US-Korea, China-Australia, etc.), bilateral applied tariffs, time-invariant natural, cultural and geographical factors, as well as within-year seasonality of supply and demand of product k. In addition to μ_{ijmk}, we also include importer-year (φ_{jt}), exporter-year (π_{it}), product-year (κ_{kt}) fixed effects, and month-year (ξ_{mt}) fixed effects, which are time varying, but not bilateral-specific, to control for changes in a country's overall inward or outward multilateral agri-food trade resistance (it, jt) and year-to-year fluctuations in global commodity prices (kt) or shifts in global agricultural trade patterns.

The direct and indirect effects of COVID-19 are captured from both the export and import side. Cov19_{imt} (Cov19_{jmt}) is an exporter-month-year (importer-month-year) specific COVID-19 variable designed to capture the influence of cases, deaths, lockdowns, and mobility impacts on an exporter's (importer's) trade with all partners. COVID-19 is a complicated multifac-

---

8. In their sensitivity analysis, Grant et al. (2021) included different degrees of fixed effects, with some specifications not including the full set of dummies (i.e., the exclusion of jt, kt, or mt). Results of their finding were generally robust to the different sets of fixed effects; however, the full set was viewed as being the most exhaustive in absorbing unobserved effects that would otherwise show up in the error term, and thus forms the basis of our estimations here. Estimates employing a smaller set of fixed effects (excluding π_{it}, φ_{jt}, and/or ξ_{kt}) were also performed and found to be largely robust to the full set of fixed effects. These estimates are available upon request.

9. For example, US-Canada, US-Mexico trade in many product lines is naturally higher than many other country-pairs in the model because of some shared border, language, cultural, and institutional similarities between USMCA/NAFTA partners. If we instead tried to leverage variation between country-pairs in the model for identification, we would miss the important fact that there are preexisting trends and trade relationships that are specific to country-pair-product and month (i.e., US exports of soybeans to China peak in the post-harvest fall season, whereas Brazilian soybean exports are counter-seasonal and peak in the US's spring planting season).

eted shock, and there is no single indicator that can reflect the entirety of its impact. Thus, we employ a battery of indicators attempting to capture different elements of its trade effect as discussed in the data section.

As suggested by Santos Silva and Tenreyro (2006), we adopt the Poisson-Pseudo-Maximum Likelihood PPML estimator because it retains the multiplicative theoretical structure of gravity type models (equation 1). It is also robust to unknown patterns of heteroskedasticity and allows the dependent variable to remain in levels (as opposed to logarithms) permitting the inclusion of zero trade flows in estimation. Zero trade flows are key in the context of assessing trade policy or pandemic-induced trade shocks at the product level, and for cases of thinner trade relationships among least developed economies for exports of certain processed food products. If the reason for zero trade is related to the COVID-19 pandemic in certain months, then omission of zero trade flows creates the classic sample selection bias leading to underestimation of trade impacts.

Finally, whereas equation (1) investigates the impact of COVID-19 on the value and volume (i.e., levels) of agricultural and non-agricultural trade, it may be the case that the pandemic's more severe disruptions occurred through supply chain logistical delays and reductions in the number of product shipments during heightened shutdown or mitigation periods to control the virus's spread. That is, the pandemic may have affected the extensive margin (number of product shipments) relatively more than the intensive margin (value or volume exported per product) of trade. US census trade data track monthly export shipments at district, port, and airport locations. In total we have monthly US export data for 353 ports and 52 airports for a total of 401 shipment localities.

Denoting ports as p, the extensive margin effect of COVID-19 is estimated as follows:

$$(2) \qquad N_{pmt} = \exp\{\mu_{pm} + \alpha_t + \gamma_1 \text{Cov19}_{smt}\} + \varepsilon_{pmt},$$

where, N_{pmt} is the extensive margin of trade defined as the count of the number of product shipments to the world market from port p, in month m and year t. All port-level exports to the global market are included for the years 2017 and 2020 of monthly data.[10] We chose 2017 as the pre-pandemic reference year when evaluating the extensive margin to mitigate any potential slowdown in some port-level shipments of agricultural products due to the US-China trade dispute. During this dispute, some agricultural shipments halted, and certain products ended up in storage as the trade dispute continued. μ_{pm} and α_t are a comprehensive set of port-month and year fixed effects, respectively. In equation (1) the COVID-19 incidence rates, lockdown

10. Because of download restrictions when accessing port level shipment data, we do not include a bilateral trade dimension (i.e., port-by-destination market), and products are defined at the HS4-digit level.

policy stringency, and mobility indicators were defined at the country level. Because port locations can be mapped directly to US states, we employ COVID-19 case and death incidence, policy stringency, and mobility indicators at the state level. Specifically, in equation (2), $Cov19_{smt}$ represents state-specific COVID-19 cases, deaths, Oxford Policy Stringency and Google Mobility indices across months, where s, m, and t denote state, month, and year, respectively. If COVID-19 affected the extensive-product margin of trade—as measured by product throughput per port—then we would expect γ_1 to be negative (positive in the case of Google Mobility indicators).

10.3.2   Data

Monthly bilateral exports from January 2016 through December 2020 reported by 93 countries to 207 importing markets are retrieved from Trade Data Monitor.[11] The sample includes 57 agricultural and related product groups as defined by USDA's Bulk, Intermediate and Consumer-Oriented products (see appendix A and appendix B for a list of country sample and commodity grouping). Thus, an observation comprises a country pair, BICO product, month, and year. We also collect aggregate non-agricultural trade data from the same source. Given the nearly 5,000 HS6-digit product codes comprising non-agriculture, we aggregate all non-agricultural products into a single sector. While this likely masks some of the pandemic's effect on individual manufacturing sectors (i.e., vehicles and parts, aircraft, electronics), it does provide a benchmark comparison from which to judge the agricultural trade effects.

US port-level exports are retrieved from the US Census Bureau.[12] For each port we observe the monthly total value and shipping weight (i.e., volume) of exports for each HS4 product. Total export values and volumes are further broken out into the value of seaborne containerized vessel exports and the value of airborne exports to the world market. We have global exports for 428 port locations in the US and a total of 501,482 port-month observations comprising the years 2017 and 2020. The extensive margin of product throughput per port is the count of the number of HS4 product exports for each month in year t. In terms of total export values, the largest ports in 2020 were New Orleans, Houston, Oakland, and Los Angeles with $19, $17.7, $15.1, and $12 billion of total agricultural export values, respectively. However, in terms of containerized vessels, Oakland, Los Angeles, Long Beach, and New York City were the largest, with 2020 agricultural exports

11. Trade Data Monitor data are available by subscription at https://tradedatamonitor.com/. Exporter reported information was selected relative to importer reported information, since the former has arguably less data lag between transaction (time when trade sale occurred) and COVID-19 events. We also tested import reported information and found the results consistent with the export reported information.

12. Accessed at: https://usatrade.census.gov/.

of $14.2, $11.3, $10.6, and $7.4 billion. New York City, Miami, Boston, and Detroit saw the largest airborne shipments in 2020.

COVID-19 indicators used in this study are collected from the following sources:

i. *Direct outbreaks*: increase in the number of coronavirus cases or deaths reported in importing country j and exporting country i per million people (Johns Hopkins University). These data are available at: https://github.com /CSSEGISandData/COVID-19.

ii. *Policy response*: Oxford Policy Stringency Index in importing country j and exporting country i. The Oxford COVID-19 Government Response Tracker (OxCGRT) systematically collects information on several different common policy responses that governments have taken to respond to the pandemic on 18 indicators such as school closures and travel restrictions. It now has data for more than 180 countries. The Oxford Stringency Index ranges from 0–100. These data are available at: https://www.bsg.ox.ac.uk /research/research-projects/covid-19-government-response-tracker.

iii. *De facto reduction in human mobility/lockdown effect*: Community Mobility indicator in importing country [deviation from pre-COVID-19 baseline] using workplace and retail people traffic are retrieved from Google Mobility data, available at: https://www.google.com/COVID-19/mobility/.

Figure 10.5 presents the distribution of COVID-19 cases and death rates per million residents, the Oxford Policy Stringency Index and Google's Workplace Mobility indicator. The mean of COVID-19 cases per million residents is 1,575 with a median of 172. Andorra, Belgium, Czech Republic, Croatia, Luxembourg, Montenegro, and Serbia experienced average monthly COVID-19 cases per million residents greater than 25,000. These more extreme cases incidences occurred in October through December of 2020. Mean COVID-19 deaths per million residents is 27 with a median of 5 and a maximum of 766. Belgium, Bulgaria, Croatia, Slovenia, and San Marino all experienced COVID-19 death rates per million residents above 500, which occurred in March, April, November, and December 2020. The government lockdown stringency index as reported by Oxford has a mean of 56 and a median of 58, a minimum of 1 and a maximum of 100 (100 indicates complete lockdown). Ten countries imposed lockdown stringencies that exceeded 90 on the index: Argentina, Azerbaijan, Guatemala, Honduras, India, Jordan, Philippines, Serbia, the State of Palestine, and Slovenia. Interestingly, China, which was often highlighted as imposing strict lockdown measures, was not on the top-10 list. China's highest Oxford Policy reading was 80, and it imposed this level of stringency for 4 out of 12 months in 2020 (i.e., a longer duration of more stringent policies to stop the viral spread). By comparison, Argentina's reading of 100 on the Oxford indicator was imposed only in April 2020.

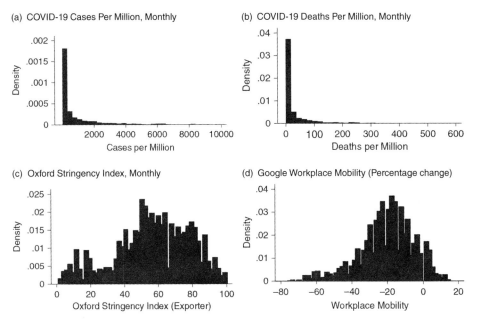

Figure 10.5   Distribution of COVID-19 cases, deaths, policy stringency and Google Mobility, March 2020 to December 2020

Source: Author calculations using cases and death rates data from Johns Hopkins University, Policy Stringency data from Oxford, and Workplace and Retail Mobility from Google. COVID-19 cases are truncated at 10,000 monthly cases per million residents to ease horizontal axis scaling. Similarly, monthly COVID-19 deaths per million residents care truncated at 600.

10.4   Econometric Results

The econometric results are organized according to different dimensions and components by which COVID-19 may be affecting international trade. Subsection one reports the overall effects on non-agriculture and agriculture. The second subsection presents the disaggregated effects on individual agricultural trade values and volumes. The third subsection examines the impacts across regions focusing in particular on how trade between low income countries were affected. In the fourth subsection we address within-year timing and dynamics of the COVID-19 trade effect. Finally, in the fifth subsection we estimate the extent to which COVID-19 indicators may have impacted the extension margin of US port shipments.

10.4.1   Estimated Sector Level Effects of Non-agricultural vs. Agricultural Trade

What is the effect of COVID-19 on global trade in 2020, holding other factors constant? Table 10.1 presents the aggregate sector level effects for

Table 10.1 Estimated impact of COVID−19 on the value of bilateral trade: non−agricultural vs. agricultural goods

VARIABLES	Non−Ag Goods value (1)	Ag value (2)	Non−Ag Goods value (3)	Ag value (4)	Non−Ag Goods value (5)	Ag value (6)	Non−Ag Goods value (7)	Ag value (8)	Non−Ag Goods value (9)	Non−Ag Goods value (10)
COVID Cases Exporter	-0.004***	0.002								
	(0.00)	(0.00)								
COVID Cases Importer	0.001	-0.003*								
	(0.00)	(0.00)								
COVID Deaths Exporter			-0.177**	-0.042					0.120*	-0.035
			(0.07)	(0.06)					(0.07)	(0.04)
COVID Deaths Importer			-0.167**	-0.248***					0.041	-0.085*
			(0.07)	(0.06)					(0.08)	(0.05)
Oxford Policy Stringency Exporter					-0.455***	-0.044			0.002	0.022
					(0.06)	(0.03)			(0.05)	(0.03)
Oxford Policy Stringency Importer					-0.144***	-0.204***			0.072*	0.012
					(0.04)	(0.05)			(0.04)	(0.03)
Google Workplace Mobility Exporter							0.396***	0.163***	0.443***	0.105**
							(0.05)	(0.04)	(0.07)	(0.05)
Google Retail Mobility Importer							0.249***	0.143***	0.299***	0.135***
							(0.03)	(0.02)	(0.05)	(0.04)
Observations	560,288	494,400	550,098	485,309	558,093	492,792	753,584	644,922	496,991	440,651

Note: The Dep. variable is value of trade estimated with PPML. Includes *ijm*, *it*, *jt*, *mt*, fixed effects. Standard errors are in parentheses and robust to clustering on *ijm*. *, **, and *** denote statistical significance at the 10, 5, and 1 percent levels, respectively. Estimated on monthly data from Jan. 2016 to Dec. 2020. Agricultural trade includes all HS codes defined under USDA's BICO definition of Agricultural and Agricultural−related goods; non-agricultural trade includes all other HS codes. Negative effect on trade is implied by a negative sign for cases and death counts and Oxford Policy Stringency and a positive sign for Google Mobility indices. Johns Hopkin's case/death counts are rescaled per a thousand, and Oxford Policy Stringency and Google Mobility indicators are rescaled to a 0−100 percent scale.

both the value of non-agricultural and agricultural trade for different indicators of the pandemic effect. All estimations include bilateral-month (i_{jm}), importer-year (i_t), exporter-year (j_t), and month-year (m_t) fixed effects. Since the estimates are performed at the overall sector level, product level fixed effects are omitted, and all standard errors are clustered by country-pair-and-month.[13]

Columns 1–4 report the estimated direct effect of the outbreak. The insignificant or small size of the coefficients suggests a very limited direct effect of the pandemic. For agricultural trade, a significant effect is found only on the death counts reported by the importing country. The coefficients in column 4 imply that each additional fatality per million people due to COVID-19 is associated with a 0.018 percent reduction in monthly agricultural trade. In our sample, the average number of new COVID-19 deaths reported per month, across all countries, is 27. Applying the estimated coefficient to the mean death count indicates that COVID-19 reduced agricultural trade by −0.5 percent, on average, throughout 2020. For non-agricultural trade, the direct COVID-19 effect for death counts is significant on both the exporter and importer side; however, the average effect implied by our coefficient estimates amounts to only a 1.1 percent reduction. The effect of COVID-19 case counts is largely negligible.

The stronger effect of the pandemic is more likely to be driven by the policy response of governments attempting to curb outbreaks and the mandatory and voluntary quarantining of individuals. The next set of results supports this. Columns 5 and 6 report the estimated impact of the Oxford Policy response. For non-agricultural trade, the coefficients are negative and statistically significant on both the exporter and importer COVID-19 indicator. A one unit increase in an importer's policy restrictiveness due to COVID-19 leads to reduction of agricultural trade of 0.2 percent. In 2020, the average importing countries' policy index was elevated to 52 percent. Applying our estimated coefficient to this average indicates that government policy response to COVID-19 reduced agricultural trade flows by 10 percent, on average. Similar to the direct effect, policy restrictions on the importer side were also negative and significant for agricultural trade, but not significant on the export side. The results may suggest that the COVID-19 effect may have been more significant through import demand channels rather than export supply. In contrast, exporter's policy response to COVID-19 is found to be much stronger for non-agricultural trade, which could be attributed to the more vulnerable supply chains occurring in non-agricultural trade that are typically longer and more complex than agricultural supply chains.

---

13. Estimates were also performed at the product level with product level fixed effects (using BICO codes). Results are provided in appendix C. The estimates on effects of the trade value with product effects are strongly robust to the estimates at the overall agricultural sector level. A separate set of estimates was also performed in terms of volumes, which was also found to be robust to the estimates in terms of value.

Columns 7 and 8 report the human mobility reduction/de facto lockdown effect of the COVID-19 using the Google Mobility indicators. Coefficients for the level of workplace mobility on the exporter side and retail mobility on the import side are positive for both non-agriculture and agriculture.[14] A 1 percent decrease in the level of workplace mobility for an exporter relative to the periods prior to COVID-19 led to a 0.4 percent reduction in non-agricultural trade and a 0.16-percent reduction in agricultural trade. In our sample the average level of workplace traffic fell by 17.8 percent under the pandemic, and retail traffic by 19.1 percent. Applying these averages to the estimated coefficients implies a 6 percent reduction in the average agricultural trade flow. By comparison, the de facto lockdown effect is about twice as large for non-agricultural trade.

Columns 9 and 10 report the results estimating all components jointly. We recognize that these variables may exhibit significant multicollinearity and thus several of the individual coefficients lose significance. Similar to the previous columns we find that the estimated effect is larger for non-agricultural than agricultural trade (twice as large). Interestingly, the COVID-19 effect seems to convey more significance on the import demand side for agricultural trade, whereas for non-agricultural trade it appears to impact export supply more severely.

It is also of interest to note the differences implied by the econometric findings relative to the simple year over year changes reported in the previous section. While year over year changes in global agricultural trade were up +2 percent in 2020, our econometric estimations (which control for other factors outside the pandemic) find statistically significant negative effects. The results suggest an approximate impact on the range of a 5–10 percent reduction in agricultural trade as predicted by the model due to COVID-19 direct and indirect factors. While two to three times smaller than non-agricultural trade, the results provide quantitative evidence that agricultural trade was not entirely resilient. Our findings also provide empirical support that policy restrictions and de facto lockdowns imposed by the importing countries are the main channels of trade loss.

10.4.2   Which Commodities Were Most Severely Impacted by the Pandemic?

In addition to some of the contrasting impacts of COVID-19 between agriculture and non-agriculture sectors, our earlier descriptive analysis also suggested noticeable differences within the agricultural sector. To understand how COVID-19 effects vary across individual product sectors, in this section we perform estimations at the commodity level as defined by USDA agricultural and agricultural-related (BICO) product groups. For these sets

---

14. Recall, Google Mobility indicators are in terms of deviations from a pre-pandemic benchmark, whereby reduced mobility implies a negative deviation. If reduced mobility is expected to decrease agricultural and non-agricultural trade, then we expect the sign on the mobility coefficients to be positive.

of estimations we estimate the joint effect of COVID-19, including direct (death counts per million), policy response (Oxford Policy Stringency), and de facto lockdown (Google Mobility) on both the importer and exporter side.[15] Case counts are not included in this specification due to the weak significance of these results found within the overall agricultural sector as reported in table 10.1.

Appendix D shows the estimation results, across individual commodities. The findings indicate very heterogeneous COVID-19 effects. In some commodities we find very large and significant negative effects, whereas others are found to carry insignificant or even positive effects. We find that 25 percent of the commodities suffered a significant negative effect from the incidence rate (death counts) impact of the pandemic, 50–55 percent from policy restrictions, and 35–40 percent from the de facto lockdown effect. In contrast, about 10 percent of the commodities are found to have experienced a positive impact from COVID-19, likely through demand shifting. Notably a slight majority of commodities (55–60 percent), were not found to be insignificantly affected by the pandemic.

Table 10.2 attempts to stratify the impacts of the pandemic across scenarios. It employs the coefficient estimates in table 10.3 and applies a one standard deviation shock to each of the COVID-19 effects (death counts, policy response, and de facto lockdown), and quantifies the resulting impact by commodities. The results are sorted from lowest to highest of the average impact across all indicators. Non-food agricultural commodities—hides and skins (−15 percent); ethanol (−10 percent); cotton (−7 percent); nursery flowers (−6 percent); rubber (−5 percent)—are found to have suffered the highest impacts. Certain meat products (−5 percent) and seafood (−5 percent), beef (−4 percent), poultry (−3 percent), and pork (−2 percent) also suffered among the most severe disruptions. Distilled spirits; tea; and sugar and sweeteners are among the other agri-food areas found to have been significantly negatively impacted.

It is of interest to note how our econometric results differ from simple year over year changes in other commodities. According to our estimates, global pork trade was reduced on average by 2 percent given a one standard deviation sized shock in COVID-19 policy restrictions and de facto lockdown effect. This stands in strong contrast to the over 20 percent increase in global growth as shown through simple year over year changes presented in section 10.2.3, which was driven by ASF. Rapeseed, which experienced an 11 percent increase in global trade in 2020, largely on confounding supply side shocks,[16] was found to be insignificantly impacted by COVID-19 in terms of the direct and indirect effects. Our estimation thus appears able to at least partially disentangle the COVID-19 effect for these commodities. For beef trade—

15. Estimations were also performed for individual sets of COVID-19 indicators and are available upon request.

16. For instance, EU rapeseed production suffered under droughts and disease, leading to a significant import demand increase in 2020 (Reuters 2020).

Table 10.2 COVID−19 trade impact across commodities

Product−group	1. Direct Effect (Deaths per million)	2. Policy Response (Oxford Stringency)	3. Human mobility reduction (Google)	4. Average (average of Direct, Policy Response, and Google Mobility effects)
Hides and skins	0%	−22%	−24%	−15%
Ethanol	−7%	−7%	−16%	−10%
Corn	0%	0%	−22%	−7%
Cotton	0%	−11%	−10%	−7%
Distilled spirits	−5%	−5%	−10%	−6%
Nursery flowers	−5%	−9%	−4%	−6%
Meat products NESOI	−3%	−8%	−5%	−5%
Essential oils	−6%	−4%	−5%	−5%
Rubber allied gums	0%	−4%	−11%	−5%
Fish products	−2%	−7%	−6%	−5%
Tea	0%	−6%	−9%	−5%
Sugars sweeteners		−6%	−7%	−5%
Forest products	0%	−3%	−9%	−4%
Beef	−3%	−3%	−6%	−4%
Cocoa beans	0%	−11%	0%	−4%
Poultry	−3%	−3%	−4%	−3%
Tobacco	−3%	−7%	0%	−3%
Snack foods NESOI	−1%	−3%	−3%	−3%
Coffee unroasted	2%	0%	−9%	−3%
Peanuts	0%	−8%	0%	−3%
Pork	−2%	−2%	−3%	−2%
Biodiesel blends	0%	0%	−6%	−2%
Wheat	−6%	0%	0%	−2%
Chocolate cocoa products	−1%	−3%	−1%	−2%
Hay	−5%	0%	0%	−2%
Eggs	0%	−4%	0%	−1%
Feeds fodders NESOI	0%	−4%	0%	−1%
Pet food	0%	−3%	0%	−1%
Processed vegetables	0%	−3%	0%	−1%
Spices	2%	−5%	0%	−1%
Food prep.	0%	−2%	0%	−1%
Other int. products	0%	−2%	0%	−1%
Fresh fruit	0%	0%	−1%	0%
Animal fats	0%	0%	0%	0%
Distillers grains	0%	0%	0%	0%
Fresh vegetables	0%	0%	0%	0%
Fruit vegetable juices	0%	0%	0%	0%
Non alcoholic bev	0%	0%	0%	0%
Palm oil	0%	0%	0%	0%
Pulses	0%	0%	0%	0%
Rapeseed	0%	0%	0%	0%
Soybean meal	0%	0%	0%	0%
Vegetable oils NESOI	0%	0%	0%	0%
Condiment sauces	1%	−2%	2%	0%
Processed fruit	1%	0%	0%	0%
Live animals	2%	0%	0%	1%
Dairy products	0%	3%	0%	1%
Oilseed meal	3%	0%	0%	1%
Tree nuts	0%	−8%	12%	1%
Coffee roasted extracts	1%	3%	0%	1%
Other bulk commodities	0%	5%	0%	2%

Table 10.2   **(continued)**

Product−group	1. Direct Effect (Deaths per million)	2. Policy Response (Oxford Stringency)	3. Human mobility reduction (Google)	4. Average (average of Direct, Policy Response, and Google Mobility effects)
Rice	4%	0%	4%	3%
Planting seeds	2%	5%	2%	3%
Soybean oil	9%	0%	0%	3%
Soybeans	0%	34%	0%	11%

Note: Impact applies cofficients estimated in table 10.2 to a one standard deviation shock of each COVID-19 indicator. One standard deviation is approximately equivalent to: Death counts-50 people per million; Oxford Policy Stringency-15 percent; and Google Mobility-10 percent. Column 4 is simple average of first three columns.

which had increased in 2020 relative to 2019—our results found a 4 percent decline given a one standard deviation shock, which is consistent with the supply chain disruptions that occurred in major producing countries.

We find that for many of the grains and oilseeds and prepared and processed foods there is a relatively small or insignificant effect. The stratification of estimated impacts seems to generally align with what has been found in the income demand elasticity literature. Non-food-related products are typically found to be the most sensitive to income shocks, followed by higher-value meat and specialty products, then staple grains and oilseeds. Consistent with the simple year over year changes, rice—a perennial staple food item—increased 4 percent given a one standard deviation COVID-19 incidence death rate or a one standard deviation in de facto lockdown effect. Soybeans are found to have a significant positive effect from the Oxford Policy restrictions. This could be attributed to increased demand driven by China's recovering herd size and thus reflecting a possible limitation in our approach to completely isolate the COVID-19 impact; however, the effect is insignificant in terms of death counts and de facto lockdown effect.

We also estimated the impact of COVID-19 on volume of trade. By focusing on volumes, we control for commodity price changes and isolate the impacts in terms of real changes in shipments.[17] Results are reported in appendix E and are found to be largely consistent with the estimations performed on values and roughly similar in magnitude.

10.4.3   Are Low Income Country Agricultural Trade Flows More Vulnerable to the Pandemic?

Concerns have been raised that COVID-19 may disproportionally affect low income countries more severely compared to high income countries. On the demand side, low income countries spend a much larger share of their

17. We note that our estimations on values do include month-time fixed effects, which at least partially controls for seasonality and price effects.

household budgets on food, and thus their purchases are more sensitive to income changes that may be caused by COVID-19. Further, low income countries may also be more vulnerable to supply chain disruptions. Ex-ante assessments indicate significant impacts on lower income countries. For example, using the USDA Economic Research Service Food Security model, Baquedano et al. (2021) found that 160 million additional people across the world may face insecurity as result of the COVID-19 pandemic.[18] Separately, the FAO estimated that an additional 118 million would become food insecure as a result of the pandemic (FAO et al. 2021). This section empirically examines whether we can detect any evidence of a disproportionate impact on low income country agricultural trade.

Table 10.3 performs the estimations according to selected subsamples which partition the data into income groups defined by the World Bank. Low income groups are defined as countries with a GNI per capita of less than $4k, middle income countries $4k–$12.5k, and high income >$12.5k. China, for example, is a middle income country. The results in table 10.4 report varying degrees of significance across the different specifications. Overall the differences across COVID-19 indicators and income groups tend to be mixed. The de facto level of lockdown for the importing country is generally larger for trade within low income countries relative to trade within high income countries. A 10 percent increase (approximately equivalent to a one standard deviation) of the de facto lockdown effect leads to a 5 percent reduction in low income to low income agricultural exports but only a 3 percent reduction for high income to high income trade. However, the effects of government policy responses is mixed. Low income to middle income agricultural exports are significant, but low income to low income agricultural exports are not significant. The overall results do not seem to provide compelling evidence that low income country agricultural trade was more severely impacted by the pandemic compared to agricultural trade between high income countries. However, we caveat that given the ongoing nature of the pandemic and rising COVID-19 outbreaks occuring in 2021 for several large developing nations, further research is warranted in assessing these differences. Finally, we also note that the coefficient on deaths per importer tends to be statistically significant (and negative) across all wealth/trade spectrums, while the coefficient on deaths per exporter is only significant in two scenarios (affecting exports to high income countries).

10.4.4   Pandemic Effects across Quarters

We also examine how COVID-19 impacted agricultural and non-agricultural trade during different periods of the pandemic. To perform

---

18. Study compares pre-pandemic forecasts from the ERS food security model to post-pandemic forecasts and finds an additional 160 million more insecure people in the post-forecast.

Table 10.3   Impact of COVID–19 on the value of bilateral agricultural trade, by country income groups

Level of Income	Low–Low (1)	Low–Mid (2)	Low–High (3)	Mid–Low (4)	Mid–Mid (5)	Mid–High (6)	High–Low (7)	High–Mid (8)	High–High (9)
COVID Deaths Exporter	-0.125	0.171	-0.080**	0.005	0.158	-0.154***	0.019	-0.020	-0.003
	(0.20)	(0.21)	(0.04)	(0.12)	(0.16)	(0.04)	(0.07)	(0.07)	(0.06)
COVID Deaths Importer	-0.077	-0.345**	-0.098**	-0.035	-0.230**	-0.138***	-0.331***	-0.327***	-0.258***
	(0.16)	(0.16)	(0.04)	(0.10)	(0.12)	(0.05)	(0.07)	(0.07)	(0.07)
Observations	184,546	194,227	255,460	241,435	249,147	297,309	319,875	325,724	358,712
Oxford Policy Stringency Exporter	-0.029	0.016	-0.094***	-0.146***	-0.064	-0.105***	0.054	0.020	-0.013
	(0.07)	(0.07)	(0.03)	(0.05)	(0.05)	(0.03)	(0.04)	(0.04)	(0.04)
Oxford Policy Stringency Importer	-0.095	-0.336***	-0.022	-0.115**	-0.235***	-0.054	-0.289***	-0.257***	-0.229***
	(0.06)	(0.09)	(0.03)	(0.05)	(0.07)	(0.03)	(0.07)	(0.06)	(0.07)
Observations	187,726	196,301	260,341	244,291	251,287	302,026	325,672	330,953	365,253
Google Workplace Mobility Exporter	0.258**	0.253***	0.166***	0.258***	0.335***	0.184***	0.077*	0.101**	0.124***
	(0.11)	(0.09)	(0.04)	(0.08)	(0.08)	(0.04)	(0.04)	(0.04)	(0.04)
Google Retail Mobility Importer	0.217***	0.096	0.077***	0.154***	0.114**	0.099***	0.193***	0.169***	0.154***
	(0.07)	(0.06)	(0.03)	(0.05)	(0.05)	(0.03)	(0.03)	(0.02)	(0.02)
Observations	289,913	251,152	318,745	346,947	308,473	364,132	449,892	427,673	467,559

Note: The Dep. variable is value of agricultural trade estimated with PPML. Includes ijm, it, jt, mt, fixed effects. Standard errors are in parentheses and robust to clustering on ijm. *, **, and *** denote statistical significance at the 10, 5, and 1 percent levels, respectively. Estimated on monthly data from Jan. 2016 to Dec. 2020. Agricultural trade includes all HS codes defined under USDA's BICO definition of Agricultural and Agricultural–related goods. Product groups defined by BICO codes. Income groups defined by World Bank Classification. High income countries have GNI per capita >$12.5k, Middle income $4–$12.5k, and Low Income <$4k. (1) Low–low means low income country exports to low income country, (2) low–mid means low income country exports to middle income country, and the rest of the columns follow accordingly. Negative effect on trade is implied by a negative sign for death counts and Oxford Policy Stringency and a positive sign for Google Mobility indices. For presentation purposes of the estimations, the Johns Hopkins case/death counts are rescaled per a thousand and Oxford Policy Stringency and Google Mobility indicators are rescaled to a 0–100 percent scale.

this analysis, we estimate quarter-specific regressions throughout 2020 for both the non-agricultural and agricultural sector. Table 10.4 reports the results. Columns 1–3 present the results using the number of deaths to explain agricultural and non-agricultural trade effects. The direct incidence rates are once again very limited and weak for both non-agricultural and agricultural trade. Columns 4–6 report the results using the Oxford Policy response. Here, the results are quite stark with a larger and more statistically significant negative COVID-19 effect under Q2 relative to Q3 and Q4. We also find that the de facto lockdown impact is most severely felt under Q2 and tends to lessen in Q3 and Q4. The joint effect indicates a similar finding.

We note that in some cases the effect is not only due to changes in the severity of COVID-19 indicators; it is also attributed to an attenuation of the COVID-19 effect across time. For instance, the coefficient results for the policy restrictiveness lessens from Q2 to Q4. We observe some similar weakening for the de facto coefficients, however, to a lesser degree. The results may suggest a learning effect whereby trade and supply chains may have adjusted to both the policy restrictions and de facto lockdown factors of COVID-19 following initial disruption in Q2.

10.4.5   Estimated Impacts along the Extensive Margin of US Agricultural Trade

In this final section, we consider whether the pandemic has impacted the number of agricultural product shipments passing through US ports. If the pandemic resulted in workers becoming ill, staying home, or mandatory shutdown of plants due to outbreaks of COVID-19, then perhaps the pandemic's effect on international trade is not necessarily through the value or volume of exports but in terms of the number of products exported as a measure of product throughput per port. US port-level data track product shipments in aggregate and by shipment method: containerized vessel versus airlifted shipments.

Table 10.6 presents the results after estimation of equation (2) using the Oxford Stringency Index of the policy response of state-level governments to the pandemic (Oxford), and percentage change in Google's Workplace Mobility (Workplace), also at the state level. Overall, the results suggest that US policy measures to contain the spread of the virus (Oxford) lead to a decrease in number of extensive product margin shipments per port (table 10.6, All Months, 2020). Across 428 port locations, the state-level Oxford Stringency index varies widely with a mean of 52 and a standard deviation of 24.[19] Thus a one (two) standard deviation increase in state governments' policy response to the de facto lockdown is representative of a 27 (92) percent increase around the mean. The results across all months in 2020 imply

---

19. The coefficient of variation is 0.46.

Table 10.4   Effects of COVID−19 on the value of non−agriculture bilateral trade by quarter

Quarter	Q2 (1)	Q3 (2)	Q4 (3)	Q2 (4)	Q3 (5)	Q4 (6)	Q2 (7)	Q3 (8)	Q4 (9)	Q2 (10)	Q3 (11)	Q4 (12)
COVID Deaths Exporter	-0.428***	-0.806***	-0.402***							0.110	-0.326**	0.126
	(0.13)	(0.17)	(0.11)							(0.11)	(0.15)	(0.08)
COVID Deaths Importer	-0.377***	-0.408*	0.108							-0.204*	-0.119	0.208**
	(0.13)	(0.24)	(0.09)							(0.11)	(0.16)	(0.09)
Oxford Policy Stringency Exporter				-0.662***	-0.473***	-0.530***				0.003	-0.004	-0.001
				(0.07)	(0.07)	(0.08)				(0.09)	(0.06)	(0.07)
Oxford Policy Stringency Importer				-0.334***	-0.095**	0.020				-0.132*	0.076*	0.013
				(0.04)	(0.05)	(0.05)				(0.07)	(0.05)	(0.05)
Google Workplace Mobility Exporter							0.458***	0.376***	0.577***	0.567***	0.367***	0.686***
							(0.07)	(0.06)	(0.08)	(0.12)	(0.09)	(0.11)
Google Retail Mobility Importer							0.360***	0.278***	-0.002	0.228***	0.292***	0.161**
							(0.04)	(0.03)	(0.04)	(0.07)	(0.05)	(0.08)
Observations	269,982	270,795	267,231	280,408	280,966	277,591	377,960	378,595	374,499	244,319	244,913	241,589

Note: The Dep. variable is value of agricultural trade estimated with PPML. Includes *ijm, it, jt, mt,* fixed effects. Standard errors are in parentheses and robust to clustering on *ijm*. *, **, and *** denote statistical significance at the 10, 5, and 1 percent levels, respectively. Estimated on monthly data from Jan. 2016 to Dec. 2020. Negative effect on trade is implied by a negative sign for death counts and Oxford Policy Stringency and a positive sign for Google Mobility indices. For presentation purposes of the estimations, the Johns Hopkins case/death counts are rescaled per a thousand and Oxford Policy Stringency and Google Mobility indicators are rescaled to a 0−100 percent scale.

Table 10.5   Effects of COVID–19 on value of agriculture bilateral trade by quarter

Quarter	Q2 (1)	Q3 (2)	Q4 (3)	Q2 (4)	Q3 (5)	Q4 (6)	Q2 (7)	Q3 (8)	Q4 (9)	Q2 (10)	Q3 (11)	Q4 (12)
COVID Deaths Exporter	-0.017	0.001	0.037							0.055	0.118	-0.042
	(0.07)	(0.13)	(0.15)							(0.06)	(0.11)	(0.08)
COVID Deaths Importer	-0.220***	-0.366**	-0.234*							-0.0836	-0.094	-0.025
	(0.07)	(0.15)	(0.13)							(0.06)	(0.16)	(0.08)
Oxford Policy Stringency Exporter				-0.123***	-0.038	-0.036				0.203***	0.077	0.000
				(0.04)	(0.04)	(0.06)				(0.06)	(0.05)	(0.06)
Oxford Policy Stringency Importer				-0.241***	-0.172**	-0.207**				-0.0012	-0.043	-0.005
				(0.06)	(0.07)	(0.10)				(0.05)	(0.05)	(0.05)
Google Workplace Mobility Exporter							0.259***	0.227***	0.244***	0.430***	0.262***	0.137
							(0.05)	(0.06)	(0.07)	(0.09)	(0.08)	(0.10)
Google Retail							0.121***	0.107***	0.058	0.091*	0.090	0.080
							(0.03)	(0.03)	(0.04)	(0.05)	(0.06)	(0.07)
Observations	237,977	238,163	235,525	247,517	247,527	245,162	323,281	323,814	320,767	216,309	216,452	214,024

Note: The Dep. variable is value of agricultural trade estimated with PPML. Includes *ijm*, *it*, *jt*, *mt*, fixed effects. Standard errors are in parentheses and robust to clustering on *ijm*. *, **, and *** denote statistical significance at the 10, 5, and 1 percent levels, respectively. Estimated on monthly data from Jan. 2016 to Dec. 2020. Negative effect on trade is implied by a negative sign for death counts and Oxford Policy Stringency and a positive sign for Google Mobility indices. For presentation purposes of the estimations, the Johns Hopkins case/death counts are rescaled per a thousand and Oxford Policy Stringency and Google Mobility indicators are rescaled to a 0–100 percent scale.

Table 10.6

Extensive margin impacts at the US port level for agricultural shipments, all months, 2017 and 2020

	No. Product Exports	No. Container Exports	No. Air Shipments	No. Product Exports	No. Container Exports	No. Air Shipments
All Months, 2020						
Oxford Policy Stringency	−0.079*** [0.010]	−0.070*** [0.019]	−0.117*** [0.017]			
Google Workplace Mobility				0.176*** [0.022]	0.126** [0.040]	0.253*** [0.034]
N	6,514	2,334	3,109	6,561	2,362	3,143
R^2	0.99	0.99	0.99	0.99	0.99	0.99
First Wave (Mar/Apr)						
Oxford Policy Stringency	−0.121** [0.037]	−0.029 [0.073]	−0.188** [0.065]			
Google Workplace Mobility				0.197*** [0.056]	0.069 [0.104]	0.298*** [0.087]
N	1,109	389	546	1,116	393	551
R^2	0.99	0.99	0.99	0.99	0.99	0.99
Second Wave (Jul/Aug)						
Oxford Policy Stringency	−0.027 [0.075]	0.121 [0.151]	−0.245 [0.162]			
Google Workplace Mobility				0.420* [0.173]	0.156 [0.290]	0.394* [0.246]
N	1,089	381	522	1,097	386	528
R^2	0.99	0.99	0.99	0.99	0.99	0.99
Third Wave (Nov/Dec)						
Oxford Policy Stringency	−0.075 [0.084]	0.039 [0.101]	−0.085 [0.148]			
Google Workplace Mobility				0.064 [0.133]	0.020 [0.249]	0.300* [0.173]
N	1,072	396	508	1,080	401	514
R^2	0.99	0.99	0.99	0.99	0.99	0.99

Note: The Dep. var. is the number of monthly agricultural product shipments per port for all US port localities including airports (No. of Product Exports); the number of containerized vessel exports per port (No. of Container Exports), and the number of airlifted shipments (No. of Air Shipments). All regressions include port−month and year fixed effects. *, **, *** denote statistical significance at the 10, 5, and 1 percent levels, respectively. Negative effect on trade is implied by a negative sign for Oxford Policy Stringency and a positive sign for Google Mobility indices.

a reduction of two (four) product shipments per port in 2020 on average for a one (two) standard deviation increase in the Oxford Stringency index. Similar results were obtained when evaluating the number of containerized product exports. For air shipments, however, the size of the coefficients is much more severe. Here, a one (two) standard deviation increase in state governments' Oxford Policy response is associated with three (six) fewer products transported by air per port.

The coefficients representing Oxford's state government response to the pandemic were generally larger during the first wave (First Wave, Mar/Apr) (with the exception of containerized exports). Thereafter, the effect of state governments' response on the extensive product margin of port-level shipments declined significantly in the second and third waves of the pandemic and became largely insignificant across modes of shipment. As reported previously, this could suggest a "learning effect" as workers and port managers better understood how to manage the policy restrictions necessitated by the pandemic. One exception is the coefficient on the policy response measured by the Oxford Stringency for air shipments during the second wave of the pandemic (-0.245). However, the coefficient is only significant beyond the 10 percent level (p-value = 0.13).

The remaining three columns in table 10.6 report the results using Google's Workplace Mobility indicator at the state level matched to port locations. Here, the pandemic's mean reduction in workplace mobility is 26 percent with a standard deviation across port-month locations of 8. The highest (absolute) reduction in workplace exceeding 60 percent occurred in Washington, D.C., Massachusetts, and New Jersey port locations. The results suggest that moving from a pre-pandemic mobility situation to the mean (-26 percent) results in five fewer product shipments per port overall and seven fewer product shipments that are transported by air. A one standard deviation move above the mean leads to two fewer shipments per port and four fewer air-transported product shipments. In contrast to the Oxford Policy impacts, the coefficient magnitudes tend to increase in the first and second waves of the pandemic. For example, during the summer wave (Second Wave, Jul/Aug) months, a further two standard deviation reduction in workplace mobility results in seven fewer product shipments per port overall and six fewer products transported by air. This translates to an approximate 10 percent contraction in the extensive margin of port-level agricultural trade in the US.

10.5   Conclusion

This study conducted a comprehensive one-year retrospective econometric assessment of the impact of the COVID-19 pandemic on global agricultural trade. Given the multifaceted nature of the pandemic's effect on domestic markets and global trade and supply chains, summarizing the pandemic's overall impact is challenging. However, several empirical findings are apparent as it relates to this pandemic and its effects on agricultural trade.

First, holding other factors constant, our estimates suggest that COVID-19 reduced overall agricultural trade by the approximate range of

5 to 10 percent, an effect two to three times smaller than our estimated effect for non-agricultural trade. The channels by which the pandemic has impacted agricultural trade is most evident through its de facto reduction in human mobility (voluntary or mandatory based) and secondly, government policy restrictions. Direct COVID-19 case and death count incidence was found to carry very limited association and quantifiable effects on trade. For agriculture trade, the negative impacts of the pandemic estimated by our model seem to be manifested more through import demand channels as opposed to export supply shocks.

Second, sharp differences in trade impacts were observed across agriculture commodities. However, the COVID-19 trade effect permeated in many non-food items (hides and skins, ethanol, rubber, cotton), which suffered the steepest trade losses. Meat products, including seafood, and higher-value agri-food products were also found to have been significantly negatively impacted. A few commodities experienced a positive impact, likely due to demand shifts for staple products (e.g., rice). Nevertheless, after an extensive empirical search the majority of agricultural commodities were not found to experience a significant trade impact from the pandemic, even when investigating quarterly within-year effects associated with various "waves" of the pandemic's more intense outbreaks and lockdown situations. We found evidence that trade flows adjusted to COVID-19 disruptions over time; however, for non-food items and some agricultural commodities, pandemic effects continued to persist through the end of 2020.

Third, several international organizations including the WTO and United Nations were concerned that the pandemic may impact low income developing countries relatively more because these countries may not be as well connected to global supply chains. However, we find limited and mixed evidence that low income and least developed countries' trade flows were more vulnerable to the COVID-19 shock, although future research should investigate this effect for key commodities of export interest to low income nations.

Finally, we found evidence that the pandemic impacted the extensive margin of agricultural trade. On average, product throughput as measured by the number of products exported per port per month fell by five overall and seven fewer products by air. At the mean, this suggests an 8 percent contraction in product shipments overall and 10 percent for products transported by air.

While this analysis shed light on the trade flow effects of the COVID-19 pandemic, the results should be put into perspective with the following caveats. First, the pandemic is still ongoing, and thus does not account for reemergence of outbreaks and ongoing surges occurring in 2021 and beyond. Second, the COVID-19 coefficients may be picking up other contemporaneous factors influencing bilateral trade not explicitly considered in this analysis. For example, several countries altered their export policies including export controls on products such as medical supplies, personal protective equipment (PPE), and some staple agricultural products. While many of these policies were temporary in nature (i.e., lasting only a month or two), the extent that these policies are correlated with the COVID-19 variables considered here could bias our estimates of the trade effects of de facto lockdown and immobility. Third, it would be interesting to disentangle monthly per capita income effects across countries in the sample that could be driving some of the results, particularly for higher valued nonfood items. For example, many of our COVID-19 government policy and de facto lockdown results were stronger on the import demand side, which could be the contemporaneous result of de facto lockdowns and declining per capita income. Although the 2020 (annual) income effect is absorbed by the importer-year fixed effect (jt), large monthly shocks to per-capita incomes are likely not well accounted for by country-time effects.[20] Additional variables that more fully describe within-year seasonality and international agricultural markets and food supply chains should improve the performance of gravity-based models at the monthly level. Finally, there may be important dynamics underlying the COVID-19 indicators and the time in which trade flows are recorded in the data. That is, there may be some incongruity between the time when COVID-19 cases, deaths, government responses, and decreased mobility indicators are surging, reflecting more serious phases of the pandemic and the time with which trade flow changes appear in countries' national statistics. On the other hand, while these lags may be important in the data and not fully captured in the current analysis, we tested alternative lag structures among the COVID-19 indicators with resulting estimates largely robust.[21]

To return to the original question posed in this article's title, Has global agricultural trade been resilient under COVID-19? The findings of our study suggest a *qualified* yes. Yes, this study did indeed find evidence of resilience, in that the econometric results found relatively small (but still statistically significant) negative effects of the pandemic that was robust along many dimensions of analysis and slices of the data—which could be interpreted as a testament of the stability of agricultural trade, at least in aggregate. However, we would also temper any broad conclusions given the high degree of evenness of impacts found by our analysis, which included evidence of severe disruptions for some sectors within agriculture. While the pandemic is still ongoing and direct and indirect effects continue to permeate across the international trading landscape, the findings summarized above offer useful empirical insights about how agricultural trade fares through a major global health crisis.

20. On the other hand, for many countries, income effects may have been stabilized, in part, through fiscal stimulus measures (IMF 2021).
21. Estimates available upon request.

Appendix A

Appendix 10A.1 List of countries in data set

Exporters			Importers			
Albania	India	Senegal	Afghanistan	Ecuador	Liberia	Saudi Arabia
Argentina	Indonesia	Serbia	Albania	Egypt	Libya	Senegal
Australia	Ireland	Singapore	Algeria	El Salvador	Lithuania	Serbia
Austria	Israel	Slovakia	Andorra	Estonia	Luxembourg	Sierra Leone
Bahrain	Italy	Slovenia	Angola	Ethiopia	Macao	Singapore
Belarus	Japan	South Africa	Argentina	Fiji	Madagascar	Slovakia
Belgium	Jordan	South Korea	Armenia	Finland	Malaysia	Slovenia
Belize	Kazakhstan	Spain	Australia	France	Maldives	Somalia
Bolivia	Kenya	Sri Lanka	Austria	French Polynesia	Mali	South Africa
Bosnia	Kosovo	Sweden	Azerbaijan	Gabon	Malta	South Korea
Botswana	Latvia	Switzerland	Bahamas	Gambia	Mauritania	Spain
Brazil	Lithuania	Taiwan	Bahrain	Georgia	Mauritius	Sri Lanka
Brunei	Luxembourg	Thailand	Bangladesh	Germany	Mexico	Sudan
Bulgaria	Macao	Turkey	Belarus	Ghana	Moldova	Swaziland
Canada	Madagascar	Ukraine	Belgium	Greece	Mongolia	Sweden
Chile	Malaysia	United Kingdom	Benin	Guatemala	Montenegro	Switzerland
China	Malta	United States	Bolivia	Guinea	Morocco	Syria
Colombia	Mauritius	Uruguay	Bosnia	Haiti	Mozambique	Taiwan
Costa Rica	Mexico	Zambia	Botswana	Honduras	Myanmar	Tajikistan
Cote d'Ivoire	Montenegro		Brazil	Hong Kong	Namibia	Tanzania
Croatia	Morocco		Brunei	Hungary	Nepal	Thailand
Cyprus	Mozambique		Bulgaria	Iceland	Netherlands	Togo
Czech Republic	Myanmar		Burkina Faso	India	New Zealand	Trinidad and Tobago
Denmark	Namibia		Cambodia	Indonesia	Nicaragua	Tunisia

(continued)

Appendix 10A.1   (continued)

Exporters			Importers		
Ecuador	Netherlands	Cameroon	Iran	Niger	Turkey
Egypt	New Zealand	Canada	Iraq	Nigeria	Turkmenistan
El Salvador	Nicaragua	Chile	Ireland	North Macedonia	Uganda
Estonia	North Macedonia	China	Israel	Norway	Ukraine
Ethiopia	Norway	Colombia	Italy	Oman	United Arab Emirates
Finland	Pakistan	Congo (DROC)	Jamaica	Pakistan	United Kingdom
France	Panama	Congo (ROC)	Japan	Panama	United States
Georgia	Paraguay	Costa Rica	Jordan	Papua New Guinea	Uruguay
Germany	Peru	Cote d'Ivoire	Kazakhstan	Paraguay	Uzbekistan
Ghana	Philippines	Croatia	Kenya	Peru	Venezuela
Greece	Poland	Cuba	Kuwait	Philippines	Vietnam
Guatemala	Portugal	Cyprus	Kyrgyzstan	Poland	Yemen
Honduras	Qatar	Czech Republic	Laos	Portugal	Zambia
Hong Kong	Romania	Denmark	Latvia	Qatar	Zimbabwe
Hungary	Russia	Djibouti	Lebanon	Romania	
Iceland	Saudi Arabia	Dominican Republic	Lesotho	Russia	

Appendix B

Appendix 10B.1   Agricultural and agricultural-related sectors defined by USDA (BICO) definition

BICO Product Category	BICO Aggregate Sector	HS6−digit Codes Comprising BICO Sectors
Coarse Grains	BULK	100200, 100290, 100300, 100390, 100400, 100490, 100700, 100790, 100820, 100829, 100840, 100850, 100860, 100890
Cocoa Beans	BULK	180100
Coffee (raw/unroasted)	BULK	090112, 090111
Corn (not for seed)	BULK	100590
Cotton	BULK	140420, 520100
Gums	BULK	130190, 400110, 400121, 400122, 400129
Oilseeds	BULK	120300, 120400, 120600, 120710, 120720, 120729, 120730, 120740, 120750, 120760, 120791, 120792, 120799
Other Bulk	BULK	100810, 100830, 121210, 121291, 121292, 121293, 140190, 140200, 140210, 140290, 140291, 140299, 140300, 140310, 140390, 140490, 400130, 500100, 500200, 530110, 530121, 530129, 530130, 530210, 530290, 530310, 530390, 530410, 530490, 530500, 530511, 530521, 530590, 530591, 530599
Peanuts/Groundnuts	BULK	120210, 120220, 120241, 120242
Pulses	BULK	071310, 071320, 071331, 071332, 071333, 071334, 071335, 071339, 071340, 071350, 071360, 071390
Rapeseed	BULK	120500, 120510, 120590
Rice	BULK	100610, 100620, 100630, 100640
Soybeans	BULK	120190
Tobacco	BULK	240110, 240120, 240130
Wheat	BULK	100110, 100119, 100190, 100199
	BULK	
Alcohol	CONSUMER	220290, 220291, 220299, 220300, 220410, 220421, 220422, 220429, 220430, 220510, 220590, 220600, 220810, 220820, 220830, 220840, 220850, 220860, 220870, 220890
Beef	CONSUMER	020110, 020120, 020130, 020210, 020220, 020230, 020610, 020621, 020622, 020629, 021020, 160250
Biodiesel	CONSUMER	382600
Cheese	CONSUMER	040610, 040620, 040630, 040640, 040690
Cocoa products	CONSUMER	180310, 180320, 180400, 180500, 180610, 180620, 180631, 180632, 180690
Coffee (roasted/processed)	CONSUMER	090121, 090122, 090140, 090190, 210110, 210111, 210112, 210130
Condiments	CONSUMER	210310, 210320, 210330, 210390, 220900
Dairy (excl. Cheese)	CONSUMER	040110, 040120, 040130, 040140, 040150, 040210, 040221, 040229, 040291, 040299, 040310, 040390, 040410, 040490, 040500, 040510, 040520, 040590, 170210, 170211, 170219, 190110, 210500, 350110, 350190, 350220, 350710, 980210

(*continued*)

BICO Product Category	BICO Aggregate Sector	HS6−digit Codes Comprising BICO Sectors
Eggs	CONSUMER	40700, 40711, 40719, 40721, 40729, 40790, 40811, 40819, 40891, 40899, 350210, 350211, 350219, 350290
Ethanol	CONSUMER	220710, 220720
Food Preparations	CONSUMER	190120, 190190, 190211, 190219, 190220, 190230, 190240, 190300, 190410, 190420, 190430, 190490, 190590, 210410, 210420, 210690
Fresh Fruit	CONSUMER	080300, 080310, 080390, 080430, 080440, 080450, 080510, 080520, 080521, 080522, 080529, 080530, 080540, 080550, 080590, 080610, 080710, 080711, 080719, 080720, 080810, 080820, 080830, 080840, 080910, 080920, 080921, 080929, 080930, 080940, 081010, 081020, 081030, 081040, 081050, 081060, 081070, 081090
Fresh Vegetables	CONSUMER	070110, 070190, 070200, 070310, 070320, 070390, 070410, 070420, 070490, 070511, 070519, 070521, 070529, 070610, 070690, 070700, 070810, 070820, 070890, 070910, 070920, 070930, 070940, 070951, 070952, 070959, 070960, 070970, 070990, 070991, 070992, 070993, 070999
Fruit/Vegetable Juice	CONSUMER	200911, 200912, 200919, 200920, 200921, 200929, 200930, 200931, 200939, 200940, 200941, 200949, 200950, 200960, 200961, 200969, 200970, 200971, 200979, 200980, 200981, 200989, 200990
Nursery	CONSUMER	060110, 060120, 060210, 060220, 060230, 060240, 060290, 060299, 060310, 060311, 060312, 060313, 060314, 060315, 060319, 060390, 060410, 060420, 060490, 060491, 060499
Other Meat	CONSUMER	20410, 20421, 20422, 20423, 20430, 20441, 20442, 20443, 20450, 20500, 20680, 20690, 20810, 20820, 20830, 20840, 20850, 20860, 20890, 21090, 21091, 21092, 21093, 21099, 41000, 50400, 160100, 160210, 160220, 160290, 160300
Petfood	CONSUMER	230910
Pork	CONSUMER	020311, 020312, 020319, 020321, 020322, 020329, 020630, 020641, 020649, 021011, 021012, 021019, 160241, 160242, 160249
Poultry	CONSUMER	020710, 020711, 020712, 020713, 020714, 020721, 020722, 020723, 020724, 020725, 020726, 020727, 020731, 020732, 020733, 020734, 020735, 020736, 020739, 020741, 020742, 020743, 020744, 020745, 020750, 020751, 020752, 020753, 020754, 020755, 020760, 160231, 160232, 160239
Processed Fruit	CONSUMER	080410, 080420, 080620, 081110, 081120, 081190, 081210, 081220, 081290, 081310, 081320, 081330, 081340, 081350, 081400, 121230, 200600, 200710, 200791, 200799, 200811, 200820, 200830, 200840, 200850, 200860, 200870, 200880, 200891, 200892, 200893, 200897, 200899

BICO Product Category	BICO Aggregate Sector	HS6−digit Codes Comprising BICO Sectors
Processed Vegetables	CONSUMER	071010, 071021, 071022, 071029, 071030, 071040, 071080, 071090, 071110, 071120, 071130, 071140, 071151, 071159, 071190, 071210, 071220, 071230, 071231, 071232, 071233, 071239, 071290, 071410, 071420, 071430, 071440, 071450, 071490, 121294, 121299, 200110, 200120, 200190, 200210, 200290, 200310, 200320, 200390, 200410, 200490, 200510, 200520, 200530, 200540, 200551, 200559, 200560, 200570, 200580, 200590, 200591, 200599
Snack Food	CONSUMER	170410, 170490, 190510, 190520, 190530, 190531, 190532, 190540
Spices	CONSUMER	090411, 090412, 090420, 090421, 090422, 090500, 090510, 090520, 090610, 090611, 090619, 090620, 090700, 090710, 090720, 090810, 090811, 090812, 090820, 090821, 090822, 090830, 090831, 090832, 090910, 090920, 090921, 090922, 090930, 090931, 090932, 090940, 090950, 090961, 090962, 091010, 091011, 091012, 091020, 091030, 091040, 091050, 091091, 091099
Tea	CONSUMER	090210, 090220, 090230, 090240, 090300, 210120
Tree Nuts	CONSUMER	080110, 080111, 080112, 080119, 080120, 080121, 080122, 080130, 080131, 080132, 080211, 080212, 080221, 080222, 080231, 080232, 080240, 080241, 080242, 080250, 080251, 080252, 080260, 080261, 080262, 080270, 080280, 080290, 200819
Distiller Dried Grains (DDGs)	INTERMEDIATE	230330
Essential Oils	INTERMEDIATE	330111, 330112, 330113, 330114, 330119, 330121, 330122, 330123, 330124, 330125, 330126, 330129, 330130, 330190, 330210
Fats	INTERMEDIATE	020900, 020910, 020990, 150100, 150110, 150120, 150190, 150200, 150210, 150290, 150300, 150500, 150510, 150590, 150600, 151610
Fodder	INTERMEDIATE	121300, 121410, 230210, 230220, 230230, 230240, 230250, 230310, 230320, 230670, 230800, 230810, 230890, 230990
Hay	INTERMEDIATE	121490
Hides & Skins	INTERMEDIATE	410110, 410120, 410121, 410122, 410129, 410130, 410140, 410150, 410190, 410210, 410221, 410229, 410310, 410320, 410330, 410390, 430110, 430120, 430130, 430140, 430150, 430160, 430170, 430180, 430190
Meal	INTERMEDIATE	120890, 230500, 230610, 230620, 230630, 230640, 230641, 230649, 230650, 230660, 230690

(continued)

BICO Product Category	BICO Aggregate Sector	HS6−digit Codes Comprising BICO Sectors
Other Intermediates (i.e., flours, yeasts, saps, waxes, hairs)	INTERMEDIATE	050210, 050290, 050300, 050510, 050590, 050610, 050690, 050790, 051000, 051110, 090130, 110100, 110210, 110220, 110230, 110290, 110311, 110312, 110313, 110314, 110319, 110320, 110321, 110329, 110411, 110412, 110419, 110421, 110422, 110423, 110429, 110430, 110510, 110520, 110610, 110620, 110630, 110710, 110720, 110811, 110812, 110813, 110814, 110819, 110820, 110900, 121010, 121020, 121110, 121120, 121130, 121140, 121150, 121190, 130211, 130212, 130213, 130214, 130219, 130220, 130231, 130232, 130239, 140410, 151911, 151912, 151919, 151920, 152190, 180200, 210210, 210220, 210230, 210610, 230110, 230700, 350300, 350400, 350510, 350520, 350790, 382311, 382312, 510111, 510119, 510121, 510129, 510130, 510210, 510211, 510219, 510220
Palm Oil	INTERMEDIATE	151110, 151190, 151321, 151329
Seed	INTERMEDIATE	100111, 100191, 100210, 100310, 100410, 100510, 100710, 100821, 120110, 120230, 120721, 120770, 120910, 120911, 120919, 120921, 120922, 120923, 120924, 120925, 120926, 120929, 120930, 120991, 120999
Soy Meal	INTERMEDIATE	120810, 230400
Soy Oil	INTERMEDIATE	150710, 150790
Honey/Sugars	INTERMEDIATE	40900, 170111, 170112, 170113, 170114, 170191, 170199, 170220, 170230, 170240, 170250, 170260, 170290, 170310, 170390
Vegetable Oil	INTERMEDIATE	150810, 150890, 150910, 150990, 151000, 151211, 151219, 151221, 151229, 151311, 151319, 151410, 151411, 151419, 151490, 151491, 151499, 151511, 151519, 151521, 151529, 151530, 151540, 151550, 151560, 151590, 151620, 151710, 151790, 151800, 152110, 291570, 291615, 292320
Biodiesel	AG RELATED	382490, 382600
Distilled Spirits	AG RELATED	2208
Ethanol	AG RELATED	220710, 220712
Forestry	AG RELATED	4401−4421
Fishery	AG RELATED	All under Chapter 3, 50800, 50900, 51191, 1504, 1604, 1605, 230120

Note: In 2021, USDA changed its previous official definition of agriculture to follow the WTO definition of agriculture. Products including ethanol, distilled spirits, industrial alcohols, and others were added whereas other products (rubber, enzymes, and others) were removed from the USDA definition.

Appendix C

Appendix 10C.1 Estimated impact of COVID-19 on agricultural trade with product group effects: values vs. volume

VARIABLES	Value (1)	Volume (2)	Value (3)	Volume (4)	Value (5)	Volume (6)	Value (7)	Volume (8)	Value (9)	Volume (10)
COVID Cases Exporter	0.002** (0.00)	0.006** (0.00)								
COVID Cases Importer	-0.003*** (0.00)	-0.005** (0.00)								
COVID Deaths Exporter			-0.037 (0.04)	-0.013 (0.09)					-0.040 (0.03)	-0.142** (0.07)
COVID Deaths Importer			-0.234*** (0.04)	-0.096 (0.07)					-0.070*** (0.03)	0.030 (0.07)
Oxford Policy Stringency Exporter					-0.030 (0.02)	0.136*** (0.05)			0.024 (0.02)	0.249*** (0.06)
Oxford Policy Stringency Importer					-0.204*** (0.03)	-0.312*** (0.05)			0.012 (0.02)	-0.050 (0.04)
Google Workplace Mobility Exporter							0.147*** (0.02)	0.462*** (0.07)	0.091*** (0.03)	0.353*** (0.07)
Google Retail Mobility Importer							0.135*** (0.01)	0.054* (0.03)	0.131*** (0.02)	0.063 (0.04)
Observations	8,296,198	8,053,593	8,103,927	7,867,905	8,287,412	8,044,391	9,731,967	9,417,002	7,418,663	7,202,455

Note: Estimated with PPML. Includes $ijkm$, it, jt, mt, kt, fixed effects. Standard errors are in parentheses and robust to clustering on $ijkm$. * , ** , and *** denote statistical significance at the 10, 5, and 1 percent levels, respectively. Estimated on monthly data from Jan. 2016 to Dec. 2020. Agricultural trade includes all HS codes defined under USDA's BICO definition of Agricultural and Agricultural–related goods. Negative effect on trade is implied by a negative sign for cases and death counts and Oxford Policy Stringency and a positive sign for Google Mobility indices. For presentation purposes of the estimations, the Johns Hopkins case/death counts are rescaled per a thousand and Oxford Policy Stringency and Google Mobility indicators are rescaled to a 0–100 percent scale.

Appendix D

Product level estimates on the value of bilateral agricultural trade

	Animal Fats	Beef	Biodiesel Blends	Chocolate Cocoa Products	Coarse Grains	Cocoa Beans	Coffee Roasted Extracts
1. Direct Effect							
COVID Deaths Exporter	0.056	−0.158	0.226	−0.192**	−0.215	−0.133	0.296**
COVID Deaths Importer	−0.254	−0.611***	−0.188	−0.098	−0.688	0.519	−0.124
Observations	76,142	116,020	25,187	211,421	78,087	34,732	167,572
2. Policy Response							
Oxford Policy Stringency Exporter	0.164	−0.118	−0.185	−0.011	0.558	−0.710*	0.184**
Oxford Policy Stringency Importer	−0.155	−0.177*	−0.507	−0.205***	−1.449***	0.170	−0.084
Observations	78,051	118,557	25,995	215,637	80,311	35,853	171,734
3. Human Mobility Reduction							
Google Workplace Mobility Exporter	0.516	0.164	−0.696	0.147	−0.637	0.211	−0.070
Google Retail Mobility Importer	0.174	0.550***	0.580**	0.115**	−0.076	−0.125	−0.064
Observations	82,228	145,598	27,767	251,375	89,451	37,674	199,910

	Pet Food	Eggs	Essential Oils	Ethanol	Feeds Fodders	Fish Products	Food Preps
1. Direct Effect							
COVID Deaths Exporter	−0.012	−0.179	0.379	−0.498	−0.159	−0.126	−0.078
COVID Deaths Importer	−0.061	−0.198	−1.149**	−1.490***	−0.077	−0.382***	0.090
Observations	105,254	80,181	184,414	68,702	173,986	227,709	303,781
2. Policy Response							
Oxford Policy Stringency Exporter	−0.212*	−0.072	−0.153	−0.487*	−0.110	−0.220***	−0.011
Oxford Policy Stringency Importer	−0.008	−0.239**	−0.290*	−0.390	−0.236***	−0.252***	−0.119**
Observations	107,947	82,153	188,919	70,566	178,237	232,835	309,756
3. Human Mobility Reduction							
Google Workplace Mobility Exporter	0.118	−0.042	0.473*	1.608***	0.155	0.317***	0.089
Google Retail Mobility Importer	−0.130*	0.092	0.526***	0.152	0.082	0.283***	0.005
Observations	117,768	97,560	216,760	80,332	199,229	271,701	382,626

	Coffee Unroasted	Condiments & Sauces	Corn	Cotton	Dairy Products	Distilled Spirits	Distillers Grains
1. Direct Effect							
COVID Deaths Exporter	0.345**	0.192*	−0.129	−1.181	−0.063	−0.955***	0.430
COVID Deaths Importer	0.225	0.020	0.032	−0.566	0.027	−0.273	−0.910
Observations	83,748	184,663	59,471	38,100	220,479	166,756	13,665
2. Policy Response							
Oxford Policy Stringency Exporter	−0.143	0.007	0.467	−0.588	0.222***	−0.134	0.049

Appendix 10D.1   (continued)

	Coffee Unroasted	Condiments & Sauces	Corn	Cotton	Dairy Products	Distilled Spirits	Distillers Grains
Oxford Policy Stringency							
Importer	−0.147	−0.138***	−0.444	−0.712**	−0.054	−0.306**	0.198
Observations	86,240	188,779	61,164	39,296	225,336	170,772	14,124
3. Human Mobility Reduction							
Google Workplace Mobility							
Exporter	0.931***	−0.182**	2.162***	−0.220	−0.127*	0.661***	−1.280
Google Retail Mobility							
Importer	−0.080	0.071*	0.273	0.969***	0.044	0.326***	0.120
Observations	92,736	221,402	70,369	42,987	275,983	202,595	16,033

	Forest Products	Fresh Fruit	Fresh Vegetables	Fruit & Veg Juices	Hay	Hides & Skins	Live Animals
1. Direct Effect							
COVID Deaths Exporter	−0.052	−0.075	0.269	−0.201	−0.989**	−0.259	0.423*
COVID Deaths Importer	−0.160	−0.116	−0.078	0.182	−0.493	−0.195	−0.208
Observations	310,180	159,241	133,451	169,014	37,533	62,204	80,024
2. Policy Response							
Oxford Policy Stringency							
Exporter	−0.201**	−0.123	−0.041	0.025	0.218	−0.848***	0.226
Oxford Policy Stringency							
Importer	−0.089	0.079	0.112	0.028	−0.108	−0.593***	0.014
Observations	316,452	162,735	136,375	172,922	38,703	64,000	82,126
3. Human Mobility Reduction							
Google Workplace Mobility							
Exporter	0.535***	0.116	−0.150	−0.084	0.443	2.385***	−0.191
Google Retail Mobility							
Importer	0.320***	0.134**	−0.035	0.000	0.113	−0.222	−0.173
Observations	380,261	185,434	151,219	200,736	42,469	69,537	95,458

	Non Alcoholic Bev	Nursery flowers	Oilseed Meal	Oilseeds NESOI	Other Bulk Commodities	Other Intermediate Products	Palm Oil
1. Direct Effect							
COVID Deaths Exporter	0.122	−0.519***	−0.386	−0.144	−0.032	0.115	−0.708
COVID Deaths Importer	−0.066	−0.566***	0.696**	0.041	−0.45	−0.043	−0.667
Observations	158,127	141,315	58,379	121,014	110,573	287,332	57,463
2. Policy Response							
Oxford Policy Stringency							
Exporter	−0.13	−0.287***	−0.106	−0.328**	0.323*	−0.052	−0.439
Oxford Policy Stringency							
Importer	−0.057	−0.341***	0.289	−0.473**	−0.103	−0.102*	−0.291
Observations	161,849	144,396	60,090	124,142	113,770	293,298	58,884
3. Human Mobility Reduction							
Google Workplace Mobility							
Exporter	−0.098	0.142	0.651*	1.103**	0.419	0.002	0.952*

(continued)

	Non Alcoholic Bev	Nursery flowers	Oilseed Meal	Oilseeds NESOI	Other Bulk Commodities	Other Intermediate Products	Palm Oil
Google Retail Mobility Importer	0.148*	0.427***	−0.074	−0.087	0.209	0.079*	0.249
Observations	193,836	159,582	65,416	136,655	122,999	348,556	68,484

	Rice	Rubber Allied Gums	Soybean Oil	Soybean meal	Soybeans	Spices	Sugars Sweeteners
1. Direct Effect							
COVID Deaths Exporter	0.896***	−0.594	1.783***	−0.53	1.044	0.415*	−0.176
COVID Deaths Importer	0.41	0.112	−0.99	0.106	0.103	0.181	−0.202
Observations	103,652	86,263	50,114	47,411	36,038	161,451	190,663
2. Policy Response							
Oxford Policy Stringency Exporter	0.352	0.091	0.603	0.273	2.269**	−0.322**	0.260**
Oxford Policy Stringency Importer	0.215	−0.245**	0.077	−0.315	−0.452	−0.025	−0.692***
Observations	105,938	88,931	51,769	48,867	37,193	165,348	194,986
3. Human Mobility Reduction							
Google Workplace Mobility Exporter	0.512	0.859***	0.024	−0.19	0.166	0.524*	0.702***
Google Retail Mobility Importer	−0.385**	0.285**	0.258	−0.099	−0.148	−0.221*	0.129
Observations	123,450	94,948	59,455	54,474	39,170	187,933	226,545

	Peanuts	Planting Seeds	Pork	Poultry	Processed Vegetables	Pulses	Rapeseed
1. Direct Effect							
COVID Deaths Exporter	−0.179	0.258	−0.242	−0.206	−0.037	−0.027	−0.714
COVID Deaths Importer	−0.038	0.318*	−0.421**	−0.620***	0.134	0.208	−0.741
Observations	41,250	134,570	102,010	115,777	215,209	112,846	22,038
2. Policy Response							
Oxford Policy Stringency Exporter	−0.12	0.312***	−0.085	−0.231**	−0.185***	0.095	−0.55
Oxford Policy Stringency Importer	−0.504*	0.005	−0.161*	−0.128	−0.046	0.144	−0.122
Observations	42,379	138,217	104,276	117,952	219,558	115,679	22,815
3. Human Mobility Reduction							
Google Workplace Mobility Exporter	0.684	0.154	0.008	0.129	−0.102	0.056	0.365
Google Retail Mobility Importer	0.065	−0.248***	0.262***	0.371***	0.065	−0.284	0.353
Observations	44,553	155,879	127,781	151,049	254,164	132,515	25,206

	Tea	Tobacco	TreeNuts	Vegetable Oils NESOI	Wheat	Processed Fruit	Snack Foods NESOI
1. Direct Effect							
COVID Deaths Exporter	−0.156	−0.012	−0.047	−0.038	−1.130**	0.253***	−0.261***

Appendix 10D.1   (continued)

	Tea	Tobacco	TreeNuts	Vegetable Oils NESOI	Wheat	Processed Fruit	Snack Foods NESOI
COVID Deaths Importer	−0.105	−0.583*	−0.164	−0.098	0.352	−0.011	−0.009
Observations	151,292	58,329	153,088	219,697	47,211	221,671	228,688
2. Policy Response							
Oxford Policy Stringency Exporter	−0.405***	−0.469*	−0.252**	0.069	−0.23	−0.051	−0.057
Oxford Policy Stringency Importer	−0.086	−0.327	−0.314**	−0.143	−0.128	−0.048	−0.217***
Observations	155,269	59,444	156,798	224,838	48,599	226,548	233,145
3. Human Mobility Reduction							
Google Workplace Mobility Exporter	0.882***	−0.595	−1.238***	−0.055	−0.274	0.058	0.338***
Google Retail Mobility Importer	−0.093	−0.039	0.278	−0.012	0.105	0.034	0.068*
Observations	176,436	64,246	180,071	260,656	57,168	258,467	278,045

Note: The Dep. variable is value of agricultural trade estimated with PPML. Includes *ijm, it, jt, mt,* fixed effects. Standard errors are in parentheses and robust to clustering on *ijm.* *, **, and *** denote statistical significance at the 10, 5, and 1 percent levels, respectively. Estimated on monthly data from Jan. 2016 to Dec. 2020. Negative effect on trade is implied by a negative sign for cases and death counts and Oxford Policy Stringency and a positive sign for Google Mobility indices. For presentation purposes of the estimations, the Johns Hopkins case/death counts are rescaled per a thousand and Oxford Policy Stringency and Google Mobility indicators are rescaled to a 0–100 percent scale.

Appendix E

Appendix 10E.1   Product level estimates on the volume of bilateral agricultural trade

	Animal Fats	Beef	Biodiesel Blends	Chocolate Cocoa Products	Coarse Grains	Cocoa Beans	Coffee Roasted Extracts
1. Direct Effect							
COVID Deaths Exporter	0.320	0.055	0.375	−0.255**	−0.542	0.004	−0.132
COVID Deaths Importer	−0.260	−0.544***	−0.299	−0.029	−0.528	0.681	−0.555**
Observations	75,471	115,877	24,898	208,712	77,651	34,222	165,981
2. Policy Response							
Oxford Policy Stringency Exporter	0.334	−0.111	0.054	0.004	0.463	−0.293	0.216**
Oxford Policy Stringency Importer	−0.271	−0.280***	−0.525	−0.226***	−1.444***	−0.023	−0.404*
Observations	77,370	118,409	25,715	212,847	79,868	35,303	170,097
3. Human Mobility Reduction							
Google Workplace Mobility Exporter	0.391	0.223	−0.849	0.231**	−0.538	−0.075	−0.314
Google Retail Mobility Importer	−0.026	0.475***	0.603**	0.071	−0.077	0.091	0.143
Observations	81,508	145,175	27,423	247,953	88,974	36,973	197,752

	Pet Food	Eggs	Essential Oils	Ethanol	Feeds Fodders	Fish Products	Food Preps
1. Direct Effect							
COVID Deaths Exporter	0.031	−0.020	0.105	0.392	−0.026	−0.117	0.240***
COVID Deaths Importer	−0.122	0.136	−0.086	−1.642***	−0.000	−0.137	0.100
Observations	104,508	75,390	179,518	53,800	172,313	223,619	299,053
2. Policy Response							
Oxford Policy Stringency Exporter	−0.083	−0.129	−0.168	0.429	0.161	−0.211***	0.081
Oxford Policy Stringency Importer	0.018	−0.211	0.151	−0.088	−0.293**	−0.106	−0.143***
Observations	107,193	77,245	183,893	55,198	176,537	228,669	304,912
3. Human Mobility Reduction							
Google Workplace Mobility Exporter	0.120	0.244	0.066	1.436***	−0.075	0.308***	−0.220**
Google Retail Mobility Importer	−0.112**	−0.151	0.085	0.119	0.001	0.262***	−0.006
Observations	116,999	91,136	210,942	63,273	196,882	265,097	376,170

	Coffee Unroasted	Condiments & Sauces	Corn	Cotton	Dairy Products	Distilled Spirits	Distillers Grains
1. Direct Effect							
COVID Deaths Exporter	0.373**	0.225*	−0.147	−1.152	−0.430*	−0.708***	0.140
COVID Deaths Importer	0.303	0.040	0.152	−0.814	0.268*	−0.178	−0.582
Observations	82,490	182,143	59,165	36,745	218,151	132,072	13,611
2. Policy Response							
Oxford Policy Stringency Exporter	−0.011	0.225**	0.582	−0.570	−0.322	0.033	0.157

Appendix 10E.1   (continued)

	Coffee Unroasted	Condiments & Sauces	Corn	Cotton	Dairy Products	Distilled Spirits	Distillers Grains
Oxford Policy Stringency Importer	−0.183	−0.069	−0.483	−0.688**	0.031	−0.201**	0.191
Observations	84,935	186,182	60,847	37,876	222,946	134,787	14,065
3. Human Mobility Reduction							
Google Workplace Mobility Exporter	0.831***	−0.475***	2.425***	−0.081	0.219	0.379**	−0.695
Google Retail Mobility Importer	−0.135	0.016	0.235	0.889***	0.136	0.256***	0.064
Observations	91,335	218,223	69,941	41,103	272,460	161,182	15,923

	Forest Products	Fresh Fruit	Fresh Vegetables	Fruit & Veg Juices	Hay	Hides & Skins	Live Animals
1. Direct Effect							
COVID Deaths Exporter	0.006	0.473***	0.250	−0.201	−1.229**	0.520*	0.682***
COVID Deaths Importer	0.057	−0.099	−0.011	0.171	−0.551	−0.284	−0.280
Observations	293,722	157,168	131,147	156,415	37,222	57,417	65,553
2. Policy Response							
Oxford Policy Stringency Exporter	−0.299***	−0.027	0.020	0.098	0.336	−0.121	0.054
Oxford Policy Stringency Importer	−0.129	0.315***	0.334**	0.051	−0.050	−0.691***	0.079
Observations	299,561	160,613	134,010	159,835	38,390	59,056	67,184
3. Human Mobility Reduction							
Google Workplace Mobility Exporter	0.564***	0.067	0.672***	0.108	0.562	0.462*	0.027
Google Retail Mobility Importer	0.348***	−0.209**	−0.433***	−0.034	−0.088	0.289**	−0.122
Observations	357,380	182,128	147,855	184,676	42,101	63,993	77,345

	Non Alcoholic Bev	Nursery flowers	Oilseed Meal	Oilseeds NESOI	Other Bulk Commodities	Other Intermediate Products	Palm Oil
1. Direct Effect							
COVID Deaths Exporter	0.216	−0.361**	−0.305	−0.178	−0.303	0.191	−0.736
COVID Deaths Importer	−0.103	−0.446***	0.706**	−0.214	−0.862**	−0.070	−0.592
Observations	126,424	128,261	57,930	118,873	108,601	282,459	57,206
2. Policy Response							
Oxford Policy Stringency Exporter	−0.047	−0.246**	−0.028	−0.079	−0.264	0.232**	−0.423
Oxford Policy Stringency Importer	−0.094	−0.268**	0.224	−0.593**	−0.089	−0.291***	−0.251
Observations	129,010	131,003	59,627	121,926	111,745	288,339	58,602
3. Human Mobility Reduction							
Google Workplace Mobility Exporter	−0.111	0.069	0.498	1.737***	1.624***	−0.010	1.155**

(continued)

Appendix 10E.1   **(continued)**

	Non Alcoholic Bev	Nursery flowers	Oilseed Meal	Oilseeds NESOI	Other Bulk Commodities	Other Intermediate Products	Palm Oil
Google Retail Mobility Importer	0.080	0.433***	−0.109	−0.283	0.376	0.116*	0.153
Observations	154,390	144,581	64,813	133,809	120,087	341,771	67,997

	Rice	Rubber Allied Gums	Soybean Oil	Soybean meal	Soybeans	Spices	Sugars Sweeteners
1. Direct Effect							
COVID Deaths Exporter	1.788***	−0.091	1.631***	−0.776**	0.842	0.677***	−0.148
COVID Deaths Importer	−0.029	0.194	−1.016	0.220	0.053	0.479	−0.455
Observations	103,151	84,451	49,791	47,268	35,888	158,987	187,684
2. Policy Response							
Oxford Policy Stringency Exporter	0.670**	0.436*	0.577	0.250	2.090**	−0.315**	0.568***
Oxford Policy Stringency Importer	0.076	−0.271**	0.187	−0.273	−0.445	−0.115	−0.858***
Observations	105,431	87,062	51,444	48,726	37,032	162,815	191,957
3. Human Mobility Reduction							
Google Workplace Mobility Exporter	0.299	0.730**	0.160	0.021	0.519	0.090	1.249***
Google Retail Mobility Importer	−0.336**	0.217*	0.187	−0.214	−0.200	−0.025	0.105
Observations	122,523	92,988	58,940	54,243	38,807	184,788	221,962

	Peanuts	Planting Seeds	Pork	Poultry	Processed Vegetables	Pulses	Rapeseed
1. Direct Effect							
COVID Deaths Exporter	0.038	0.671	−0.199	−0.076	0.152	0.144	−0.211
COVID Deaths Importer	−0.003	−0.810*	−0.395*	−0.466***	0.426**	−0.245	−0.538
Observations	40,676	129,348	101,945	115,185	212,389	112,412	21,620
2. Policy Response							
Oxford Policy Stringency Exporter	−0.178	0.023	0.022	−0.072	−0.154	−0.315	−0.401
Oxford Policy Stringency Importer	−0.802***	−0.080	−0.231***	−0.117	−0.043	0.120	−0.146
Observations	41,776	132,826	104,202	117,341	216,644	115,222	22,391
3. Human Mobility Reduction							
Google Workplace Mobility Exporter	0.934*	0.608	−0.115	0.331**	0.111	0.111	0.096
Google Retail Mobility Importer	0.038	−0.289	0.338***	0.323***	0.083	−0.082	0.168
Observations	43,628	149,616	127,431	149,903	250,330	131,302	24,787

	Tea	Tobacco	TreeNuts	Vegetable Oils NESOI	Wheat	Processed Fruit	Snack Foods NESOI
1. Direct Effect							
COVID Deaths Exporter	0.110	0.193	0.073	−0.109	−1.285***	0.312***	0.041

Appendix 10E.1   (continued)

	Tea	Tobacco	TreeNuts	Vegetable Oils NESOI	Wheat	Processed Fruit	Snack Foods NESOI
COVID Deaths Importer	0.219	−0.544*	−0.319	0.052	0.454	−0.039	0.164
Observations	148,026	58,344	151,071	216,926	46,993	218,665	226,046
2. Policy Response							
Oxford Policy Stringency Exporter	−0.418***	−0.342	−0.207	0.106	−0.230	−0.133	0.101
Oxford Policy Stringency Importer	0.016	−0.401*	−0.617***	−0.119	−0.142	−0.211**	−0.302***
Observations	151,949	59,477	154,729	222,019	48,378	223,406	230,382
3. Human Mobility Reduction							
Google Workplace Mobility Exporter	0.985***	0.180	−1.381***	−0.081	−0.333	−0.115	−0.096
Google Retail Mobility Importer	−0.279**	0.128	0.164	−0.116	0.081	0.085	0.085
Observations	172,140	62,633	176,547	256,879	56,823	254,670	274,546

Note: The Dep. variable is value of agricultural trade estimated with PPML. Includes ijm, it, jt, mt, fixed effects. Standard errors are in parentheses and robust to clustering on ijm. *, **, and *** denote statistical significance at the 10, 5, and 1 percent levels, respectively. Estimated on monthly data from Jan. 2016 to Dec. 2020. Negative effect on trade is implied by a negative sign for cases and death counts and Oxford Policy Stringency and a positive sign for Google Mobility indices. For presentation purposes of the estimations, the Johns Hopkins case/death counts are rescaled per a thousand and Oxford Policy Stringency and Google Mobility indicators are rescaled to a 0−100 percent scale.

References

Ahn, S., and S. Steinbach. 2021. "COVID-19 Trade Actions in the Agricultural and Food Sector." *Food Distribution Research Society* 52 (2): 51–75. https://www.fdrsinc.org/wp-content/uploads/2021/09/JFDR-July-2021-Full-Issue.pdf #page=55.

Amiti, M., S. J. Redding, and D. Weinstein. 2019. "The Impact of the 2018 Trade War on US Prices and Welfare." *Journal of Economic Perspectives* 33 (4): 187–210. https://www.aeaweb.org/articles?id=10.1257/jep.33.4.187.

Anderson, J. E., and Y. V. Yotov. 2016. "Terms of Trade and Global Efficiency Effects of Free Trade Agreements, 1990–2002." *Journal of International Economics* 99: 279–98. https://www.sciencedirect.com/science/article/pii/S0022199615001531.

Arita, S., J. Grant, and S. Sydow. 2021. "Has COVID-19 Caused a Great Trade Collapse? An Initial Ex Post Assessment." *Choices* Quarter 3. https://www.choicesmagazine.org/choices-magazine/theme-articles/agricultural-market-response-to-covid-19/has-covid-19-caused-a-great-trade-collapse-an-initial-ex-post-assessment.

Baldwin, R., and D. Taglioni. 2006. "Gravity for Dummies and Dummies for Gravity Equations." NBER Working Paper No. 12516. Cambridge, MA: National Bureau of Economic Research. https://www.nber.org/papers/w12516.

Baquedano, F., Y. Zereyesus, C. Christensen, and C. Valdes. 2021. "International Food Security Assessment, 2020–2030: COVID-19 Update and Impacts on Food Insecurity." USDA Economic Research Service: COVID-19 Working Paper

#AP-087. https://www.ers.usda.gov/webdocs/publications/100276/ap-087.pdf?v
=3889.4.
Beckman, J., and A. Countryman. 2021. "The Importance of Agriculture in the
Economy: Impacts from COVID-19." *American Journal of Agricultural Economics*
103 (5): 1595–1611. https://doi.org/10.1111/ajae.12212.
Binkley, J. K., and Y. Liu. 2019. "Food at home and away from home: commodity
composition, nutrition differences, and differences in consumers." Agricultural
and Resource Economics Review 48 (2): 221–252. DOI: https://doi.org/10.1017
/age.2019.1.
Bown, C. P. 2018. "Trump's Trade War Timeline: An Up-to-Date Guide." Trade and
Investment Policy Watch (blog). Peterson Institute for International Economics, April 19. https://www.piie.com/blogs/tradeinvestment-policy-watch/trump
-trade-war-china-date-guide.
Bown, C. P. 2019. "US-China Trade War: The Guns of August." Trade and Investment Policy Watch (blog). Peterson Institute for International Economics, September 20. https://www.piie.com/blogs/trade-andinvestment-policy-watch/us
-china-trade-war-guns-august.
Brahmbhatt, M., and A. Dutta. 2008. "On SARS Type Economic Effects during
Infectious Disease Outbreaks." World Bank Policy Research Paper No. 4466.
Washington, DC: World Bank. https://openknowledge.worldbank.org/handle
/10986/6440.
Carter, C. A., and S. Steinbach. 2020. "The Impact of Retaliatory Tariffs on Agri-
cultural and Food Trade. NBER Working Paper No. 27147. Cambridge, MA:
National Bureau of Economic Research. https://www.nber.org/papers/w27147
#:~:text=The%20results%20indicate%20that%20these,reorientation%20of
%20international%20trade%20patterns.
Chenarides, L., M. Manfredo, and T. J. Richards. 2020. "COVID-19 and Food
Supply Chains." *Applied Economic Perspectives and Policy* 43 (1): 270–79. doi
.org/10.1002/aepp.13085.
Crowley, M. A. 2019. *Trade War: The Clash of Economic Systems Threatening Global
Prosperity*. London: CEPR Press. https://voxeu.org/content/trade-war-clash
-economic-systems-threatening-global-prosperity.
Evenett, S., M. Fiorini, J. Fritz, B. Hoekman, P. Lukaszuk, N. Rocha, M. Ruta,
F. Santi, and A. Shingal. 2022. "Trade Policy Responses to the COVID-19 Pan-
demic Crisis: Evidence from a New Data Set. The World Economy 45 (2): 342–364.
Fajgelbaum, P., A. Khandelwal, W. Kim, C. Mantovani, and E. Schaal. 2020. "Opti-
mal Lockdown in a Commuting Network." NBER Working Paper No. 27441.
Cambridge, MA: National Bureau of Economic Research. https://www.nber.org
/papers/w27441.
FAO, IFAD, UNICEF, WFP, and WHO. 2021. *The State of Food Security and Nutri-
tion in the World 2021. Transforming Food Systems for Food Security, Improved
Nutrition and Affordable Healthy Diets for All*. Rome: FAO. https://doi.org/10.4060
/cb4474en.
Friedt, F., and K. Zhang. 2020. "The Triple Effect of COVID-19 on Chinese Exports:
First Evidence of the Export Supply, Import Demand and GVC Contagion
Effects." Center for Economic Policy Analysis, Covid Economics: Vetted and
Real Time Papers. https://www.econbiz.de/Record/the-triple-effect-of-covid-19
-on-chinese-exports-first-evidence-of-the-export-supply-import-demand-and
-gvc-contagion-effects-friedt-felix/10012311905.
Grant, J., and S. Arita. 2017. "Sanitary and Phyto-sanitary Measures: Assessment,
Measurement, and Impact." No. 938–2017–1828. International Agricultural

Trade Research Consortium (IATRC). https://iatrc.umn.edu/sanitary-and-phyto
-sanitary-measures-assessment-measurement-and-impact.

Grant, J. H., S. Arita, C. Emlinger, R. Johansson, and C. Xie. 2021. "Agricultural Exports and Retaliatory Trade Actions: An Empirical Assessment of the 2018/2019 Trade Conflict." *Applied Economics Perspectives and Policy* 43 (2): 619–40. https://doi.org/10.1002/aepp.13138.

Head, K., and T. Mayer. 2014. "Gravity Equations: Workhorse, Toolkit, and Cookbook." *Handbook of International Economics* 4: 131–95. Elsevier. https://doi.org/10.1016/B978-0-444-54314-1.00003-3.

International Monetary Fund (IMF). 2020. World Economic Outlook Update, June. https://www.imf.org/en/Publications/WEO/Issues/2020/06/24/WEOUpdateJune2020.

International Monetary Fund. 2021. World Economic Outlook: Managing Divergent Recoveries. https://www.imf.org/en/Publications/WEO/Issues/2021/03/23/world-economic-outlook-april-2021.

Kejzar, K. Z., and A. Velic. 2020. "COVID-19, Trade Collapse, and GVC Linkages: European Experience." Center for Economic Policy Analysis, Covid Economics: Vetted and Real Time Papers. https://cepr.org/content/covid-economics-vetted-and-real-time-papers-0.

Luckstead, J., R. M. Nayga Jr., and H. A. Snell. 2021. "Labor Issues in the Food Supply Chain amid the COVID-19 Pandemic." *Applied Economic Perspectives and Policy* 43 (1): 382–400. doi.org/10.1002/aepp.13090.

Lusk, Jayson L., Glynn T. Tonsor, and Lee L. Schulz. 2021. "Beef and pork marketing margins and price spreads during COVID-19." Applied Economic Perspectives and Policy 43 (1): 4–23.

Mallory, M. L. 2020. "Impact of COVID-19 on Medium-Term Export Prospects for Soybeans, Corn, Beef, Pork, and Poultry." *Applied Economic Perspectives and Policy* 43 (1): 292–303. doi.org/10.1002/aepp.13113.

Ning, X., and J. H. Grant. 2019. "New Estimates of the Ad-valorem Equivalent of SPS Measures: Evidence from Specific Trade Concerns." Working paper. https://vtechworks.lib.vt.edu/handle/10919/95217.

Peterson, E., J. Grant, D. Roberts, and V. Karov. 2013. "Evaluating the Trade Restrictiveness of Phytosanitary Measures on US Fresh Fruit and Vegetable Imports." *American Journal of Agricultural Economics* 95 (4): 842–58. https://onlinelibrary.wiley.com/journal/14678276.

Reuters. 2020. "Rain to Help EU Rapeseed But Too Late to Avert French Area Drop." October. 2. https://www.reuters.com/article/us-europe-grains-sowing/rain-to-help-eu-rapeseed-but-too-late-to-avert-french-area-drop-idUSKBN26N27F.

Santos Silva, J. M. C., and S. Tenreyro. 2006. "The Log of Gravity." *The Review of Economics and Statistics* 88 (4): 641–58. https://direct.mit.edu/rest/article/88/4/641/57668/The-Log-of-Gravity.

United Nations Conference on Trade and Development (UNCTAD). 2016. Key Indicators and Trends in International Trade 2016. https://unctad.org/en/PublicationsLibrary/ditctab2016d3_en.pdf.

World Bank. 2021. "Global Economic Prospects." World Bank Global Economic Prospects Report, January. https://www.worldbank.org/en/publication/global-economic-prospects.

World Trade Organization (WTO). 2020a. Methodology for the WTO Trade Forecast of April 8 2020. https://www.wto.org/english/news_e/pres20_e/methodpr855_e.pdf.

World Trade Organization (WTO). 2020b. "COVID-19 and Agriculture: A Story of

Resilience." Information Note, August 26. https://www.wto.org/english/tratop_e/COVID-19_e/agric_report_e.pdf.

World Trade Organization (WTO). 2021. "World Trade Primed for Strong but Uneven Recovery after COVID-19 Pandemic Shock." Press Release, March 31. https://www.wto.org/english/news_e/pres21_e/pr876_e.pdf.

Yaffe-Bellany, D., and M. Corkery. 2020. "Dumped Milk, Smashed Eggs, Plowed Vegetables: Food Waste of the Pandemic." *New York Times*, April 11. https://www.nytimes.com/2020/04/11/business/coronavirus-destroying-food.html.

Yotov, Y. V., R. Piermartini, J. A. Monteiro, and M. Larch. 2016. "An Advanced Guide to Trade Policy Analysis: The Structural Gravity Model." Geneva: World Trade Organization. https://www.wto.org/english/res_e/booksp_e/advancedwto unctad2016_e.pdf.

Contributors

Pol Antràs
Department of Economics
Harvard University
1805 Cambridge Street
Cambridge, MA 02138

Shawn Arita
Office of the Chief Economist
US Department of Agriculture
1400 Independence Avenue, SW
Washington, DC 20250

Jayson Beckman
Economic Research Service
US Department of Agriculture
1400 Independence Avenue, SW
Washington, DC 20250-0002

Michael Delgado
Department of Agricultural
  Economics
Purdue University
403 West State St.
West Lafayette, IN 47907

Barry K. Goodwin
Departments of Economics and
  Agricultural
and Resource Economics
North Carolina State University
Box 8109
Raleigh, NC 27695

Jason Grant
Department of Agricultural and
  Applied Economics
Virginia Tech
Blacksburg, VA 24061

Mildred M. Haley
US Department of Agriculture
805 Pennsylvania Avenue
Kansas City, MO 64105

Geoffrey Heal
Graduate School of Business
Columbia University
665 West 130th Street
New York, NY 10027

A. G. Kawamura
Orange County Produce LLC
210 W. Walnut Avenue
Fullerton, CA 92832

Sunghun Lim
Department of Agricultural
  Economics and Agribusiness
Louisiana State University
Baton Rouge, LA 70803

Liang Lu
Agricultural Economics and Rural
   Sociology
University of Idaho
875 Perimeter Drive
Moscow, ID 83844

Jayson L. Lusk
Department of Agricultural
   Economics
Purdue University
403 West State St.
West Lafayette, IN 47907

Meilin Ma
Department of Agricultural
   Economics
Purdue University
403 West State St.
West Lafayette, IN 47907

Ruby Nguyen
Idaho National Laboratory
1955 N. Fremont Avenue
Idaho Falls, ID 83415

Md Mamunur Rahman
Idaho National Laboratory
1955 N. Fremont Avenue
Idaho Falls, ID 83415

A. Ford Ramsey
Department of Agricultural and
   Applied Economics
Virginia Tech
250 Drillfield Drive
Blacksburg, VA 24061

Thomas Reardon
Department of Agricultural, Food, and
   Resource Economics
Michigan State University
East Lansing, MI 48824-1039

Sandro Steinbach
Agribusiness and Applied Economics
Center for Agricultural Policy and
   Trade Studies
North Dakota State University
1230 Albrecht Blvd
Fargo ND 58102

Sharon Sydow
Office of the Chief Economist
US Department of Agriculture
1400 Independence Avenue, SW
Washington, DC 20250

Charles A. Taylor
Department of Agricultural and
   Resource Economics
University of California
Berkeley, CA 94720

H. Holly Wang
Department of Agricultural
   Economics
Purdue University
403 West State St.
West Lafayette, IN 47907

Jason Winfree
Agricultural Economics and Rural
   Sociology
University of Idaho
875 Perimeter Drive
Moscow, ID 83844

David Zilberman
Department of Agricultural &
   Resource Economics
207 Giannini Hall, #3310
University of California
Berkeley, CA 94720-3310

Author Index

Subject Index